"Kat's personal stories weaved throughout this special book probably resonate with many third-culture kids like myself. She has the ability to create such nostalgic, classic cookies but introduce them in creative ways that are a true reflection of her identity and that are approachable at the same time." **—CALVIN ENG, chef and owner of Bonnie's and author of *Salt Sugar MSG***

"Kat Lieu is a leading voice in home cookery today, and in her fantastic third cookbook, she celebrates the beloved cookie like no one has done before. Whimsical, daring, proudly Asian, and utterly delicious, Kat's recipes and storytelling are bound to make anyone smile. You're in for a treat!" **—CATHY ERWAY, James Beard Award–winning writer and author of *The Food of Taiwan***

"*108 Asian Cookies* speaks to the heart of third-culture experience—the feeling of being caught between worlds. Through delicious, not-too-sweet recipes, she transforms that in-between place from one of stigmatization into one of delicious inspiration." **—J. KENJI LÓPEZ-ALT, author of *The Food Lab* and *The Wok***

"Kat's *108 Asian Cookies* is a testament to her baking prowess and the deep love she has for her family. I adore the explosion of colors and flavors that you can find among these pages. It's very refreshing to see so many third-culture ingredients come together so cohesively. If you are lucky enough to read her cookbook, you will have dessert inspiration for years to come!" **—ABI BALINGIT, baking blogger at The Dusky Kitchen and James Beard Award–winning author of *Mayumu: Filipino American Desserts Remixed***

108 ASIAN COOKIES

108 ASIAN COOKIES

NOT-TOO-SWEET Treats from a Third-Culture Kitchen

KAT LIEU
Founder of Subtle Asian Baking

VORACIOUS
LITTLE, BROWN AND COMPANY
New York Boston London

Voracious / Little, Brown and Company
Hachette Book Group
1290 Avenue of the Americas, New York, NY 10104
voraciousbooks.com

First Edition: October 2025

Voracious is an imprint of Little, Brown and Company, a division of Hachette Book Group, Inc. The Voracious name and logo are trademarks of Hachette Book Group, Inc.

The publisher is not responsible for websites (or their content) that are not owned by the publisher.

The Hachette Speakers Bureau provides a wide range of authors for speaking events. To find out more, go to hachettespeakersbureau.com or call (866) 376-6591.

Little, Brown and Company books may be purchased in bulk for business, educational, or promotional use. For information, please contact your local bookseller or the Hachette Book Group Special Markets Department at special.markets@hbgusa.com.

Photographs by Charity Burggraaf
Author headshot by Heather Willensky
Personal photos by Kat Lieu, Jake Young, and contributors
Styled by Theresa Gilliam and Tyler Hill
Book interior design by Toni Tajima

ISBN 9780316579162
Library of Congress Control Number: 2025935170

10 9 8 7 6 5 4 3 2 1

PCF

Printed in Malaysia

TO MY DEAR AH MA (paternal grandmother), who introduced me to baking. I love and miss you so much, every day. I wish we got to say goodbye.

TO AH GONG (maternal grandfather), the "Great Alexander." I wish I had baked for you, at least once. You once told me I'd be a 女強人 (career woman) and that I'd achieve anything I set my heart on, and you were right.

◂ Ah Gong holding Philip in Manhattan, 2014

TO ZEZE (paternal grandfather), who made me the foodie I am today. I wish I had picked your brilliant mind more. Thank you for telling me how "even kings need advisors." Because of your words, I never hesitated to ask for help when needed.

TO AH PO (maternal grandmother), who cooked the most delicious meals for her family and gave me quarters every time she saw me. I love and miss you.

And as always, I dedicate this book **TO YOU**, dear reader.

CONTENTS

III. BROWNIES, BLONDIES, AND BARS (Plus One Biscotti) 124

IV. SUGAR AND SPICE AND EVERYTHING NICE: Cookies with a Kick 168

V. UMAMI UNLEASHED 210

VI. MODERN ALCHEMY AND DELIGHTFUL FUSIONS 252

VII. SPECIAL OCCASION AND HOLIDAY COOKIES 302

VIII. LIFE IS A BOX OF NOT-TOO-SWEET TREATS 342

INTRODUCTION

Dear friend,

One night when I was eleven years old, I put together a most peculiar treat: Chips Ahoy! cookies sandwiched with a mountain of Reddi-wip, rolled in pork floss (or dried shredded pork). I didn't realize it then, but each sweet, savory, and chaotic bite reflected my third-culture identity. If you're not familiar with the term "third-culture," it means growing up caught between two (or more) cultures: one being from the homeland of your parents and the other being the environment where you were raised. In my case, I was born in Canada to a Chinese mother from Hong Kong and a Chinese Vietnamese father from Vietnam. They found each other in Montreal and raised me in the rougher parts of Coney Island.

Every week, my parents took me and my younger sister food shopping. It was always Pathmark for Western groceries and Chinatown for Asian staples. Our kitchen was a blend of cultures and collision of flavors. It became my creative, safe space. Outside, the world during the nineties often felt too unkind.

Racists would mock the shape and size of my eyes, tell me to "go back to China" (even though I'd never even visited China as a child), or assume I didn't speak any English. During these moments, I honestly hated being Asian. Then there were times when I felt I wasn't Asian enough. I couldn't read Chinese characters or speak fluent Vietnamese. I wasn't thin like my cousins or all the Asian celebrities my relatives idolized, the same relatives who called me an ABC (American-born Chinese), like it was a bad thing. (And technically, I was born in Canada.)

All that toxicity weighed heavily on my young mind, but one bite of that sweet-savory cookie sandwich melted my worries and sadness away that night.

Even though my moment of solace was brief, it was a sweet one. That's the quiet power of cookies, formidable little warriors in the baking world. Beyond bringing comfort, cookies are compact powerhouses. Why? Because the cookie is a shapeshifter as much as it is a storyteller. Dress it up or keep it simple. Load it with nuts, mochi, or chocolate chips or strip it back to just its basic, buttery goodness. This very adaptability endears the cookie to the masses, and it's no wonder that everyone I've polled has a favorite cookie (or two).

Some people prefer the basics: they'll immediately say their favorite cookie is the classic chocolate chip. Snickerdoodles have many fans, and I have one for you (page 73) where five spice powder, not cinnamon, is the star. Personally, the cookies I find hardest to resist are the delicious and chewy Taiwanese Snowflake Crisps, Your Way (page 58). They're QQ (or boba-chewy, in texture) and not-too-sweet (the ultimate East Asian compliment!).

Admittedly, I also love a good ol' chocolate chip cookie, but it can't be basic. I'm a chaotic kitchen wizard, after all, someone who thrives on pushing boundaries when developing new recipes (hello, pork floss whipped cream cookie sandwich!). I also love adding unexpected flair to classic recipes. For example, you'll find non-traditional ingredients and hints of umami in my Fudgy Soy Sauce-Chocolate Chip Cookies (page 216) and my Bourbon and Fish Sauce Cookies (page 246), both chocolate chip cookies with savory, Asian twists.

You might think that with all these fun recipes and three cookbooks under my belt in just four years, that I've been baking my whole life. I wish I could tell you I had a formative "cookie phase" or that growing up I had baked cookies on Sunday mornings with a gentle mother. Or that I had discovered a treasure trove of handwritten cookie recipes in an attic one magical afternoon.

Well, I never lived in a house with an attic and the truth is, I only started baking in 2017, deep into my thirties when I unearthed a vintage Sunbeam Mixmaster tucked away in our garage. It was a cherished heirloom from my 阿嫲 (Ah Ma, my paternal grandmother), a mixer that had traveled with me from Montreal to NYC to Seattle. Even then, it wasn't until 2020 that I baked my very first cookie from scratch.

I know this will sound cliché, but baking has not only healed me: it saved me. During the height of the COVID-19 pandemic, I felt so burnt out as a doctor of physical therapy, thirteen years into a career my parents had chosen for me shortly after high school.

Then in 2020, I watched my beloved father, once so full of life and energy, take one final sharp exhale, and then he was gone. You always believe you will have more time with the people you love, but that is rarely true. His sudden passing plunged me into a deep depression.

I mourned, tears running deep, in my kitchen. Some days, I would call Ah Ma, who lived in Montreal, and talk to her about my father, her son. We would commiserate and cry, then take turns telling each other not to cry.

"Nothing hurts more than when a white-haired person mourns a black-haired person," she told me in Cantonese, meaning it's painful when an older person grieves the death of a younger person.

"But Dad also had white hair," I replied, hoping humor would quell her tears. It did. To lighten the mood, we'd talk about food. Ah Ma used to bake and cook a lot when she was younger, especially back in Hanoi. I told her I was learning to bake on my own, using her mixer, and she encouraged me to keep going at it. And I did.

When her Mixmaster eventually tripped the circuits in my kitchen and broke down, I mourned it for a while before replacing it with a KitchenAid. Then with each milk bread, chiffon cake, and cookie I taught myself to bake, I felt myself healing as I stirred my dreams into batter and molded them into dough. I tested recipes, played around with ingredients, and filled notebook after notebook with my own treasure trove of recipes, which I now share with you in *108 Asian Cookies*.

Throughout these pages, I've left you pieces of my spirit and parts of my soul. Sprinkled bits of my heart ❤️. Some of the cookies here reflect my experience as a third-culture kid, like that pork floss cookie sandwich and my Black Sesame and Brown Butter Rice Krispies Treats (page 136). Rice Krispies Treats are classic American snacks I enjoyed as a child, and one of the only Western snacks my mother made. As an adult, I've given them an Asian twist, incorporating miso, black sesame (my mother's favorite), and sesame oil.

Other cookies in the book mesh flavors and stories from across Asia and its diasporas. And some recipes, like Sharon's Sakura and Strawberry Biscotti (page 163) and the Ondeh-Ondeh Macarons (page 282), are by members of Subtle Asian Baking (SAB), the global online group I founded in 2020. SAB began as a small virtual community of passionate bakers. Today it has grown into a vibrant platform for sharing Asian-inspired creations, fostering creativity, celebrating culinary heritage, and fundraising for causes important to our community.

Like how SAB isn't just about sharing recipes, this book isn't just about introducing black sesame, pandan, miso, and ube into the cookie lexicon. Some cookies here are new creations while others are timeless recipes passed down through generations. I must admit, however, that I have only scratched the surface here. It is important to acknowledge that this cookie book is not an exhaustive encyclopedia of *all* Asian and Asian-inspired cookies. Rather, it is a necessary

▲ Subtle Asian Baking members at the 2023 Very Asian Sunday Funday in Bellevue, WA

first step, and I'm glad to have taken this step with a truly dream-come-true project.

I wrote *108 Asian Cookies* for two main reasons. First, to address the homogeneity and lack of diversity in baking cookbooks, especially cookie-themed ones. When I pitched this book in 2023, I filled two pages of my proposal with photos of cookie cookbook authors. I kid you not, they were all white. It's important to uplift and support diverse voices, and while we've made incredible strides, there's still a long way to go. And second, to celebrate and showcase ingredients like furu, star anise, cardamom, yuzu, and butterfly pea flower beyond their mislabeled "exotic" or "alien" tags. Instead, they are warm, familiar, and increasingly accessible. They deserve to be the star ingredients on a diverse culinary stage. Likewise, I deserve to be a star in the food world and it's time for voices like mine to shine.

In baking cookies, developing new recipes in the kitchen, and pouring my heart into my cookbooks, I've found my true calling, a destiny that began to unfold the night I created those Chips Ahoy! and creamy pork floss cookie sandwiches. Cookies had brought me solace and comfort as a child, and as an adult, baking has mended some of the wounds I've carried. I've also found it gently coaxing out my inner child and nurturing her.

I wish the same for you, that whenever you're in need of a little comfort or healing, you'll find it in baking. The whisk is your wand, and *108 Asian Cookies* your spell book. I am so honored you've welcomed us into your precious space. As we bake these sweet (and not-too-sweet) cookies together, I hope you'll find what you're looking for: be it solace, to create new memories, to celebrate victories, or just to satiate a craving. We're here for you. So, let's get ready to bake something beautiful together.

◂ I always wanted to be a writer. I think this was my 20th birthday when my friends bought me *The Complete Idiot's Guide: Getting Published.*

WHY 108 (一百零八)?

DAD always loved the number eight and I've inherited his fondness for the number. In Cantonese, the term for "eight" (八, pronounced "baat") is a homonym for the word for "fortune" (發, pronounced "faat"), making it an auspicious number.

Whenever Dad balanced his checkbook, he always made small adjustments, transferring money around so he'd always end up with the number eight. The first home he purchased in Brooklyn with my mother? Its address was 2838 West 25th Street. On weekends, Dad would wager on racehorses, and he would always pick the ones that bore the number eight. He played the lottery religiously and would always choose the numbers 8, 18, 28, and so on.

After Dad passed away in 2020, I got a tattoo. I had the number 8 etched into my left bicep. If you see it, you'll probably think of the infinity sign, a symbol of my everlasting love for my father. And as a further homage to Dad's lifelong love for the number eight, this book presents precisely 108 sweet and not-too-sweet cookies split across eight lucky chapters. 🧡

> 唔係太甜 or "not too sweet," by the way, is quite the compliment, especially in Cantonese mom- or auntie-speak, especially for sweet treats, including the salty-sweet kinds.

MSG AND COOKIES?

IF YOU'RE wondering whether monosodium glutamate (MSG) belongs in cookies, my answer is *heck yes*. I even have an entire chapter called Umami Unleashed that is dedicated to sweet and savory cookies, many of which use MSG. While MSG is as safe as common pantry staples like salt, sugar, and pepper, society has unfairly demonized and stigmatized it for decades. The root of this? Misinformation, xenophobia, and simply, racism.

In 1968, *The New England Journal of Medicine* published a letter titled "Chinese Restaurant Syndrome." This publication started a chain effect that built mistrust around MSG and Chinese cuisine. The letter speculated that MSG consumption may have caused symptoms like numbness, heart palpitations, and headaches, even though the doctor writing to the journal pointed out that he had also consumed cooking wine and salt. Then a flawed study in 1969 linked these symptoms exclusively to MSG, branding it as a toxin. It wasn't until 2020 that Merriam-Webster updated its definition of "Chinese restaurant syndrome," finally labeling it as "offensive" and "outdated." Despite this change, the enduring misconceptions had already cast a long shadow of stigma over MSG, and subsequently, Chinese and other Asian cuisines for decades.

MSG's demonization is emblematic of a broader pattern of discrimination and misunderstanding in food culture, particularly against non-Western or "foreign" cuisines. Non-Western cuisines are frequently left out of the conversation of "healthy" eating or are always seen as "cheap eats," reflecting a form of systemic racism. In America, it is common to pay $31 for a plate of pasta, but people often balk at an $18 bowl of pho. This inherently implies that Asian cuisine is inferior to Western cuisine. This also mirrors history, like when French colonizers in Vietnam pushed their European cuisine as superior, forcing the Vietnamese, like my grandparents, to learn to cook Western foods. The colonizers saw Vietnamese local dishes as dirty and subpar.

The cookbook industry historically compounds this problem. There's a notable disparity in representation, leading to homogeneity and a society that favors Western cuisines and white authors who often, mostly unintentionally, whitewash, misrepresent, appropriate, or oversimplify non-Western ingredients and cuisines. You get "bánh mì bowls" made with Thai ingredients and rice-less, fish-less "sushi." There's also a cascading effect on how the wider public perceives and accepts "foreign" foods. An ingredient like pandan is trivialized as "the vanilla of Asia," downplaying the unique characteristics of a traditional Southeast Asian ingredient while also ignoring the complex, often problematic history of vanilla cultivation involving child slavery. (Few people know the origins of vanilla in America and the ingenuity of an enslaved child named Edmond Albius, who discovered the painstaking way to hand-pollinate and proliferate vanilla flowers.)

Before I digress further, let's get back to pandan. Pandan can turn food vibrantly green and it adds a distinct floral and young coconut flavor that's very different from vanilla. Therefore, pandan is so much more than the "vanilla of Asia." This minimization of Asian ingredients seems to happen every time an ingredient goes mainstream.

Aside from ingredients, even specific dishes such as Taiwanese snowflake crisps are oversimplified and stripped of their cultural context, being labeled merely as "Asian Rice Krispies Treats."

These examples illustrate the broader trend of cultural reductionism, homogeneity, and commodification in food publishing and food media. In 2023, I watched, agape, as two well-known white chefs ridiculed fish sauce on a live taping of a television show. I was livid. All this just continues to cast Asian food and ingredients as undesirable or inferior.

When I confronted one of the chefs, his answer was, "I love fish sauce!" If this were the case, why did he compare fish sauce to "gym socks," while not making similar comments about the other pungent ingredients, like the Parmesan cheese and balsamic vinegar, on the table?

These days, my use of ingredients like fish sauce and MSG goes beyond being a trend or enhancing flavors; it's about challenging stereotypes, altering perceptions, erasing stigma, and reclaiming a narrative. I hope to dismantle outdated norms and elevate diverse, often overlooked voices and narratives in the culinary world. Through this book, I aim to break free from the conventional norms, one Asian-inspired cookie at a time. And I thank you for being here on this incredible journey with me. ❤️

HOW TO USE THIS BOOK

WHETHER you are a wizard with the whisk or just started baking cookies from scratch, you'll find (I hope!) that these recipes are approachable and adaptable, as well as fun and exciting. Of course, some recipes will be more step-packed and time-intensive than others (turn to page 377 for Cute Pineapple Tarts if you're looking for a challenge). I make note of this so there are no surprises. Each recipe also comes with a difficulty rating, as well as prep and cook times.

1–Read the recipe and practice mise en place.

Before preheating the oven or reaching for the flour, take a moment to read through the entire recipe. By first reading the recipe from start to finish, you will avoid unexpected surprises, like realizing halfway through you're missing a pan, don't have enough time to complete the dish, or have run out of brown sugar. Then, practice what the French call mise en place—getting all your ingredients gathered, measured, sifted, and chopped, and finally readying all your tools.

2–Line your baking pans and sheets.

To make your life easier, always line your baking pans and sheets with parchment paper (not wax paper). While I prefer parchment paper, reusable silicone mats work just as well.

3–Mix the dry ingredients together first. Same goes for the wet ingredients.

Unless otherwise specified, first combine all dry ingredients, including chemical leaveners like baking soda and baking powder, to ensure they're evenly dispersed. The exception is sugar, which is usually creamed with butter separately. Similarly, mix all wet ingredients together before combining them with the dry mix. This method ensures an even and quick mix for the final batter or dough, resulting in uniformly textured cookies.

4–Be flexible when it comes to the flavors, ingredients, and tools.

If you do find yourself missing a particular ingredient, I've included variations and substitutions for flexibility. I designed my cookbooks as friendly guides meant to spark your creativity. After you try one of my recipes for the first time, I encourage you to tweak it to make it your own. Since we all have different baking tools and environments (like humidity, altitude, or a hotter oven), your results might vary from mine, and that's perfectly okay. For this reason, you'll see I use the word "about" in my recipes.

5—Be precise with the measurements.

While each recipe in this book comes with measurements in both cups and grams, using a scale to measure ingredients significantly enhances the accuracy, consistency, and quality of your cookies. A cup of flour can differ in weight depending how you scoop it, or if it's packed in the measuring cup. In contrast, 100 grams of flour is always 100 grams, regardless of these variables. (Unless, of course, Earth's gravity suddenly shifts!)

6—Remember that I'm here to help guide you.

I've structured my recipes in clear, easy-to-follow steps, with each stage of the process detailed enough to help even the most novice bakers produce great cookies. With stories, pictures, and tips sprinkled throughout, you are never baking alone.

7—Store the cookies properly.

You can store most of my cookies in an airtight container at room temperature for 3 to 5 days, and up to a week in the refrigerator. Cookie dough and cookies, when properly covered, can be frozen months to a year. If you freeze baked cookies, thaw them on the counter in their storage container, then enjoy. Or you can warm them in the microwave for 10 seconds or reheat them in the toaster oven for a few minutes.

8—Ready, set, bake!

Baking with a new cookbook is always a fun journey, filled with fresh discoveries and lots of learning along the way. Not everything will pan out the first time. And that's okay. Above all, have fun creating, tasting, and sharing these 108 delicious Asian cookies with loved ones!

TOOLS AND EQUIPMENT

- Baking sheets (two or three 18 by 13-inch half-sheets)
- Bench knife or scraper
- Candy thermometer or digital thermometer
- Chopsticks
- Containers (airtight) for cookie storage
- Cookie cutters and scoopers
- Cooling racks (one or two wire racks)
- Digital scale
- Food processor or blender
- Frying pan or skillet
- Knife
- Mortar and pestle
- Measuring cups and spoons
- Mixing bowls (two or three different sizes)
- Mooncake molds
- Offset spatula
- Oven mitt
- Parchment paper (not wax paper)
- Pastry brush
- Piping bag and tips
- Rolling pin (roller)
- Rubber/silicone spatula (two)
- Sifter or sieve
- Stand mixer
- Steamer basket
- Whisk
- Wooden spoon

MY ASIAN COOKIE PANTRY ESSENTIALS

I STILL feel like a kid whenever I step into an Asian supermarket. It seems like there's always something new and trendy from Asia, from ice cream shaped like peaches and mangoes to frozen mochi bread that looks like purple sweet potatoes. Then, there are the staples I recognize from my childhood, like the soy sauce and chicken powder from Lee Kum Kee, Huy Fong's sriracha, Three Crabs' fish sauce, Ajinomoto's MSG, Koda Farm's mochiko, and Kikkoman's panko.

Once only available in large cities like Montreal, New York, and San Francisco, Asian supermarkets and grocery stores have become more widespread in the West. If perusing Asian groceries feels overwhelming, here's my tip to you: Ask a friendly Asian auntie or uncle for their recommendations. I still do this when I'm struggling to decide between different types or brands of noodles or rice paper. You also can't go wrong with a little experimentation, so be like a kid in a candy store while in an Asian supermarket.

DRY INGREDIENTS and LEAVENING AGENTS

Baker's ammonia
Due to its strong odor, the Chinese call baker's ammonia "stinky powder" or 臭粉. Most, if not all, of the stench dissipates in a hot oven. Still, only use a scant amount when you bake with baker's ammonia to make Cantonese-style cookies (like the Chinese Walnut Cookies on page 93 and Old-Fashioned Cantonese Shortbread on page 105) extra crispy and flaky, or sung faa (鬆化). You can find baker's ammonia online.

Baking powder vs. baking soda: For crispy cookies that spread, use baking soda. For puffier cookies with more volume, use baking powder. I like to use a mix of both in my cookies. Be aware that too much baking soda can leave a bitter, metallic aftertaste.

Custard powder
A light-yellow powder popularly used in many East Asian desserts, this ingredient is shelf stable and adds creamy, eggy flavor.

Glutinous rice flour
Not to be confused with rice flour, this gluten-free flour is made from ground sticky rice (mochigome). When mixed with liquid and cooked, the resulting texture is gummy and glue-like, hence, "glutinous." Glutinous rice flour is a must for making mochi and desserts with a mochi texture, like mochi brownies.

Panko
Crispy, crustless milk bread breadcrumbs from Japan, panko can be mixed into cookie batter or used as a topping to add crunchiness. Kikkoman produces a gluten-free version.

Rice flour
Made from finely ground long- or medium-grain rice, rice flour can be used as a gluten-free substitute for wheat flour. While you can use rice flour as a thickener, you will never achieve the mochi consistency or texture you get with glutinous rice flour.

Sago
A gluten-free starch made from the spongy pith of palm stems, sago is usually found as a powder, pearl, or flour.

Tapioca flour (or starch)
Commonly used to make boba and other chewy goodies, tapioca flour is gluten-free and made from cassava root. It can be somewhat tricky to work with: when you add too much liquid it can become a Newtonian fluid, or something that looks like it came out of a horror movie (like *The Blob*).

FATS

Butter
Throughout this book, we'll use unsalted butter unless otherwise indicated. I prefer baking with high-fat European-style butter, like Plugrà.

Lard
Commonly used before butter became accessible, it makes baked goods tender and flaky. You should be able to buy rendered lard in the supermarket or from local butchers.

Margarine
Usually made from plant or vegetable fats, margarine is commonly used in Asian baking, especially as a spread or filling for desserts.

Neutral cooking oils
These include canola, vegetable, corn, and safflower oils. Unlike sesame oil and extra-virgin olive oil, neutral oils impart little to no flavor.

CHAOKOH
COCONUT MILK
ชาวเกาะ
ese Five Spice
PACKED ON
Mar 19, 2024
WORLD SPICE
der
PACKED ON
Mar 19, 2024
WORLD SPICE
良友牌
葉荔枝
MABUHAY
UBE HALAYA
(Sweet Purple Yam Jam)
GLUTINOUS RIC
水磨白糯米
FARINE DE RIZ GL
BỘT NẾP TỈNH K
LORANN
AMMONIUM CARBONATE
Baker's Ammonia
CARBONATE D'AMMONIUM
Ammoniaque du boulanger
AmeriColor
120
SUPER RED
ARMOUR
LARD
BHA, PROPYL GALLATE AND CITRIC ACID ADDED TO PROTECT FLAVOR
NET WT 16 OZ (1 LB) 454 g

ALL NATURAL
YUZU EXTRACT
KODA FARMS
A Family Legacy in California Farming Since 1928
Gluten-Free
Sweet Rice
もちこ
자연나라
꿀유자차
Honey
Yuzu Tea
Nestle
MILO
Pocky
CHOCOLATE
CHOCOLATE CREAM COVERED BISCUIT STICKS
Share happiness! Pocky
Glico
Nutrition Facts

FRUITS, VEGETABLES, and HERBS

Calamansi
Green when young and orange when ripe, calamansi has notes of mandarin orange and lime and subtly bitter undertones.

Curry leaves
Native to India, curry leaves are aromatic, citrusy, and a little spicy with notes of star anise. I love frying curry leaves or drying them to add to snacks and savory bakes, like my Salted-Egg-Yolk Cornflake Haystacks (page 348).

Durian
My favorite fruit, period. From Southeast Asia, durian is fragrant, creamy, and rich, like nature's ice cream. If you can get past the aroma, you'll be a forever fan, like me.

Haw flakes
I ate these as a child. They're thin, disc-shaped candies made from sweet and tangy hawthorn berries. You can find them in many Chinese supermarkets, especially during Lunar New Year time, as they are popularly given to children during the holidays.

Lychee
Native to China, this juicy, fleshy fruit (with a large seed in the middle) tastes a little like grapes, pears, and rose. In the US, Hawaiian farmers are the predominant growers of lychee.

Pandan
A fragrant and aromatic leaf found in Southeast Asia, pandan imparts sweet, young coconut, and vanilla notes. You can usually find leaves in the frozen aisle or look for extracts in an Asian supermarket.

Sakura
Japanese for cherry blossom, sakura is the pink flower of cherry trees, commonly used in making desserts and drinks in Japan. You can find sakura online in powder, pickled (petals and stem), or dried petal forms.

Taro
A little nutty, with earthy and chestnut notes, taro, a starchy root vegetable, becomes lightly purple and gray when cooked and is delicious when made into lattes, cookies, fillings, and frostings.

Thai basil
Native to Southeast Asia and with reddish-purplish stems and dark green leaves, Thai basil has peppery-tasting notes of anise and licorice. It retains more flavor than Italian basil after cooking and baking. Thai basil really shines in my Chocolate Sandwich Cookies with Thai Basil (page 67).

Ube
The heirloom produce of the Philippines, ube is a purple yam that has subtle vanilla and nutty notes. Fresh ube is hard to find, even in the Philippines, and you'll probably only be able to access ube in extract, powder, frozen, or halaya (jam) forms in the West. Note that ube extract has food coloring that will turn your treats a vibrant, striking purple. You can find ube halaya in Asian supermarkets or online. My cookbook *Modern Asian Baking at Home* has a great ube halaya recipe.

Yuzu
Floral and aromatic, this citrus fruit blends lemon, tangerine, and grapefruit notes and is common in Japanese cuisine. You won't find fresh yuzu in American supermarkets due to import laws, but you can find yuzu extract and juice to incorporate into your baking and cooking.

NUTS and SEEDS

Black sesame paste
A strikingly black, rich, velvety spread usually made from ground black sesame seeds, sugar, and sometimes a touch of oil.

Nuts
I like to use a mix of nuts such as cashews, peanuts, walnuts, almonds, pecans, and pistachios to make my cookies. Feel free to use your favorite nuts.

Sesame seeds
Packed with nutty flavor, these crunchy seeds come in white or black. Toast or dry-roast them for more flavor.

Tahini
A staple in Middle Eastern and Asian cuisines, tahini is a creamy, rich, nutty paste made from ground white sesame seeds.

SAVORY SEASONINGS

Chicken powder (or bouillion): Made from dehydrated chicken stock, salt, and other flavor enhancers like MSG, this seasoning has been a staple in my household for decades. The vegan alternative is mushroom powder.

Doenjang
This Korean fermented soybean paste is brackish and chunky, and like miso, can be used as an umami booster in cookies and desserts.

Fish sauce
After using fish sauce to make glaze and caramels, I'm a strong believer that this umami bomb belongs as much in desserts as it does in pho broth and dipping sauces. Quite pungent, it's made from fermenting fish or krill with salt.

Furikake
A Japanese seasoning blend that reminds me of crunchy sweet and salty sprinkles, furikake tastes amazing as a dessert mix-in or topping. Some blends are vegan, while others may include salmon and bonito flakes. Try a sprinkle over popcorn, or swap out sea salt flakes with furikake when garnishing cookies.

Furu (fermented bean curd): Salty, subtly sweet, pungent, and soft, furu is fermented bean curd. Growing up in Hong Kong, my mother had no access to cheese, so she would pretend furu was the cheese she so yearned to eat. I love using it in my marinades and stir-fry sauces, and now as the salt component in my desserts. If you find red furu, it's actually nam yu, and the redness is due to red yeast rice added during the fermentation process.

Hoisin sauce
Fragrant, sweet, and umami-laden, hoisin sauce can bring flavor and balance to very sweet glazes or frosting.

Miso
A smooth, fermented soybean paste from Japan, miso adds a pleasant salinity. If you're gluten sensitive, look at the labels because not all store-bought miso is gluten-free.

Monosodium glutamate (MSG): A naturally occurring food additive, a dash of MSG can bring out salty and umami notes in your savory-sweet desserts.

Salted duck egg yolks
Savory and full of umami, salted duck egg yolks can be grated over cookies, incorporated into fillings, and used as fillings themselves. You can find whole salted duck eggs and ones packed in salted charcoal, but I usually only buy the vacuum-pack sealed precooked salted duck yolks.

Soy sauce
Some soy sauces, like kecap manis from Indonesia, are sweeter than others. For the recipes in this book, use the all-purpose or light soy sauce you normally use to cook with or to make dumpling dipping sauces, like a bottle of Kikkoman or Lee Kum Kee. You can also swap soy sauce one-to-one with tamari.

SPICY SEASONINGS and CONDIMENTS

Chili crisp (aka chili crunch): A versatile spicy condiment made from hot oil, spices, aromatics, chilis, and crispy shallots (or garlic or onion), chili crisp tastes amazing when drizzled over ice cream, mixed with chocolate, or incorporated into desserts.

Doubanjiang
Spicy, umami-rich, and salty, this paste made from fermented broad beans, chilis, and soybeans is a Sichuan staple and commonly used to make mapo tofu.

Gochugaru
Korean red pepper flakes that also come in powdered form, gochugaru adds a vibrant redness, gentle heat, and subtle sweetness, making them perfect for dusting over or incorporating into cookies and other baked goods. You can also dust spicy desserts with gochugaru, like I do with my recipe for Chocolate Mochi Bars with Sambal Oelek (195).

Gochujang
A Korean fermented chili paste, gochujang has notes of sweetness and caramel, along with potent heat and umami. Gochujang adds rich depth to desserts, especially chocolate ones.

Laksa paste
You can find jars of laksa paste, a concentrated blend of shrimp paste, garlic, lemongrass,

S&B
ORIENTAL
CURRY
白味噌
WHITE TYPE
李錦記
LEE KUM KEE
鮮味生抽
SOY SAUCE
香辣脆
油辣椒
LAOGANMA
SPICY CHILI CRISP
NET WT:7.41OZ(210G)
KADOYA
純淨上等
PRODUCT OF JAPAN
11 FL.OZ
(327ml)
HOT CHILI SAUCE
No.1
해찬들
GOCHUJANG
HOT PEPPER PASTE
골드
고추장

turmeric, and other spices in Asian supermarkets.

Sambal oelek
The Vietnamese lady in me says you can never have enough spicy condiments at home, and you should definitely not skip stocking up on sambal oelek, a flavorful raw Indonesian chili paste made from crushed chili peppers, salt, and vinegar. A little goes a long way in cookies and desserts.

Sriracha
A bright red chili sauce from Thailand, sriracha has complex flavors, making it the perfect condiment to mix with chocolate or add to cookie dough, frosting, or even whipped cream to add heat.

Thai chili sauce
Garlicky, tangy, packing a little heat, and predominantly sweet, Thai chili sauce is a popular Southeast Asian dipping sauce. Try using it as a glaze or to add heat to icing or frosting.

Wasabi
You're probably thinking about sushi now. A paste made from grated Japanese horseradish, wasabi doesn't numb the tongue or taste like hot sauce; instead, it clears the sinuses with a shocking sensation that goes away as quickly as it comes.

SPICES

Cardamom
This aromatic Indian spice has notes of mint and citrus. It adds an unforgettable depth and warmth to desserts. We'll mostly be using ground cardamom versus the whole green or black pods.

Five spice
A spice blend usually made of ground star anise, cloves, cinnamon, fennel seeds, and a fifth spice, like Sichuan peppercorns, five spice originated in China and represents the five fundamental flavors: sweet, bitter, sour, salty, and savory. The aromatic blend adds a warm, complex, and distinctive flavor to baked goods.

Garam masala
A blend of ground spices used in Indian cuisine, garam masala typically includes cinnamon, cardamom, cloves, cumin, and coriander.

Vietnamese cinnamon
Bold, sweet-spicy, and warm, Vietnamese cinnamon is a cassia cinnamon and is stronger than Ceylon cinnamon, which is sweeter and brighter.

SWEETENERS

Gula aren (palm sugar)
Made from palm tree sap, this sweetener is an essential ingredient in many dishes and desserts across Southeast Asia.

Sweetened condensed milk: Usually made from cooking down milk or coconut milk with sugar, this thick sweetener is creamy and rich. For the recipes in this book, you can use the vegan and dairy versions interchangeably.

TEA POWDERS

Hojicha
A roasted green tea from Japan, hojicha is toasty with light caramel notes, lending warmth and depth to lattes and baked goods. It is one of my favorite teas, after Earl Grey.

Matcha
The Japanese grind dried young green tea leaves into a fine vibrant green powder that is rich, nutty, and earthy in flavor. You can use matcha to make cookies, frosting, cakes, and glazes. Honestly, there are few desserts that matcha can't be a part of.

Milk tea powder
Boba tea made milk tea powder popular across East Asia and Asian diasporas. Usually, the powder comes sweetened and can be mixed with hot water or milk to make instant milk tea.

Thai tea
Made from a blend of black tea and star anise, Thai tea is warmly spiced and rich. You can find Thai tea mixes in Asian grocery stores or online, and order iced Thai tea in many Asian restaurants and cafes.

RECIPE NOTES

Unless otherwise specified:

All eggs are large (about 2 ounces, or 50 grams, each).	Always sift your dry ingredients, such as flour, confectioners' sugar, and larger amounts of cornstarch, milk powder, or cocoa powder, before using.
All dairy milk, cream cheese, Greek yogurt, and crème fraîche are whole or full fat.	Instead of vanilla extract, I use Japanese whisky, bourbon, or rum. If you can't use alcohol, or don't like the flavor, it is okay to omit it.
All butter is unsalted (unless otherwise noted). I prefer European-style butters with 82% butterfat.	Leave your butter out on the counter for 20 to 30 minutes before creaming it. This way, it will come to room temperature and soften to the right consistency for creaming. If your kitchen runs warm, the butter will soften quicker.
All salt, other than sea salt flakes, is non-iodized kosher or table salt (e.g., Morton).	For consistency and accuracy, all ingredients in the recipes, including liquids, are measured in grams using a digital scale. I recommend following the weight measurements, as they are more precise than their approximate volumetric conversions. When no quantity is specified, quantities are flexible and discretionary to your taste.
All food coloring is gel.	For perfectly round cookies, immediately after baking, place a round cookie cutter or biscuit cutter slightly larger than the cookie over it and gently move it in circular motions to shape the edges while the cookie is still warm.
When I bake and cook, I mainly use red miso. For baking, white is okay too. If you don't have miso, swap it out with a pinch of kosher salt instead.	**→ ADDITIONALLY . . .** **A Note About Chinese Characters** Because I am Chinese and fluent in Cantonese, I've included Chinese characters in the titles of the Chinese dishes I grew up eating, but I didn't do the same for the Korean and Japanese recipes, as I don't have the same personal cultural or linguistic connection to those cuisines.

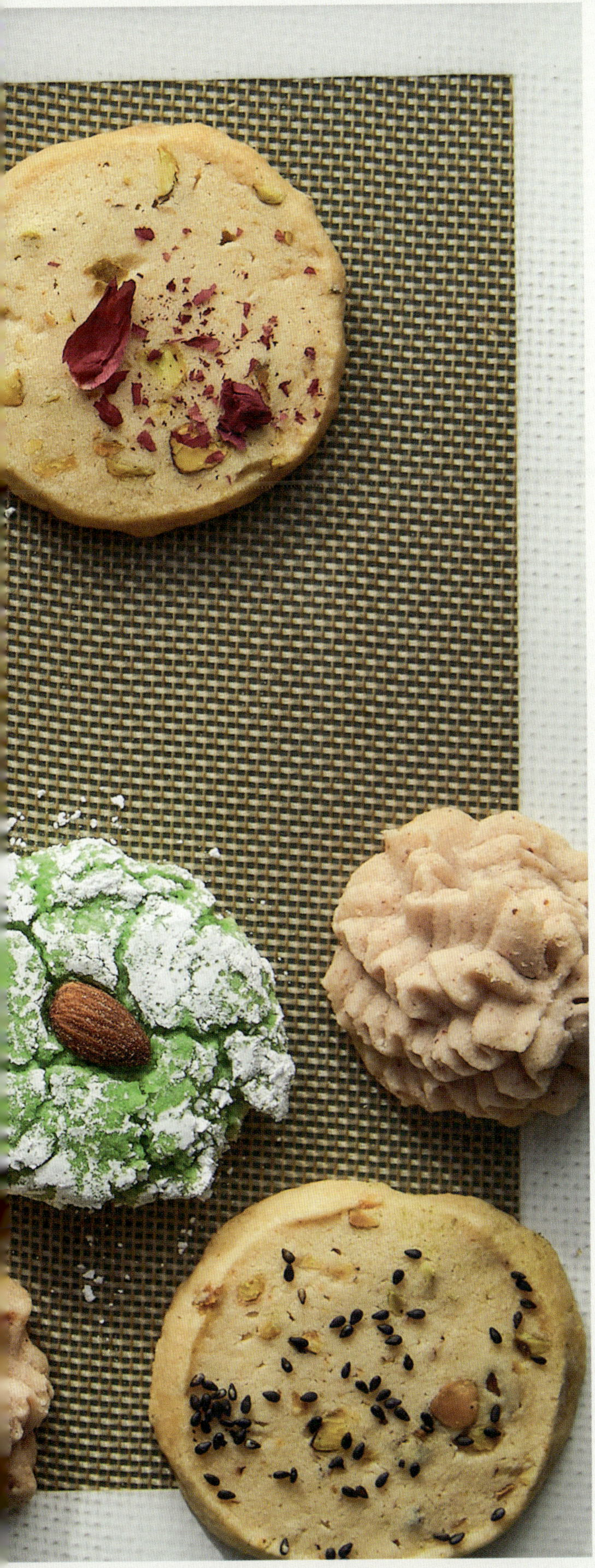

1

COOKIE BOX ESSENTIALS

Essential and everyday cookie recipes, perfect for a cookie box worth gifting.

When I dreamed up this chapter, I imagined a cookie box filled with some of the best cookies the world has to offer, all with Asian twists and spins, some subtle and others bold. For example, you'll use ube halaya, a Filipino jam and staple, to make Ube Linzer Cookies (page 52). You'll add Thai basil, a popular Southeast Asian herb usually added to pho or other noodle soups, to Chocolate Sandwich Cookies (page 67) to give them a different kind of minty spin.

Each cookie here is familiar, yet surprising. You'll find crunchy white mulberries, which are native to China, in my Oatmeal Cookies (page 79). Five spice powder is the star of my Snickerdoodles (page 73). As you explore these recipes, you'll discover how miso is a key ingredient in many of my cookies, replacing salt to add balance and temper sweetness.

The cookies in this chapter are also not too complicated to make. While baking is a science, it's meant to be fun and as stress-free as possible. Make one or two of the recipes when you have a craving or explore a few to build a cookie box. My goal here is that when you do build that box, the person you gift the cookies to will greet it with eyes full of wonder. Everyone will have warm and fuzzy feelings. Oh, and you might not hear it, but their inner child will be squealing with delight.

COWBOY COOKIES, BUT ASIAN

Makes
about 21 large cookies

Prep Time
15 minutes

Inactive Time
At least 1 hour

Cook Time
16 to 17 minutes

Difficulty
★★☆☆☆
(It's a relatively forgiving cookie.)

- 1 cup (120 g) all-purpose flour
- 1 teaspoon baking powder
- 1 teaspoon baking soda
- 1 teaspoon ground cardamom
- 1 teaspoon ground ginger (optional)
- ½ cup | 1 stick (113 g) unsalted butter, softened
- ½ cup (100 g) granulated sugar
- ½ cup (110 g) packed brown sugar
- 1 tablespoon red miso
- 1 large egg
- 1 cup (170 g) semisweet or dark chocolate chips
- 1 cup (about 100 g) broken Pocky sticks
- ⅔ cup (75 g) toasted walnuts, chopped
- ⅔ cup (50 to 55 g) sweetened or unsweetened coconut flakes
- Sea salt flakes, for topping

Think of a cowboy. He's probably wearing a wide-brimmed hat, jeans, and boots, walking into a saloon and asking for a whiskey with a drawl. But no matter what you pictured him wearing or doing, you probably didn't envision him as an Asian dude. For much of my childhood, I didn't either. Leafing through American history textbooks at school, I never saw vivid portrayals of the diverse cultures that shaped the Old West. But I later learned that Asians, including Chinese migrants and laborers, were instrumental in building the Transcontinental Railroad. There were, in fact, Asian cowboys. Even today, you can find Asian American cowboys in the Midwest.

I dedicate these cookies to the unsung heroes who played a key role in the United States' westward expansion. According to legend, cowboy cookies sustained the cowboys of the Old West. To give the oat- and pecan-packed treats an Asian spin, I include aromatic cardamom and ground ginger to add fragrant depth. Miso replaces salt, bringing subtle umami. The choice of walnuts, a major Chinese export, is a departure from the traditional pecans. I like to imagine these big and chewy cookies might have comforted the forgotten migrants and laborers. This recipe is my small way of celebrating Chinese railroad workers and Asian cowboys. (Pictured on page 37.)

1. Whisk the flour, baking powder, baking soda, cardamom, and ground ginger, if using, together in a medium bowl. Set aside.

2. Using a stand mixer fitted with the paddle attachment (or in a large bowl with a hand mixer, whisk, or spatula), cream the butter, sugars, and miso together until light and fluffy. Scrape down the sides and bottom of the bowl. Add the egg and mix until well incorporated. Add the flour mixture and mix on low speed just until a cookie dough forms. Fold in the chocolate chips, broken Pocky sticks, walnuts, and coconut flakes. Cover the dough with plastic wrap and refrigerate for at least 1 hour, or overnight.

Cookie Tip
Dry-roast or toast the walnuts first in a frying pan for more flavor.

Variation
Instead of the crushed Pocky sticks, use 1 cup crushed hard pretzels or old-fashioned rolled oats.

Storage
Store the cookies in an airtight container at room temperature for up to 3 days.

3. About 25 minutes before baking, adjust two racks to the upper- and lower-middle positions of the oven. Preheat the oven to 350°F. Line two baking sheets with parchment paper.

4. Scoop about 3 tablespoons (or up to ¼ cup) of dough per cookie and shape roughly into a ball, making about 21 balls. Place on the prepared baking sheet, spacing at least 2 inches apart.

5. Bake all the cookies, switching the sheets between the top to bottom racks and rotating front to back once halfway through, until the cookie edges begin to brown, 16 to 17 minutes.

6. Let the cookies set for 5 minutes on the baking sheet, then transfer to a wire rack to cool completely. Finish with a sprinkle of sea salt flakes.

BEST CHOCOLATE CHIP COOKIES EVER

Makes
about
24 cookies

Prep Time
15 minutes

Inactive Time
30 minutes

Cook Time
10 to 12 minutes

Difficulty
★★☆☆☆
(The hardest part is putting these down!)

- 1 cup (120 g) all-purpose flour
- ¼ cup (35 g) Milo or Ovaltine chocolate malt mix
- ½ teaspoon cream of tartar
- ½ teaspoon baking powder
- ¼ teaspoon baking soda
- 6 tablespoons (85 g) unsalted butter, softened
- ⅓ cup (71 g) packed dark brown sugar
- ⅓ cup plus 1 tablespoon (76 g) granulated sugar
- 1 tablespoon molasses or honey
- 1½ teaspoons red miso
- 1 large egg
- 1½ cups (255 g) semisweet chocolate chips
- Sea salt flakes (optional)

My son, Philip, has declared these to be my best cookies ever. They're his absolute favorite. During one taste test, he channeled his inner food critic mid-bite and said, "You need to put this recipe in your cookbook so other people can try it, Mom." Philip didn't have to tell me twice. It is, after all, unthinkable to write a whole cookie book without a standout chocolate chip cookie recipe.

While I dedicate this recipe to my son, these cookies are an homage to members of the Asian diasporas who, like me, grew up on the rich, malty goodness of Milo or Ovaltine. During the wintertime, my mom always ordered those hot drinks for me. I wanted to maintain this tradition with Philip, but even when it's cold, he only wants boba tea! So, these cookies are my way of sneaking the flavors of my childhood into his favorite treat.

Thus, these really are my best chocolate chip cookies ever, not just because my son loves them, but also because they have everything I adore in one bite. The middles are melty. There's umami from miso and a subtle tang from vinegar that slices through all the sweetness. You'll find these rich, layered cookies not only live up to my child's high praise but can delight almost every palate.

1. Line two baking sheets with parchment paper.

2. Whisk the flour, Milo or Ovaltine, cream of tartar, baking powder, and baking soda together in a medium bowl. Set aside.

3. Using a stand mixer fitted with the paddle attachment (or in a large bowl with a hand mixer, whisk, or spatula), cream the butter, sugars, molasses or honey, and miso together until light and fluffy. Scrape down the sides and bottom of the bowl. Add the egg and mix until well incorporated. Add the flour mixture and mix on low speed just until a cookie dough forms. Fold in the chocolate chips.

RECIPE *continues* →

BEST CHOCOLATE CHIP COOKIES EVER, *continued*

Cookie Tip
Do not overbake these cookies; they set quickly once out of the oven.

Substitutions
Swap out the Milo or Ovaltine for cocoa powder or Horlicks (a malted milk powder) one-to-one.

Storage
Store the cookies in an airtight container for up to 2 days.

4. Transfer the dough by the tablespoonful onto the prepared baking sheets, spacing them about 3 inches apart, and making about 24 cookies. These cookies like to spread, so chill in the refrigerator for 30 minutes.

5. While the dough is chilling, adjust two racks to the upper- and lower-middle positions of the oven. Preheat the oven to 375°F.

6. Bake all the cookies, switching the sheets between the top to bottom racks and rotating front to back once halfway through, until the edges are golden brown, 10 to 12 minutes.

7. Allow the cookies to set on the baking sheet for about 5 minutes, then transfer to a wire rack: You can let them cool completely, although these cookies are best when warm and the insides are gooey.

BUTTER FLOWER COOKIES

Makes
18 to 24 cookies, depending on how big you pipe them.

Prep Time
20 minutes

Inactive Time
About 30 minutes

Cook Time
About 25 minutes

Difficulty
★★★½☆
(The hardest part is piping the cookies.)

- 1 cup (120 g) cake flour
- About ½ cup (65 g) bread flour
- About ½ cup (65 g) cornstarch
- ½ teaspoon baking soda
- ½ teaspoon baking powder
- 2 tablespoons freeze-dried strawberry powder (optional)
- About ⅔ cup | 1⅓ sticks (150 g) unsalted butter, softened
- About ¼ cup (50 g) lard
- ½ cup (57 g) confectioners' sugar
- 3 tablespoons (45 g) heavy cream
- 1 teaspoon miso (red or white)

Established in 2005, Jenny Bakery quickly became an iconic Hong Kong landmark, known for its ridiculously long queues, famously terrible customer service (that's the Cantonese way!), and delicious, worth-the-wait cookies—especially Butter Flower Cookies. These cookies have not only captivated locals and tourists alike, but have even fueled bootleg Jenny Bakery shops, cookie hawking, and a cookie "black market" across Hong Kong and Shenzhen.

Whenever friends or family visit Hong Kong, they never fail to return with a cartoon-bear-adorned tin of Butter Flower Cookies from Jenny Bakery. My mom, who is from Hong Kong, treasures these cookies, which inspired me to re-create their acclaimed, buttery, melt-in-your-mouth magic. (I may be in my 40s, but I still live to please my mother!) Jenny Bakery offers three flavors: original, coffee, and chocolate. Here, I've added personal flair by infusing the dough with freeze-dried strawberry powder for a subtle pink blush color (my favorite).

Tuck these in an elegant cookie jar or tin that reflects the spirit of Jenny Bakery's revered originals, perfect for gifting to loved ones. Or, of course, you could also always keep them for yourself.

Cookie Tip
If you can't find strawberry powder, pulse about a cup of freeze-dried strawberries in a food processor until a fine, dusty powder forms. You can also use a mortar and pestle. Store any extra powder you have in an airtight container as long as it remains dry or for up to one week.

Variations and Substitutions
For the strawberry powder, you can swap in matcha, black sesame powder, or cocoa powder for different flavors. If you don't have lard handy, substitute an additional 4 tablespoons (50g) unsalted butter.

Storage
Store the cookies in an airtight container at room temperature for up to 3 days.

1. Line two baking sheets with parchment paper.
2. Whisk the cake flour, bread flour, cornstarch, baking soda, baking powder, and strawberry powder, if using, together in a medium bowl. Set aside.
3. Using a stand mixer fitted with the paddle attachment (or in a large bowl with a hand mixer, whisk, or spatula), cream the butter, lard, sugar, cream, and miso together until smooth and well incorporated. Scrape down the sides of the bowl as needed. Add the flour mixture and mix on low speed until a smooth dough forms.

RECIPE *continues* →

4. Transfer the dough to a lightly floured work surface and knead with your warm hands until pliable and smooth. This step helps soften the dough, making it easier to pipe later. Divide the dough into two equal portions.

5. Fit a piping bag with a ½-inch Ateco or Wilton closed star tip and fill with half of the dough.

6. Hold the bag vertically about 2 inches above one baking sheet and pipe the dough into 1½-inch wide and tall cookies, using a wavy motion for height. If the dough is too stiff to pipe, warm it in your hands—or use a cookie press for easier handling. Repeat with the remaining dough, spacing the cookies an inch apart on the sheets. Chill in the freezer, uncovered, for at least 30 minutes.

7. About 25 minutes before baking, adjust two racks to the upper- and lower-middle positions of the oven. Preheat the oven to 300°F.

8. Bake all the cookies, switching the sheets between the top and bottom racks and rotating front to back once halfway through, until the bottoms and the edges of the cookies turn golden brown, about 25 minutes. Remove from the oven (and note, it's natural for the cookies to spread and deflate). Allow the cookies to set on the baking sheets for 5 minutes, then cool completely on a wire rack.

SIMPLE SHORTBREAD WITH MISO

Makes	**Prep Time**	**Cook Time**	**Difficulty**
about 32 cookies	10 minutes **Inactive Time** About 30 minutes	30 to 35 minutes	★☆☆☆☆ (A good beginner cookie to try.)

- 1 cup (226 g) unsalted butter or ¾ cup (about 170 g) vegan butter
- ⅔ cup (135 g) granulated sugar
- 1 tablespoon miso (red or white)
- 2 cups (240 g) all-purpose flour
- 1 tablespoon yuzu or calamansi juice (optional, to add subtle citrus flavor)
- ½ cup (60 g) roasted, unsalted pistachios (or any other nuts of your choice), chopped or pulsed (optional)
- Granulated or turbinado sugar for sprinkling (optional)

To me, shortbread is the ideal cookie canvas. It's beautifully simple in composition, and all you need to start are three foundational ingredients: fat, sugar, and flour. Some people will subsequently add salt and eggs (or at least the yolks), but let's just Keep It Simple, Silly (KISS). As a novice physical therapist, I remember one of my managers telling me to KISS whenever I explain new exercises to my patients. Keeping things simple these days translates to what I do in my kitchen. For this simple shortbread, however, miso replaces the salt for a subtly Asian twist on the classic cookie. Miso's umami also serves to balance the shortbread's sweetness. For a pop of color and added texture, let's toss in chopped pistachios, which resemble little jade fragments.

Once you've mastered the basic shortbread, you can make almost any variation. Introducing mix-ins can diversify the flavor, texture, and appearance of your shortbread cookies. Honestly, I could make 107 other cookies using this base recipe and call it a day, but Vivian, my editor, would have a heart attack, LOL.

1. Using a stand mixer fitted with the paddle attachment (or in a large bowl with a hand mixer, whisk, or spatula), cream the butter, sugar, and miso together until light and fluffy, about 2 minutes. Scrape down the sides and bottom of the bowl.
2. Add the flour and yuzu or calamansi juice (if using). Mix on low speed just until the mixture starts to form large crumbs and clumps. If you like, fold in the chopped pistachios or other nuts.
3. **For cookie rounds**, divide the dough into two equal portions and shape each into a log about 8 inches long and 1½ inches in diameter. Use your hands to more firmly press the dough into log shape if it's too crumbly.
4. Cover the dough with plastic wrap and refrigerate for at least 30 minutes.

RECIPE *continues* →

SIMPLE SHORTBREAD WITH MISO, *continued*

5. About 20 minutes before baking, adjust a rack to the middle position and preheat the oven to 300°F.

6. Line two baking sheets with parchment paper. Slice the chilled dough logs into slices approximately ¼ inch thick. Place on the prepared baking sheets, leaving about 1 inch between each cookie.

7. Bake the shortbread (one sheet at a time for the cookie rounds) until golden brown around the edges, 30 to 35 minutes. Halfway through, rotate the baking sheet or baking pan for even baking.

8. Transfer the cookies to a wire rack to cool completely. If you like, sprinkle the cookies with some sugar while still warm.

Variations
To change the base flavor of the cookie, substitute 2 tablespoons of the flour with 2 tablespoons of any of the following food powders: butterfly pea flour, black sesame, cocoa, matcha, or any other food powder of your choice, really. With butterfly pea flower, you'll get a subtly blue and nutty-flavored cookie, and it tastes beautiful with the touch of citrus. For rectangular shortbread cookies, line a 9-inch square cake pan with parchment paper and press the dough evenly into the pan. Score the top to indicate your desired cookie sizes. Optionally, you can also use the tines of a fork to prick even rows of holes into the top of the shortbread dough, but this is solely for aesthetic reasons. After baking, transfer to a cutting board and allow to cool for 10 minutes. Then slice along the scored lines for clean cuts.

Storage
Store the cookies in an airtight container at room temperature for up to 5 days.

MATCHA, MACADAMIA NUT, AND WHITE CHOCOLATE MONSTERS

Makes
about 8 large cookies

Prep Time
About 10 minutes

Inactive Time
About 15 minutes

Cook Time
About 32 minutes

Difficulty
★★½☆☆
(Not very difficult, but the dough is a bit chunky.)

- 1½ cups (180 g) all-purpose flour
- 1½ cups (180 g) cake flour
- 1 teaspoon baking powder
- 1 tablespoon culinary-grade matcha, or to taste
- 1 cup | 2 sticks (226 g) unsalted butter, softened
- About ¾ cup (170 g) packed brown sugar
- About ¼ cup (50 g) granulated sugar
- 1 tablespoon red miso
- 2 large eggs
- 1 cup (170 g) white chocolate chips
- 1 cup (170 g) semisweet chocolate chips
- ½ cup (65 g) chopped macadamia nuts

I've always regretted moving away from New York City before trying Levain Bakery's famous gargantuan cookies. Their rise to fame was the first time I realized just how significant baking can be—how a single cookie could make someone, or a brand, famous.

While not exactly a copycat recipe, these cookies are inspired by Levain's iconic chunky style. I aptly named these chonky cookies "monsters," a nod to both their size and bold flavors. Matcha, with its distinct earthy notes and subtle umami, complements the sharp sweetness of white chocolate, while the macadamia nuts add a satisfying crunch.

1. Adjust a rack to the middle position and preheat the oven to 400°F. Line two baking sheets with parchment paper.

2. Whisk the all-purpose flour, cake flour, baking powder, and matcha together in a medium bowl. Set aside.

3. Using a stand mixer fitted with the paddle attachment (or in a large bowl with a hand mixer, whisk, or spatula), cream the butter, sugars, and miso together until light and fluffy, about 2 minutes. Scrape down the sides and bottom of the bowl. Add the eggs and mix until well incorporated. Add the flour mixture and mix on low speed just until a cohesive dough forms. Fold in the white and semisweet chocolate chips and the nuts.

4. These are gargantuan cookies, so use a scoop or tablespoon to form eight balls of dough, about ¼ cup each. Place the balls on the baking sheets, leaving about 2 inches between each. Chill in the freezer, uncovered, for 15 minutes.

RECIPE *continues* →

Cookie Tip
If you worry these cookies will be underbaked since they are so thick, you can flatten them a little with your hands before baking.

Variation
Substitute 1 teaspoon pandan extract for the matcha. Pandan goes perfectly with white chocolate and will also make the cookies green.

Storage
Store the cookies in an airtight container at room temperature for up to 3 days.

5. Bake one sheet at a time until the tops are golden, and the edges are golden brown, about 16 minutes. As these are thick, chunky cookies, allow them to set and cool directly on the baking sheet, which takes about 15 minutes.

UBE LINZER COOKIES

Makes about 30 individual cookies, or 15 sandwich cookies, when assembled

Prep Time 25 minutes

Inactive Time 1 hour or longer

Cook Time 12 to 15 minutes

Difficulty: ★★★★☆ (Multiple rolling and chilling stages and assembly required.)

1 ¼ cups (150 g) all-purpose flour

½ cup (48 g) almond flour

½ cup |1 stick (113 g) unsalted butter, softened

½ cup (57 g) confectioners' sugar

1 teaspoon red miso

1 large egg yolk

1 tablespoon calamansi, yuzu, or lemon juice, plus optional grated zest for garnish

About ⅓ cup (90 g) ube halaya (jam)

Confectioners' sugar, for dusting (optional)

Linzer cookies are Old World treats from Linz, Austria. Growing up, my younger sister Evelyn and I would only enjoy these cookies during American holiday parties, be it at the Christmas party at the company my father toiled for, or at his only white American friend's house. Linzer cookies have always been a beloved holiday staple, but they often go unnoticed and overlooked, like a wallflower, or like me throughout my childhood.

It was time to give these traditional cookies a makeover, so they shine all year long: creamy, custardy ube halaya sits inside the heart of these cookies, a far cry from the typical syrupy fruit fillings. Feel free to get creative with the shapes and peekaboo cutouts. Whether you opt for classic circles, fluted rounds, festive stars, or playful hearts, each shape can add appeal to these already delightful treats, a beautiful fusion of East and West. Hopefully, these ube Linzer cookies will be a new favorite in your baking repertoire, not just during the holidays but for all seasons. They won't go unnoticed or overlooked.

1. Whisk the all-purpose flour and almond flour together in a medium bowl. Set aside.

2. In a stand mixer fitted with the paddle attachment (or in a large bowl with a hand mixer), cream the butter, confectioners' sugar, and miso together until light and fluffy. Scrape down the sides and bottom of the bowl. Add the egg yolk and citrus juice, then mix until well incorporated. Add the flour mixture and mix on low speed just until a dough forms.

3. Divide the dough in half and shape each into a disc about 1 inch thick. Wrap each disc in plastic wrap and chill in the refrigerator for at least 1 hour.

4. Line two baking sheets with parchment paper. Adjust a rack to the middle position and preheat the oven to 350°F.

RECIPE *continues* →

UBE LINZER COOKIES, *continued*

Cookie Tip
You'll benefit from having a Linzer cookie cutter set, but you can also use other cookie cutters and piping tips for this recipe.

Variation
After creaming the butter, add about 1½ teaspoons ube extract to add more ube flavor and turn the cookies purple, as pictured.

Storage
Store the assembled cookies in an airtight container at room temperature for up to 2 days.

5. On a lightly floured surface, or between two sheets of parchment paper, roll out each chilled dough disc to about ⅛ inch thick. Using a 2½-inch round or fluted round cookie cutter, cut out rounds. Gather the scraps, re-roll, and continue cutting until all the dough is used to make 30 to 32 rounds. Place 15 or 16 cookies on each of the prepared baking sheets. If the dough becomes sticky, refrigerate again for about 20 minutes before continuing.

6. Refrigerate half of the cookies for 30 minutes. Meanwhile, cut peekaboo shapes in the center of the remaining cookies using a smaller cutter or the end of a piping tip. Refrigerate these as well. (As for the cutout shapes, you can gather them to re-roll, or reserve to bake bite-sized sandwich cookies.)

7. Bake the cookies, one sheet at a time (while the other sheet chills in the fridge), until the edges begin to brown, 12 to 15 minutes. Let the cookies set on the baking sheet for a few minutes, then transfer to a wire rack to cool completely.

8. To assemble the Linzer cookies, spread 1 to 2 teaspoons ube halaya on the flat side of each of the whole cookies. If you like, sift confectioners' sugar over the cookies with the peekaboo cutouts. Top the cookie bottoms with peekaboo cutout cookies to make sandwiches. Garnish the tops with lemon or calamansi zest, if using, for added color and flavor.

CHEESECAKE COOKIES WITH BLACK SESAME

Makes
about 12 filled cookies

Prep Time
25 minutes

Inactive Time
About 60 minutes

Cook Time
16 minutes

Difficulty
★★★★☆
(Assembling the cookies can be tricky, plus lots of steps involved.)

For the cheesecake filling

- One 8-ounce (226 g) block full-fat cream cheese, softened
- 1 teaspoon red miso, or ¼ teaspoon fine salt
- 1 tablespoon lemon or yuzu juice
- ½ cup (57 g) confectioners' sugar
- 1 to 2 tablespoons Japanese whisky (optional)
- Cooking spray or neutral oil

For the cookie dough

- 2 ¼ cups (270 g) all-purpose flour
- ¼ cup (30 g) black sesame powder
- ½ teaspoon baking soda
- ½ teaspoon baking powder
- ½ cup | 1 stick (113 grams) unsalted butter, softened
- ½ cup (100 grams) granulated sugar, plus more for coating the bottom of a glass or measuring cup
- ⅓ cup (71 grams) packed light brown sugar
- 1 heaping teaspoon red miso
- ¼ cup (60 grams) Greek yogurt
- 1 large egg
- 2 tablespoons black sesame paste
- ⅓ cup (40 g) black sesame seeds, plus more to sprinkle on top of the cookies
- Sea salt flakes (optional)

Whenever I use black sesame and they go viral on social media, I receive comments ranging from "looks like mold" to "is that lint?" or even "kinda looks like cement." Oddly enough, I never see this kind of talk about cookies and cream or Oreo desserts, which these look similar to at first glance. So, I whipped up these cookies as a sort of delicious third-culture ambassador for black sesame.

I cherish black sesame for its deep, nutty flavor and the striking dark gray, almost black color it imparts to desserts. Traditionally used in Asian cuisines, like in fillings for mooncakes or mochi and in Chinese black sesame soup and my beloved sweet steamed bao, it is now growing in popularity in Western recipes.

When working with black sesame, toasting the seeds before grinding them into powder or paste can enhance their rich flavor. For those who haven't yet had the pleasure of enjoying anything with black sesame, I hope these cookies will show them what they're missing out on. Plus, I hid a surprise at the heart of these soft, buttery, toasty cookies: a layer of gooey cheesecake awaits within.

1. **Make the cheesecake filling:** In a medium bowl, mix the cream cheese, miso or salt, lemon or yuzu juice, confectioners' sugar, and Japanese whisky, if using, until smooth.

2. Spray or grease a standard 12-cup muffin tin with cooking spray or neutral oil. Drop a heaping tablespoonful of the cheesecake filling mixture into each cup of the muffin tin to make 12 portions of filling. Freeze, uncovered, until frozen solid, at least 45 minutes.

3. **Make the cookie dough:** Whisk the flour, black sesame powder, baking soda, and baking powder together in a medium bowl. Set aside. Using a stand mixer fitted with the paddle attachment (or in a large bowl with a hand mixer, whisk, or

RECIPE *continues* →

Cookie Tips

If you don't have a muffin tin, drop the tablespoonfuls of cheesecake filling onto a parchment-lined baking sheet.

If you end up with extra cookie dough, bake unfilled cookies for a treat for yourself.

Variation

To brighten the flavors, consider adding about 1 teaspoon grated lemon zest to the cookie dough, in step 3.

Storage

Store the cookies in an airtight container at room temperature for up to 2 days.

spatula), cream the butter, sugars, and miso together until light and fluffy, about 2 minutes. Scrape down the sides and bottom of the bowl. Add the yogurt, egg, and black sesame paste and mix until well incorporated. Again, scrape the bowl as needed. Add the flour mixture and mix until a dough forms. Fold in the black sesame seeds.

4. **Form the cookies:** Use a tablespoon to scoop two 1½-tablespoon dough portions onto a work surface. Lightly flour your clean hands and flatten the dough with your hands to approximately 2½-inch rounds. Add a frozen piece of cheesecake filling to the center of one, and top with the second portion of dough. Roll and shape the dough into a ball, making sure it covers all the filling. Repeat with the remaining dough and filling to make twelve cookies in total. If the dough feels unmanageable, refrigerate it so it's easier to shape and work with.

5. Line two baking sheets with parchment paper. Place six filled dough balls evenly on each baking sheet. Sprinkle sesame seeds on the tops of each ball and slightly flatten with the bottom of a glass or measuring cup coated in sugar. Chill the assembled cookies in the refrigerator, uncovered, for 30 minutes.

6. About 30 minutes before baking, adjust two racks to the upper- and lower-middle positions of the oven. Preheat the oven to 350°F.

7. Bake all the cookies, switching the sheets between top and bottom racks and rotating front to back once halfway through, until the cookie edges are set and begin to brown lightly, about 16 minutes.

8. Let the cookies set and cool on the baking sheets. If you like, garnish with sea salt flakes. It's best to enjoy these cookies warm, so the cheesecake filling is still melty.

KAT'S FAVORITE COOKIE: TAIWANESE SNOWFLAKE CRISPS, YOUR WAY

Makes
24 to 30 crisps, depending on how big or small you cut them.

Prep Time
10 minutes

Inactive Time
30 minutes

Cook Time
10 minutes

Difficulty
★☆☆☆☆
(Clean up will be the hardest part, due to sticky marshmallows in the pot, as well as resisting these snacks.)

- ⅓ cup (75 g) unsalted butter
- About 4 cups (225 g) mini marshmallows
- 1 teaspoon pandan or ube extract (with color) (optional)
- 1 tablespoon milk powder or buttermilk powder, plus more for dusting
- About 40 (130 g) buttery snack crackers, like Ritz
- ½ cup (65 g) salted roasted pistachios, or nuts of your choice
- ½ cup (65 g) dried cranberries, or dried berries and fruits of your choice

These delightful treats were created in a store in Yilan City in Taiwan around 2015 and reached peak popularity around 2020. Known also as milk nougat bites, or 雪花酥 (xǔe hūa sū) and 雪Q餅 (xǔe Q bǐng), the cookies hold a special place in my heart—and soon, perhaps, in yours, too.

I first learned about snowflake crisps around 2018 when my neighbor Mindy Zhou made pistachio and cranberry crisps for me. One chewy (or, as the Taiwanese say, "QQ"), crispy, sweet, and salty bite later, I was in love. Mindy showed me how to make them using marshmallows and Ritz crackers. Despite having beautiful layers and looking factory-manufactured, the crisps are deceptively simple to make by hand, which makes them a little dangerous.

1. Crumple, then uncrumple a large sheet of parchment paper, then use it to line an 8-inch square cake pan with some overhang. Smooth and press down the parchment paper with your hands.

2. In a heavy saucepan or frying pan, heat the butter over medium heat until it begins to brown lightly. Add the marshmallows and turn off the heat. Stir until all the marshmallows have melted into one thick fluff, like melty mozzarella cheese. (If the marshmallows aren't melting into one big fluff, turn the heat back on to low, then immediately turn off the heat once all the marshmallows have melted together.) Add the pandan or ube extract, if using, and stir until fully incorporated. Stir in the milk or buttermilk powder until incorporated.

RECIPE *continues* →

Variations and Substitutions

The beauty of this recipe lies in its adaptability. Swap in freeze-dried strawberries or cashews for the dried cranberries and pistachios, and you'll still end up with a snack that vanishes before you know it. Instead of the pandan or ube extract, which makes the treats green or purple, respectively, you can add about 1 tablespoon matcha or cocoa powder to the melted marshmallows to change up the flavor. Dust the cookies with confectioners' sugar instead of milk powder, and top with edible sprinkles or glitter, if desired.

Storage

The crisps keep in an airtight container at room temperature for up to 4 days.

3. Add the crackers, nuts, and dried berries or fruits. Using a spatula, stir and mix until all the ingredients are coated with the melted marshmallows. Try not to break the crackers too much.

4. Once the mixture is cool to the touch, lightly oil your hands, and pull, stretch, and knead the mixture. Transfer to the prepared pan and press it down with your hands. (Adding parchment paper on top of the mixture will make it easier to press down.) Flatten into a leveled square about 1 inch thick. Cover and let it rest on the counter at room temperature for about 30 minutes to fully set.

5. Use a sharp knife to cut into 24 to 30 equal pieces. Dust with milk powder to create the crisps' signature snowy appearance.

LACE COOKIES WITH MISO CARAMEL AND SESAME

Makes about 36 cookies

Prep Time 20 minutes

Cook Time About 20 minutes, including making the caramel

Difficulty (Multiple steps are involved.)

For the miso caramel sauce

½ cup (100 g) granulated sugar

7 tablespoons (100 g) unsalted butter, cubed

¼ cup (60 g) coconut milk

1 tablespoon miso (red or white)

Pinch of MSG (optional)

For the lace cookies

6 tablespoons (85 g) unsalted butter

1 tablespoon honey

6 tablespoons (75 g) granulated sugar

½ cup (48 g) almond flour

Black or white sesame seeds, or both, for topping

Sea salt flakes, for topping (optional)

Growing up, I ate a lot of sesame candy (芝麻糖 jī màh tóng), a traditional Chinese treat passed around during Lunar New Year. Memories of snacking on those crunchy, sweet candies inspired this Asian version of Florentine lace cookies. They possess a complex flavor that belies their ease of preparation, making them a go-to when I want a quick cookie fix. Fair warning though, they are not the typical not-too-sweet treats like many of the others in the book, but rather they are perfect for those with a strong sweet tooth.

This recipe allows for a playful, choose-your-own-adventure approach: You can make a cookie sandwich with a layer of salted miso caramel in the center, or choose to simply drizzle the caramel over the top. (You might wonder why I've added caramel sauce to an already sweet cookie. This miso caramel sauce is worth it, and it's actually not *too* sweet when layered with other flavors. People have told me to sell this sauce, but I'm more of a passive-income type of gal.) The sesame seeds, a nod to the candies I consumed so much of as a kid, provide crunch and a hint of nuttiness to subtly balance out the sweetness.

1. Adjust a rack to the middle position and preheat the oven to 350°F. Line two baking sheets with parchment paper.

2. **Make the miso caramel sauce.** Heat the sugar in a saucepan over low heat, swirling the pan gently every 30 seconds, until melted and caramelized, about 15 minutes. It should form clumps before fully melting. Once melted, remove from heat and stir in the butter; the mixture should bubble rapidly and violently. Whisk vigorously but carefully to dissipate the foam and bubbles, until combined, a few minutes. Then, over low heat, stir in the coconut milk, miso, and MSG, if using, while continuously whisking the mixture until well combined but

RECIPE *continues* →

still runny. If using a candy or digital thermometer, the caramel should register at 225°F (107°C). The caramel sauce will thicken more when cooled. Avoid overcooking the caramel, as it will taste burnt. Remove the pan from the heat and set aside.

3. **Make the lace cookies.** In a medium microwave-safe bowl, combine the butter and honey and microwave in 30-second bursts until melted. Whisk in the sugar until dissolved, then mix in the almond flour until smooth. Microwave for 20 seconds and stir again. Drop 1-teaspoon portions of batter directly onto the parchment-lined baking sheets, making 36 cookies and spacing them at least 2 inches apart. Top with sesame seeds. Bake the cookies, one sheet at a time, until shiny, flat, and golden brown all over, about 10 minutes.

4. While warm, you can gently manipulate the cookies' shapes, folding them or curling them. Transfer the cookies to a wire rack to cool completely. Drizzle the tops with the miso caramel. Alternatively, to enjoy as a caramel cookie sandwich, spread the caramel evenly over the bottom of a cookie. Sandwich the caramel with another cookie. Drizzle more caramel over the top and enjoy. Of course, these cookies are equally delightful on their own, without any caramel.

Cookie Tips

If almond flour isn't readily available, pulse whole almonds in the food processor until finely chopped, if you like chunkier cookies.

Store any leftover caramel sauce in an airtight container in the refrigerator for up to 2 weeks.

Variations and Substitutions

Substitute either light corn syrup or agave syrup for the honey.

Instead of the almond flour, mix rolled oats into the batter, which will hold the oats together.

Storage

Unknown because they never last in my home.

花生餅 CHEAT CODE CHINESE PEANUT COOKIES

Makes
12 to 15 cookies

Prep Time
15 minutes

Inactive Time
30 minutes

Cook Time
About
16 to 18 minutes

Difficulty
★★☆☆☆
(My husband—who swears he can't bake—can probably make these with ease.)

¾ cup (100 g) all-purpose flour
½ teaspoon baking soda
½ teaspoon baking powder
½ teaspoon five spice powder (optional)
1 tablespoon unsalted butter, softened
¼ cup (50 g) granulated sugar
3 tablespoons (45 g) brown sugar
1 tablespoon red miso
1 large egg
1 cup (250 grams) natural (non-hydrogenated) peanut butter (crunchy or smooth)
1 tablespoon Japanese whisky (optional)
¼ cup (about 50 g) coarse, granulated, or demerara sugar, placed in a shallow bowl
12 to 15 shelled peanuts (salted or unsalted), for topping
1 large egg yolk, beaten and mixed with 2 teaspoons milk or water, for egg wash

These peanut cookies, called 花生餅 (fā sāng béng), are a popular Lunar New Year staple. In Chinese, the word peanut means "flower born" and peanuts symbolize blooming life and health. They're also a symbol of prosperity and fertility; hence, their popularity during holiday celebrations. You'll find peanuts not just in cookies like these, but in candies, savory dishes, and enjoyed as appetizers.

Though prized during Lunar New Year, I find myself seeking comfort in these cookies all year long. They're traditionally made with ground peanuts, but due to the daily whirlwind that is life, I've adapted this classic by using peanut butter as a cheat to save time. The cookies carry a hint of warmth from the five spice, while miso introduces an additional depth of umami. Each melt-in-the-mouth bite is deeply satisfying.

P.S.: Don't skip the cute little peanut on top.

1. Whisk the flour, baking soda, baking powder, and five spice powder, if using, together in a medium bowl. Set aside.

2. Using a stand mixer fitted with the paddle attachment (or in a large bowl with a hand mixer, whisk, or spatula), cream the butter, sugars, and miso together until light and fluffy. Scrape down the sides and bottom of the bowl. Add the egg, peanut butter, and Japanese whisky, if using, and mix until well incorporated. Again, scrape the bowl as needed. Add the flour mixture and mix until a dough forms. Cover and chill in the refrigerator for 30 minutes.

3. While the dough is chilling, adjust a rack to the middle position and preheat the oven to 350°F. Line a baking sheet with parchment paper.

RECIPE *continues* →

CHEAT CODE CHINESE PEANUT COOKIES, *continued*

Cookie Tips
If the dough is a bit dry to handle, add additional peanut butter, about a teaspoon at a time.

Substitutions
Five spice powder can be an acquired taste in desserts, so it's okay if you swap it out for another spice of your choice, like cinnamon or cardamom.

Storage
Store the cookies in an airtight container at room temperature for up to 3 days.

4. Divide the dough into 12 to 15 portions, each about a heaping tablespoon. Shape and smooth each into a ball and toss in the bowl of coarse sugar to coat thoroughly. Place on the prepared baking sheet about an inch apart (these cookies don't spread much).

5. To the center of each ball, press in a whole peanut. Brush all the tops with the egg wash to add shine and color. Bake, rotating the baking sheet halfway through baking, until the tops shine and the edges are browner, 16 to 18 minutes.

6. Out of the oven, the cookies will appear crumbly, so allow them to set and cool directly on the baking sheet.

CHOCOLATE SANDWICH COOKIES WITH THAI BASIL

Makes
about
25 cookies

Prep Time:
30 minutes

Inactive Time:
About
10 minutes

Cook Time:
About
20 minutes
for two batches

Difficulty:
★★★☆☆
(Some assembly required; plus melting chocolate can be a little tricky.)

For the cookies

- 1 ¼ cups (150 g) all-purpose flour
- ¼ cup (25 g) unsweetened Dutch-processed cocoa powder, sifted
- ½ teaspoon baking soda
- ⅔ cup (about 15 g) Thai basil leaves (no stems), washed
- 2 tablespoons pine nuts or chopped walnuts
- 2 tablespoons extra-virgin olive oil
- ½ cup | 1 stick (113 g) unsalted butter, softened
- 1 cup (200 g) granulated sugar
- 2 tablespoons Greek yogurt or crème fraîche
- 1 teaspoon red miso
- 1 large egg

For the filling

- ½ cup plus 2 tablespoons (150 g) heavy cream
- ⅓ cup (about 8 g) Thai basil leaves (no stems), washed
- ¼ cup (50 g) granulated sugar
- 1 ¾ cups (283 g) chopped semisweet or milk chocolate
- 1 tablespoon neutral oil
- 1 teaspoon red miso

For topping the cookies

- Thai basil leaves, minced (optional)
- Edible gold foil (optional)

If you're like me and a fan of decadence and double chocolate desserts, these are the cookies for you. I initially set out to make a minty chocolate sandwich cookie, but I only had Thai basil in the fridge. (The night before, we had homemade pho for dinner.) I popped a piece of dark chocolate in my mouth, then a Thai basil leaf, and the flavor combo was divine! Thus, these cookies were born.

You'll add Thai basil to both the cookie dough and filling to infuse them with its unique, aromatic flavor. If desired, you can also garnish the assembled cookies with minced Thai basil for an extra burst of freshness and color. As Thai basil tastes very different from the basil you use to make pesto or add on top of pizza margherita, I would argue the two are not interchangeable. Making a trip to your local Asian supermarket or grocery store to pick up some Thai basil will be well worth your while. Oh and by the way, Thai basil also freezes well, so you can reserve some to use the next time you make pho or other noodle soups.

1. Line two to three baking sheets with parchment paper.

2. **Make the cookies.** Whisk the flour, cocoa powder, and baking soda together in a medium bowl. Set aside. In a food processor, pulse the Thai basil leaves and pine nuts or walnuts together until finely chopped. Add the olive oil and pulse until a thick paste forms. Using a stand mixer fitted with the paddle attachment, cream the butter, sugar, yogurt or crème fraîche, and miso together until smooth and well incorporated. Scrape down the sides of the bowl as needed. Add the egg and mix until combined. Add the Thai basil mixture and flour mixture and mix on low speed just until a well-incorporated dough forms.

RECIPE *continues* →

Substitution
Use chocolate chips instead of chopped chocolate.

Storage
Store the cookies in an airtight container at room temperature for up to 2 days. You can also store them in the refrigerator for up to 1 week.

3. Drop the dough by the tablespoonful onto the prepared baking sheets, making about 25 cookies and spacing them 2 inches apart. Wet a clean finger to smooth out the top of each cookie. Chill in the refrigerator for 30 minutes.

4. Adjust a rack to the middle position and preheat the oven to 350°F.

5. One sheet at a time, bake the cookies until they are set and the tops flatten out, about 10 minutes. Remove from the oven and cool completely on wire racks.

6. **Make the filling.** While the dough chills, bring the cream to a boil in a small saucepan. Remove from heat and add the Thai basil leaves. Give it a good stir, then let the leaves steep for about 30 minutes. Remove the leaves and compost them. Add the sugar to the cream and bring to a boil again. Remove from the heat, add the chocolate, and cover the saucepan with a lid. Let this rest for 10 minutes. Add the neutral oil and miso and whisk until the ganache is glossy and no chocolate lumps remain. The filling should be soft and smooth and easy to spread over the cookies.

7. **Assemble the cookies.** Spread 1 tablespoon filling evenly across a completely cooled cookie. Add a second cookie on top of the filling to make a sandwich. If you like, garnish with minced Thai basil leaves or edible gold foil. Repeat to assemble the remaining cookies.

LYCHEE FROSTED SUGAR COOKIES

Makes
9 large cookies

Prep Time
About
15 minutes

Inactive Time
About
30 minutes

Cook Time
About
12 minutes

Difficulty
★★★★☆
(Multiple steps are involved.)

For the cookies

2½ cups (300 g) all-purpose flour

⅔ cup (85 g) cake flour

¼ teaspoon baking soda

¼ teaspoon cream of tartar

½ cup | 1 stick (113 g) unsalted butter, softened

6 tablespoons (90 g) neutral oil

½ cup plus 2 tablespoons (120 g) granulated sugar, plus more for pressing the cookies

About ½ cup (60 g) confectioners' sugar

1 teaspoon red miso

1 large egg

1 tablespoon freshly grated lemon zest

1 teaspoon lychee extract

For the frosting

6 tablespoons (85 g) unsalted butter, softened

1 cup plus 2 tablespoons (140 g) confectioners' sugar, divided

4 teaspoons (20 g) heavy cream

1 teaspoon lychee extract

Pink or red food coloring gel (optional, but if you use it, we want light pink, not a hot magenta pink)

For decorating the cookies (optional)

About ⅓ cup (110 g) store-bought strawberry jam

5 to 6 fresh or canned lychees, chopped

Edible pearl sprinkles or gold foil

At first glance, these sugar cookies appear humble when unfrosted, like any other ordinary sugar cookie, like those you would find at the supermarket. But don't be fooled. These charming sugar cookies shine even on their own with their rich buttery base, tender crumb, bright refreshing citrus notes, and a slight chew. Then, when topped with a luxurious buttercream infused with lychee extract, a bit of berry compote or jam, and finally crowned with chopped canned lychees, they undergo a *bibbidi-bobbidi-boo* moment. The more you bite into this layered and regal cookie, the more you'll feel like royalty.

1. **Make the cookies.** Whisk both flours, the baking soda, and cream of tartar together in a medium bowl. Using a stand mixer fitted with the paddle attachment (or in a large bowl with a hand mixer, whisk, or spatula), cream the butter, oil, both sugars, and miso together until light and fluffy. Scrape down the sides and bottom of the bowl. Add the egg, lemon zest, and lychee extract and mix until well incorporated. Again, scrape the bowl as needed. Add the flour mixture and mix on low speed just until a dough forms. Cover and chill the dough in the refrigerator for 30 minutes, or up to overnight.

2. About 25 minutes before baking, adjust a rack to the middle position and preheat the oven to 350°F. Line two baking sheets with parchment paper.

3. Use a large cookie scoop to create nine portions of dough, each about 3.2 ounces (½ cup, 90 g), placing them 3 inches apart on the prepared baking sheets. Press each ball with the bottom of a sugar-lined glass or measuring cup until the cookie edges begin to crack.

RECIPE *continues* →

LYCHEE FROSTED SUGAR COOKIES, *continued*

Cookie Tip
When pressing the dough portions, slightly wet the bottom of a glass or measuring cup, then dip into a shallow bowl of sugar to coat the bottom.

Variation
You can skip the jam and add the lychees directly to the frosting.

Storage
Store the cookies in an airtight container at room temperature, each separated by parchment paper, for up to 3 days.

4. Bake the cookies one sheet at a time (while the other sheet chills in the fridge), until the edges are crispy and golden brown, about 12 minutes. Let the cookies set on the baking sheet for a few minutes before transferring to a wire rack to cool completely.

5. **Make the frosting.** In a stand mixer fitted with the paddle attachment, mix the butter on high speed until fluffy, about 2 minutes. Scrape the bowl as needed. Add about half of the confectioners' sugar and mix on medium speed until incorporated. Add the remaining confectioners' sugar and mix until incorporated as well. Add the cream, lychee extract, and food coloring, if using, and mix until combined and spreadable. Note that you will have just enough frosting for the nine large cookies. If you love the frosting, I recommend making more for these cookies.

6. **Frost and decorate the cookies.** Spread the frosting evenly over the cooled cookies. If you like, add about a teaspoon of jam on top and garnish with chopped lychees and edible pearl sprinkles or edible gold foil.

SNICKER-DOODLES WITH FIVE SPICE

Makes	*Prep Time*	*Cook Time*	*Difficulty*
24 cookies	15 minutes *Inactive Time* Up to 30 minutes	8 to 10 minutes	★★½☆☆ (Overall it's a simple recipe, with multiple steps involved.)

For the cookies

2 ¾ cups (330 g) all-purpose flour

2 teaspoons cream of tartar

1 teaspoon baking soda

½ teaspoon five spice powder

½ cup (92 g) vegetable shortening

½ cup | 1 stick (113 g) unsalted butter, softened

1 ¼ cups (250 g) granulated sugar

1 tablespoon red miso

2 large eggs

For the spiced sugar

⅓ cup (67 g) granulated sugar

1 tablespoon ground cinnamon

1 teaspoon five spice powder

Can you believe I didn't try a snickerdoodle until my early 20s? I was a physical therapist when a coworker brought homemade ones to work, and with just one chewy zingy bite, I was smitten. It's no wonder the snickerdoodle is one of America's favorite cookies.

To add an Asian twist to this classic, I included five spice and miso. Miso, as you know, brings a balancing pop of umami and savoriness to sweet treats. Although more commonly used in cooking, particularly in Chinese recipes, five spice in cookies delivers warmth, spice, and aroma, enhancing the overall flavors.

If you adore complex, nuanced flavors like I do, feel free to incorporate some minced ginger, or lemon or calamansi zest, or even gochujang to the cookie dough (see variations on page 75). The ginger adds a spicy kick, while the citrus zest lends a refreshing tang that beautifully complements the vinegary essence of cream of tartar, the key to a snickerdoodle's signature chew.

1. Line two baking sheets with parchment paper.

2. **Make the cookies.** Whisk the flour, cream of tartar, baking soda, and five spice together in a medium bowl. Set aside.

3. Using a stand mixer fitted with the paddle attachment (or in a large bowl with a hand mixer, whisk, or spatula), cream the shortening, butter, sugar, and miso together until smooth and well incorporated. Scrape down the sides and bottom of the bowl as needed. Add the eggs, one at a time, and mix until well incorporated. Add the flour mixture and mix on low speed just until a dough forms. The cream of tartar makes this a very soft dough, but it's manageable.

4. Use a cookie scoop or a tablespoon to scoop out 24 dough balls, each about 1 ½ inches in diameter. Roll each ball between your palms to smooth out, then place on the prepared baking

RECIPE *continues* →

Cookie Tip
Cream of tartar is an acid that stops sugar from crystallizing in cookies, making snickerdoodles chewy instead of crispy while also imparting tanginess.

Variations
Mix 2 teaspoons grated lemon or calamansi zest into the dough in Step 3 for an even tangier cookie. Alternatively, mix in 1 teaspoon finely minced ginger for a spicy spin. For an even spicier spin, omit the miso and add 1 tablespoon gochujang.

Substitution
Classic snickerdoodles typically call for shortening, but if you don't have any on hand, substitute butter one-to-one, using a total of 1 cup (2 sticks) butter.

Storage
Store the cookies in an airtight container at room temperature for up to 3 days.

sheet, spacing them 2 inches apart. Chill, uncovered, in the refrigerator for 15 to 30 minutes.

5. About 25 minutes before baking, adjust a rack to the middle position and preheat the oven to 350°F.

6. **Make the spiced sugar.** Mix the sugar, cinnamon, and five spice together in a shallow bowl.

7. Briefly roll each chilled ball between your palms to smooth it out again. Then, roll a few balls at a time in the bowl of spiced sugar, ensuring they are evenly and completely coated. If the spiced sugar doesn't adhere well, wet your fingers to lightly dampen the balls with water before coating. Repeat this process until all the balls are coated, placing them back on the baking sheet and spacing them at least an inch apart. Flatten each ball to about ½-inch thickness using the bottom of a cup or glass.

8. Bake the cookies, one sheet at a time (while the other sheet chills in the fridge), until golden brown around the edges and slightly golden on top, 8 to 10 minutes.

9. Allow the cookies to set and cool on the baking sheets for a few minutes, then transfer to a wire rack to cool completely. These cookies are even chewier the next day.

AMARETTI COOKIES WITH PANDAN AND PISTACHIOS

Makes
about 18 cookies

Prep Time
15 minutes

Cook Time
About 25 minutes

Difficulty
★★★☆☆
(Whipping egg whites to stiff peaks takes practice.)

For the cookies

- 2 ¼ cups (225 g) almond flour
- ¾ cup (150 g) granulated sugar
- 3 large egg whites
- ¼ teaspoon cream of tartar
- 1 ½ teaspoons green pandan extract
- 1 teaspoon almond extract
- 1 tablespoon red miso (gluten-free if that is a concern)
- ⅓ cup (43 g) pistachios, chopped finely

For coating and topping the cookies

- ⅓ cup (67 g) granulated sugar, in a shallow bowl or plate
- ½ cup (57 g) confectioners' sugar, in a shallow bowl or plate, plus more as needed to dust the cookies
- 18 whole, roasted almonds
- Culinary-grade matcha

A not-too-sweet amaretti cookie that's jade green on the inside and, at first glance, resembles a snowy Chinese almond cookie? Why not! This playful twist on the classic Italian amaretti, a gem dating back to the Renaissance, blends almond and pistachio flavors (two of my favorites) into a delightfully chewy bite. Enjoy them with hot tea, coffee, or on their own whenever you need a whimsical treat to brighten your day.

1. Line two baking sheets with parchment paper. Adjust two racks to the upper- and lower-middle positions of the oven. Preheat the oven to 325°F.

2. **Make the cookies.** Whisk the almond flour and granulated sugar together in a medium bowl. Set aside.

3. Using a stand mixer fitted with the whisk attachment, beat the egg whites and cream of tartar on high speed until frothy. Add the pandan and almond extracts and whip on high speed until stiff peaks form, 2 to 3 minutes.

4. Transfer the almond flour mixture to the bowl of the stand mixer, along with the miso and chopped pistachios. Mix on low speed until a thick and cohesive dough forms. Scrape down the sides and bottom of the bowl as needed.

5. Scoop about 2 tablespoons of the dough and roll into a ball. Toss in the granulated sugar, then repeat with the confectioners' sugar to coat thoroughly. Repeat to make 18 balls, spacing them at least 2 inches apart on the prepared baking sheets. Press each dough ball with the bottom of a sugar-coated glass or measuring cup until the cookie edges begin to crack, about ½ inch in thickness. Alternatively, skip the flattening step and

RECIPE *continues* →

Variation
Swap out the almonds for your favorite nut.

Storage
Store the cookies in an airtight container at room temperature for up to 3 days.

keep the balls of dough rounded. Press a whole almond into the center of each dough ball.

6. Bake all the cookies, switching the sheets between top and bottom racks and rotating front to back once halfway through, until lightly browned around the edges and cracked, about 25 minutes.

7. Let the cookies set and cool on the baking sheet for a few minutes, then transfer to a wire rack to cool completely. Dust the tops with a little more confectioners' sugar, then some matcha.

OATMEAL COOKIES WITH WHITE MULBERRIES

Makes	Prep Time	Cook Time	Difficulty
about 23 cookies	15 minutes	About 10 minutes	★★☆☆☆ (For me, folding mix-ins into cookie dough is challenging since we want all the ingredients evenly distributed.)

1½ cups (135 g) thick rolled or old-fashioned oats (not quick oats)

¾ cup (90 g) all-purpose flour

¼ cup (36 g) toasted white sesame seeds

½ teaspoon five spice powder

½ teaspoon ground Vietnamese cinnamon

½ teaspoon baking soda

½ cup | 1 stick (113 g) unsalted butter, softened

⅔ cup (142 g) unpacked light brown sugar

¼ cup (50 g) granulated sugar

1 tablespoon red miso

1 large egg

⅓ cup (about 50 g) dried white mulberries

⅓ cup (about 50 g) golden raisins

⅓ cup (56 g) semisweet or dark chocolate chips (optional)

For coating the dough balls

¼ cup (36 g) toasted white sesame seeds

¼ cup (50 g) granulated sugar

Sea salt flakes, for garnish (optional)

White mulberries are native to China and were once the sole source of food for silkworms across Asia. I'm surprised it's not more common to use white mulberries in desserts and cookies. They're sweet and crunchy (unlike dried cherries, raisins, or dried cranberries) and are perfect in my subtly Asian oatmeal cookies. It turns out, the plant itself is considered an invasive species in the United States. The berries, however, are sold in health food stores and online. Their fruity sweetness is perfect when paired with the warmth from five spice and Vietnamese cinnamon (or Saigon cinnamon). Compared to other cinnamons, like Ceylon and cassia, Vietnamese cinnamon is spicier, sweeter, and bolder.

Growing up, I've always loved oatmeal cookies but always wished they included more Asian ingredients. So here they are! Oh, and if you've never been a fan of oatmeal cookies, I bet you will be now.

1. Adjust two racks to the upper- and lower-middle positions of the oven. Preheat the oven to 375°F. Line two baking sheets with parchment paper.

2. Whisk the oats, flour, sesame seeds, five spice powder, cinnamon, and baking soda together in a medium bowl. Set aside.

3. Using a stand mixer fitted with the paddle attachment (or in a large bowl with a hand mixer, whisk, or spatula), cream the butter, sugars, and miso together until light and fluffy. Scrape down the sides and bottom of the bowl. Add the egg and mix until well incorporated. Add the flour mixture and mix on low speed just until a cookie dough forms. Fold in the mulberries, raisins, and chocolate chips, if using.

RECIPE *continues* →

Cookie Tips
If your dried mulberries are a little large, chop them first. If you're a chocolate lover, don't omit the chocolate chips in these cookies.

Storage
Store the cookies in an airtight container at room temperature for up to 2 days.

4. Scoop 1½ tablespoons (35 grams) of dough for each cookie and roll into a ball. You should have enough dough to make about 23 balls.

5. **Coat and bake the dough balls.** Combine the sesame seeds and granulated sugar in a shallow bowl. Toss and roll each ball in the sugar and sesame seeds until thoroughly coated. Place on the prepared baking sheets, spacing 2 inches apart.

6. Bake all the cookies, switching the sheets between top and bottom racks and rotating front to back once halfway through, until they are slightly puffed and the edges and tops brown lightly, about 10 minutes. The centers should remain soft and chewy.

7. Allow the cookies to set for a few minutes on the baking sheets, then transfer to a wire rack to cool completely. If you like, sprinkle sea salt flakes over the tops of the cookies before serving.

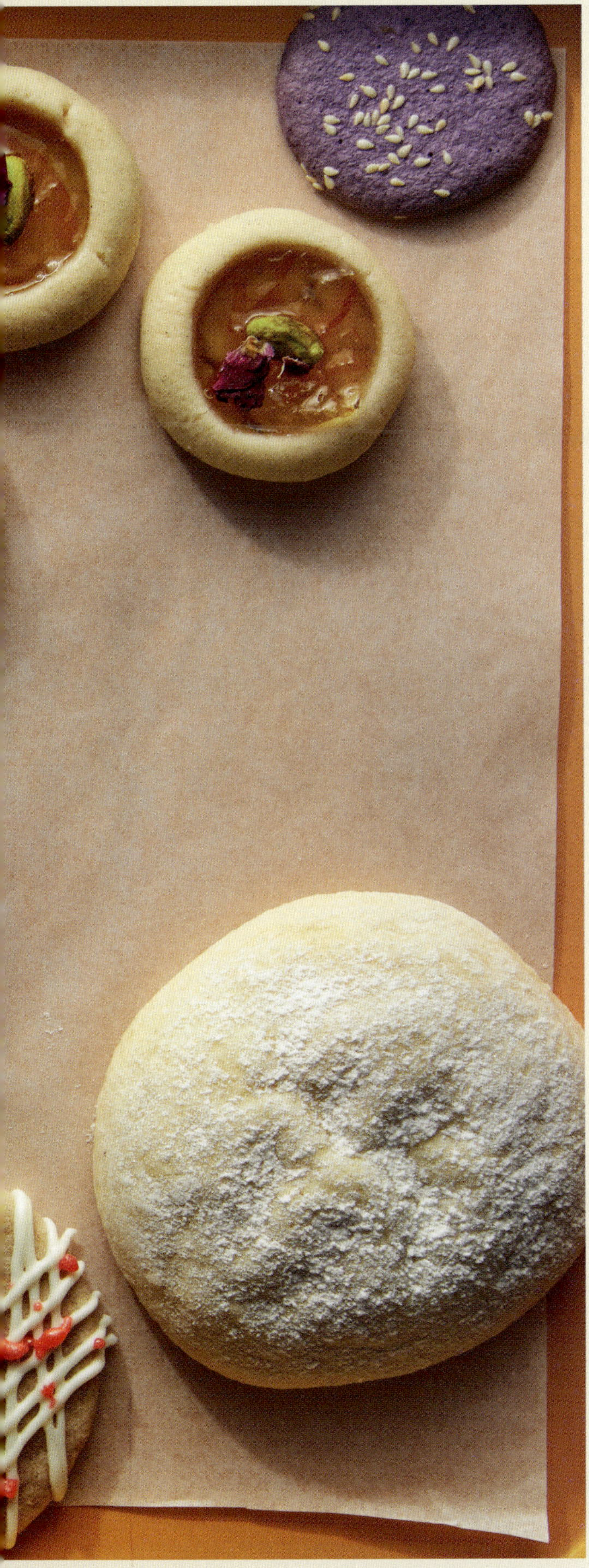

II

SILK ROAD SWEETS

CLASSIC ASIAN COOKIES AND TREATS

Classic cookies found across Asia and Asian diasporas

When Paul Hollywood visited Japan and explored the bakeries there for the first time, it genuinely shocked him to discover that the Japanese baked and that they're good bakers, too. I wondered if Paul would've been surprised to learn that other Asians baked and made cookies as well, for centuries. The history of Asian baking is rich and diverse, harking back to the ancient trade routes like the Silk Road, which moved ingredients and techniques across continents. Then, of course, there was colonization, which introduced European pastries and baking techniques to Asia. So, Paul, yes, Asians bake, and we're quite good at it, too.

For as long as I can remember, I've enjoyed Asian-style cookies, especially the classics like the somewhat savory Kampar Little Chicken Biscuits (page 87) from Malaysia. It's a cookie that requires more than a bite or two to appreciate, thanks to all its nuanced flavors and pronounced umami notes, and I personally love them. Then, there's the Old-Fashioned Cantonese Shortbread (page 105), cookies my mother wanted to eat throughout her youth in Hong Kong but couldn't afford, as that would mean she wouldn't get a more filling meal for lunch or dinner. Here, I also have two Indian treats for you, the Pandan, Coconut, and Cardamom Ladoo (page 102) and Easy Cashew Burfi (page 90). Both are no-bake treats and sweeter than the rest. They're two of my favorite Indian desserts and can easily shine on any cookie platter. These cookies and the other sweet treats in this chapter are my modern little love letters to the diverse flavors and rich history that the Silk Road has brought us.

ONE-BOWL RICE CAKE BARS OR COOKIES (Chapssaltteok)

Makes
12 to 16 cookie bars

Prep Time
10 minutes

Inactive Time
About 30 minutes

Cook Time
15 to 20 minutes

Difficulty
★☆☆☆☆
(My husband could probably make these with his eyes closed. Okay, maybe not.)

- 2 cups (300 g) mochiko (glutinous rice flour)
- 2 tablespoons granulated sugar
- 1 tablespoon culinary-grade matcha
- 1½ teaspoons baking powder
- 1 cup (240 g) plain plant-based milk, like oat milk or soy milk
- ⅔ cup (160 g) water
- ⅓ cup (104 g) maple syrup or agave syrup
- 2 tablespoons (28 g) extra-virgin olive oil
- 1 teaspoon red miso
- ½ cup (75 g) dried berries or fruits of your choice
- ½ cup (71 g) mixed nuts of your choice
- ⅓ cup (57 g) semisweet chocolate chips (optional)

Variations
For individual round cookies, place 2-tablespoon portions of batter on a parchment-lined baking sheet, spacing them 2 inches apart. Bake at 350°F until the cookies are crispy, about 12 to 15 minutes. You can make about 8 large round cookies.

For different flavors, swap out the matcha for another food powder, like 1 tablespoon cocoa powder or black sesame powder, or about 1 teaspoon ube or pandan extract.

Storage
Store the cookies in an airtight container at room temperature for up to 3 days, but note that they will soften over time.

Whenever I'm craving something a little crispy but predominantly chewy and satisfying, I turn to these bar cookies, inspired by the crispy, chewy, and not-too-sweet LA chapssaltteok, a delightful baked rice cake full of nuts and fruits. This confectionery was born in the kitchens of South Koreans who had immigrated to California in the 20th century and were nostalgic for their homeland's flavors. Generally, chapssaltteok is easy to whip up: Just toss all the ingredients into a large bowl and mix. The glutinous rice flour absorbs the milk and water, and while the batter appears runny, just trust the process. The bars will bake up just fine, crispy on the outside, chewy on the inside, albeit a little flat, as they're meant to be. (Some people online have equated these to mousepads when I bake them as round cookies, LOL!) This recipe is also versatile; it practically begs you to play around with a variety of flavors and inclusions. (Pictured on page 85.)

1. Whisk the glutinous rice flour, sugar, matcha, and baking powder together in a large mixing bowl. Make a well in the center with a cup or a measuring cup. Pour in the plant-based milk, water, maple or agave syrup, olive oil, and miso and mix until thoroughly combined and cohesive. (Note that this cookie batter is meant to be wet and runny.) Fold in the dried berries or fruit, nuts, and chocolate chips, if using. Cover and rest the batter for about 30 minutes, at room temperature or refrigerated.

2. Adjust a rack to the middle position and preheat the oven to 425°F. Crumple, then uncrumple a large sheet of parchment paper and use to line a 9 by 13-inch baking dish with some overhang.

3. Pour the batter into the prepared baking dish. Bake until set and the top and edges are crispy and golden brown, 15 to 20 minutes.

4. Cool in the baking dish for a few minutes, then lift the parchment paper to transfer the slab to a wire rack to cool completely. Cut into 12 to 16 equal bars.

雞仔餅 KAMPAR LITTLE CHICKEN BISCUITS

Makes
about 70 small and thin cookies, or more or less depending on the size of your cookie cutter(s)

Prep Time
20 minutes

Inactive Time
30 minutes

Cook Time
10 to 12 minutes

Difficulty
★★★☆☆
(Not too difficult, but there are many different processes involved.)

For the dry ingredients

- 2 ½ cups (300 g) all-purpose flour
- About ⅓ cup (50 grams) white sesame seeds
- About ⅓ cup (50 grams) black sesame seeds
- 1 teaspoon ground white pepper
- 1 teaspoon five spice powder
- 1 teaspoon chicken powder
- ½ teaspoon ground black pepper
- ½ teaspoon baking powder
- ½ teaspoon baking soda
- Dash of MSG

For the wet ingredients

- ½ cup (109 g) neutral oil
- 1 large egg
- 2 cubes nam yu
- 2 tablespoons nam yu sauce (red sauce from the jar of nam yu)
- 1 tablespoon honey
- ½ cup (100 g) fine granulated sugar
- About ½ cup plus 2 tablespoons (150 g) candied winter melon or candied pineapple
- 2 garlic cloves, minced

Gāi jái béng (雞仔餅), found across Malaysia and Guangdong, are savory-sweet treats that usually contain no chicken, other than some chicken powder. Their name in Cantonese translates as "little chicken biscuit," probably because they either used to resemble chicks, or because "little chicken" in Cantonese also means cute. The Cantonese version, which I grew up eating and loving, is more like savory pastries or mooncakes. They could also take over a day to make, involving multiple ingredients, which felt beyond the scope of this book. But I do highly recommend you seeking them out at a Chinese bakery.

You'll find a similar flavor profile in cookie form when you make these Malaysian chicken biscuits, though. These cookies are savory, crispy, and a little caramelly. The nam yu (fermented red bean curd, made with red rice and chilis) imparts a unique savory and slightly tangy taste to the cookies, adding depth and complexity. Plus, they are garlicky and more savory than sweet. If at first bite, you're a fan, you'll be a forever fan, like me.

1. Whisk all the dry ingredients together in a large bowl and set aside.

2. Combine all the wet ingredients in a food processor and pulse until a well-incorporated and cohesive mixture forms. Transfer the mixture to the bowl with the dry ingredients and fold with a rubber spatula until a cohesive dough forms. Cover and chill the dough in the refrigerator for 30 minutes.

3. About 20 minutes before baking, adjust two racks to the upper- and lower-middle positions of the oven. Preheat the oven to 350°F. Line two baking sheets with parchment paper.

RECIPE *continues* →

Substitutions
I'd like to keep this recipe as true to the taste as I can, so don't omit the nam yu.

Storage
Store the cookies in an airtight container at room temperature for up to 3 days.

4. Lightly flour a work surface. Roll the dough into a rectangle about ⅛ to ⅙ inch thick. Use a cookie cutter, like a chicken-shaped one (or a circle or fluted circle), to cut out cookie shapes. Gather the scraps, re-roll, and continue cutting until all the dough is used. Carefully place the cutouts on the prepared baking sheets, spacing them 1 inch apart.

5. Place both baking sheets in the oven and mist the oven and the tops of the cookies with a little water. Bake the cookies, switching the sheets between the top to bottom racks and rotating front to back once halfway through, until they are golden brown and the edges are crispy, 10 to 12 minutes.

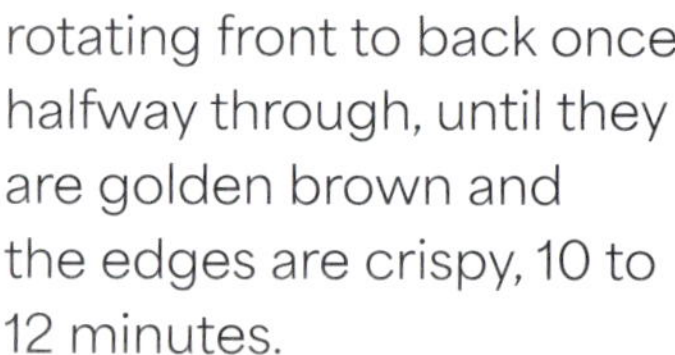

6. Let the cookies set and cool on the baking sheets for a few minutes before transferring to a wire rack to cool completely. Note the cookies should get crispier as they cool down.

EASY CASHEW BURFI (Indian Fudge)

Makes
16 to 20 burfi

Prep Time
15 minutes

Inactive Time
1 hour

Cook Time
About 10 minutes

Difficulty
★★☆☆☆
(A bit of patience is needed, waiting for the burfi to set.)

- 1 cup (120 g) cashew flour (finely ground)
- 2 tablespoons milk powder
- ½ teaspoon ground cardamom
- ¼ teaspoon kosher salt
- Pinch of nutmeg
- ⅓ cup (79 g) whole milk or plain plant-based milk
- ⅓ cup (67 g) granulated sugar
- 2 teaspoons unsalted butter or ghee
- ½ teaspoon lemongrass paste (optional)
- ¼ cup (36 g) finely chopped pistachios (optional, for a pop of color and layered flavor)
- 1 teaspoon rose water or orange blossom water
- Edible gold or silver leaves, for garnish (optional)
- 16 to 20 whole cashews, for garnish (optional)

One Saturday when I was having lunch at my friend Suraj Chetnani's house, I asked him what his favorite Indian cookies and sweets were while he made us his signature chai. Suraj kept reflecting but could not come up with one Indian cookie, so I told him how much I liked the gulab jamun and burfi that my neighbors, Mary Usha and her family, would gift us during Diwali. Suraj grinned and replied, "They're too sweet." We joked that his palate belonged more to an East Asian than a South Asian.

Suraj went on to mention that back in India, his grandmother would mix ingredients like chickpea or nut flour, sugar, milk, and ghee together to make sweets, or reduce milk down to make fudge, like the burfi that I so loved. Our chat inspired me to develop this recipe, an easy, highly customizable burfi that doesn't require reducing milk into condensed milk, which takes hours. This burfi, made with cashew flour and milk powder, is still melt-in-the-mouth fudgy while being not-too-sweet. Including lemongrass paste is an homage to Suraj's chai, which you'll learn more about on page 333, when you make my Lemongrass and Masala Gingerbread Cookies.

1. Sift the cashew flour into a medium bowl. Whisk in the milk powder, ground cardamom, salt, and nutmeg. Set aside.

2. Combine the milk, sugar, butter or ghee, and lemongrass paste, if using, in a heavy saucepan and stir. Cook over medium heat, constantly stirring with a rubber spatula or whisk, until the sugar dissolves and the mixture boils, a few minutes. Reduce the heat to low and carefully dump in the cashew flour mixture. Whisk until combined and no lumps remain. If you like, fold in the chopped pistachios. Then cook, using a rubber spatula to mix and "knead" the mixture until it becomes a smooth, non-sticky dough that no longer sticks to the saucepan, about 10 minutes. Avoid overcooking, as the burfi will be dry if you do.

RECIPE *continues* →

You can tear off a little piece and see if you can knead it into a small and smooth ball. If yes, remove the pan from heat and mix in the rose or orange blossom water.

3. Transfer the burfi to a large sheet of parchment paper. Cover with another sheet of parchment paper and cool for a few minutes. With the parchment still on top, use a rolling pin to roll the burfi into a flat rectangle about ⅙ inch thick. (If you prefer it thicker, roll to ¼-inch thickness.) Let the burfi set at room temperature for 1 hour. You can also chill the burfi in the refrigerator until ready to serve.

4. Remove the top sheet of parchment paper and cut the burfi into 16 to 20 equal pieces. Alternatively, cut them into any fun shape you'd like, like diamonds. If you like (and I highly recommend this), garnish with edible gold or silver leaves and then press a cashew into the center of each piece of burfi.

Burfi Tips
You want a soft texture for burfi—one that's not too hard or dry—but also make sure not to undercook it or the burfi will not set properly.

Substitutions
For the granulated sugar, you can substitute ½ cup jaggery powder. Almond flour can be a one-to-one substitute for cashew flour.

Storage
Store the burfi in an airtight container in the refrigerator for up to 1 week.

CHINESE WALNUT COOKIES

Makes
16 cookies

Prep Time
15 minutes

Inactive Time
30 minutes

Cook Time
18 to 20 minutes

Difficulty
★★☆☆☆
(It'll be a bit of an adventure sourcing the ingredients.)

About 1 ⅓ cups (164 g) cake flour
½ teaspoon baking soda
Pinch of baker's ammonia
⅓ cup plus 1 tablespoon (84 g) lard
⅓ cup plus 1 tablespoon (84 g) granulated sugar
1 teaspoon red miso
1 large egg
1 to 2 cooked salted duck egg yolks, mashed with a fork (optional)
1 large egg, beaten, for egg wash
16 walnuts, for topping
Sesame seeds, for garnish (optional)

There are several variations of Chinese walnut cookies (hahp tòuh sōu or 合桃酥), but my favorite is this golden-yellow, crispy-crumbly version with a big, fat walnut on top. These are the cookies you'd find in Chinese bakeries back in the olden days (which, according to my kiddo Phil, includes the 1990s and earlier, before baking with lard fell out of fashion).

Another key ingredient in these cookies is baker's ammonia, known in Chinese as "stinky powder" or 臭粉. Due to its strong odor and limited use as a baking ingredient, it, like lard, is rarely used these days in Western baking. However, the two work beautifully together to give these cookies the crispy, airy, and crumbly texture I adore, known in Chinese as sūng fa (鬆化), which roughly translates to "loose." You can usually find lard in supermarkets, while baker's ammonia can be sourced online.

As fond as I am of the original, I have always felt that these cookies could benefit from a pop of flavor. Hence, I add umami-rich miso and mashed salted egg yolk to the dough. As my mother says, salted egg yolk makes everything better.

1. Whisk the cake flour, baking soda, and baker's ammonia together in a medium bowl.

2. Using a stand mixer fitted with the paddle attachment (or in a large bowl with a hand mixer, whisk, or spatula), cream the lard, sugar, and miso together until light and fluffy. Scrape down the sides and bottom of the bowl. Add the egg and salted duck egg yolks, if using, and mix until well incorporated. Add the flour mixture and mix on low speed just until a cookie dough forms. Cover the dough and chill in the refrigerator for 30 minutes.

3. While the dough is chilling, adjust a rack to the middle position and preheat the oven to 350°F. Line two baking sheets with parchment paper.

RECIPE *continues* →

CHINESE WALNUT COOKIES, *continued*

Cookie Tip
Look for vacuum-sealed cooked salted duck egg yolks from brands like Asian Taste, Red Plum, and Ocean Champ at your local Asian supermarket; avoid whole, shell-on salted duck eggs. You'll have to remove the yolk from the shell and have very salty egg white leftover. Cover with a wet paper towel and microwave for 15 seconds to soften the duck eggs.

Substitutions
If you don't have baker's ammonia, use 4 grams of baking powder instead.

Although baked goods made with lard are usually flakier and less dense than those made with butter, substituting lard for butter in baking is not always a straightforward one-to-one replacement. A good starting point is using about 20 percent less lard than butter if you're substituting by volume (not by weight) and then adjust as necessary based on the dough or batter consistency. So for this recipe, you'd need about ½ cup butter to substitute for the lard.

Storage
Store the cookies in an airtight container at room temperature for up to 3 days. They start losing crispness after prolonged storage.

4. Portion the dough into 16 equal pieces, about 24 grams each. Shape each piece into a small ball and place 1 inch apart on the prepared baking sheets. Gently flatten each ball with your palm to form a thick disc. Create a small indentation in the center of each disc. Brush the top of each cookie evenly with egg wash, then center a walnut in each indentation. If you like, garnish the cookies with sesame seeds.

5. Bake until the tops are golden brown, crackly, and glossy, 18 to 20 minutes. Transfer the cookies to a wire rack to cool completely. The cookies will be crispier once set and cooled.

TAMAGO BORO (Japanese Egg Biscuits)

Makes a few dozen tiny cookies, depending on how big you make them

Prep Time 15 minutes

Cook Time 18 minutes

Difficulty ★★★½☆ (This recipe can be a little tricky. The dough can quickly become crumbly and dry.)

- 2 large egg yolks
- 3 tablespoons plus 1 teaspoon (70 g) sweetened condensed milk, plus more as needed
- 3 tablespoons (42 g) unsalted butter, softened
- 1 teaspoon Japanese whisky
- 1 cup plus 1 tablespoon (140 g) cornstarch, sifted, plus more if needed
- 1 teaspoon milk powder
- 1 teaspoon baking powder
- ½ teaspoon freeze-dried strawberry powder, plus more for dusting
- ½ teaspoon sakura powder, plus more for dusting
- Pinch of kosher salt

Tamago boro are tiny Japanese egg biscuits that melt in your mouth and are meant to be eaten by the dozen. They're not-too-sweet and super light, almost like eating air. Jake and I remember having these growing up, which makes sense as tamago boro are meant to be snacks for children. You'll even see the words "baby cookies" on the packaging. Nowadays, Jake likes to pop a few between video calls, delighting his inner child, and I enjoy making them at home. While you can find different variations in Asian supermarkets, I think you should try baking them at least once. They're fun and therapeutic to make. The store-bought versions usually feature plain egg flavor, but recently, I've seen strawberry and matcha varieties.

These cookies have a history dating back to 19th-century Japan, when the Portuguese introduced bolo, a confectionery that the Japanese adapted into these light, airy, not-too-sweet treats. They remain popular today for their simplicity and texture. Typically made with cornstarch or potato starch, tamago boro crumble and melt in your mouth. Some people find them a bit "powdery" or "chalky." To counteract that, you can swap out some of the cornstarch for bread flour, though I prefer to keep the cookies gluten-free.

1. Adjust a rack to the middle position and preheat the oven to 325°F. Line a baking sheet with parchment paper.

2. Using a rubber spatula, mix the egg yolks, condensed milk, butter, and whisky together in a medium bowl until fully incorporated. Add the cornstarch, milk powder, baking powder, strawberry powder, sakura powder, and salt. Mix until a smooth dough that's no longer sticky forms. Take a small portion of dough and shape into a ball. If it holds its shape, it's ready. If it crumbles and falls apart, mix a teaspoon of milk or a little more sweetened condensed milk into the dough. Conversely, if the dough is too sticky, add a little more cornstarch, a scant

RECIPE *continues* →

福

Cookie Tip
Please save the egg whites for another recipe, like the Ondeh-Ondeh Macarons on page 282, Paciencia Galletas on page 99, or Laura's Matcha Langues de Chat on page 293.

Variations
For matcha-flavored tamago boro, swap out the whisky for 1 teaspoon almond extract or other flavored extract, and instead of the sakura and strawberry powder, mix in 1 teaspoon matcha in step 2.

Storage
Store the cookies in an airtight jar or container at room temperature for up to 3 days.

teaspoon at a time. If you add too much, the dough will become very crumbly and dry.

3. Turn the dough out onto a lightly floured surface. Divide into three equal portions and roll each into a long rope about 1 cm in diameter. Keeping any unused dough covered and working with one rope at a time, cut the dough into 1-cm pieces and shape each piece into a smooth ball. Work with wet hands so the balls will be smoother. Place the balls on the prepared baking sheets, spacing them evenly together, as the cookies don't spread or expand much. Continue until all the dough is used.

4. Spray or mist water over the tops of the cookies and in the oven. This keeps the exterior crispy. Bake for 5 minutes, then spray the tops of the cookies with water again. Bake for another 5 minutes and spray the tops with water once again to prevent the tops from over-cracking and to keep the interior light and airy. Rotate the baking sheet and bake until the edges and bottoms are golden brown and the cookies are crispy, 8 minutes.

5. Place the baking sheet on a wire rack and allow the cookies to cool completely. If you like, dust the cookies with a little strawberry or sakura powder, or both.

PACIENCIA GALLETAS (Filipino Meringue Cookies)

Makes
about
20 cookies

Prep Time
10 minutes

Cook Time
18 to 20 minutes

Difficulty
★★★☆☆
(Whipping egg whites with more added sugar takes patience, even with a stand mixer. Not overmixing the final cookie batter also takes a little skill. If you've made macarons before, your macaronage skills will come in handy here.)

¼ cup (30 g) all-purpose flour or 1:1 gluten-free flour

2 tablespoons finely ground cashews or almond flour

¼ teaspoon baking powder

¼ teaspoon kosher salt

2 large egg whites

¼ teaspoon cream of tartar

½ cup (100 g) granulated sugar

1 teaspoon ube extract (with color)

2 teaspoons rum

For optional toppings

Slivered almonds

Toasted sesame seeds

Sweetened shredded coconut

"Paciencia" means patience in Spanish, and making these Filipino meringue galletas (or cookies) used to require a lot of it, especially before stand and hand mixers became commonplace in the home. I honestly believe recipes like these were meant to keep housewives of the olden days occupied. But jokes aside, some Filipino galletas trace their origins back to the Spanish colonization of the Philippines, which spanned over 300 years and left a lasting influence on Filipino cuisine. These paciencia galletas are light, crispy, and chewy, reminding me of crunchy marshmallows and the delicate cookie layers that make up sylvanas. Jake told me how these cookies also remind him of all the ones he enjoyed with his grandmother back in Bacolod City.

Since we now have modern tools and more time to make these cookies, I figured why not add a fun modern twist to a traditional recipe? I've included ground cashews and ube extract in the cookie batter to add purple color, ube and nutty flavor, and texture. I'm not sure Jake's grandmother, who rests in peace now, would approve of my rendition, but I wanted to make something new out of a recipe from the Old World for Philip to enjoy. Both he and Jake love these and, between the two of them, twenty of these galletas can disappear rather quickly.

1. Adjust two racks to the upper- and lower-middle positions of the oven. Preheat the oven to 350°F. Line two baking sheets with parchment paper.

2. Whisk the flour, ground cashews or almond flour, baking powder, and salt together in a medium bowl. Set aside.

3. Using a stand mixer fitted with the whisk attachment, beat the egg whites and cream of tartar on high speed until white and frothy, about 2 minutes. Add the sugar in increments and whisk on high speed until stiff, glossy peaks form,

RECIPE *continues* →

Cookie Tips
Instead of piping, you can use a teaspoon to drop spoonfuls of batter onto the baking sheets and bake these as drop cookies. They will just look more rustic.

Variation
Rum is popular in the Philippines; however, not everyone has alcohol at home, so it's fine to omit it.

Storage
Store the cookies in an airtight container in a cool, dry place or refrigerate for up to 3 days.

8 to 10 minutes. Add the ube extract and rum, if using, and mix on low speed until combined. Use a rubber spatula to fold in the flour mixture until thoroughly combined, but don't overmix.

4. Transfer the batter to a piping bag fitted with a medium round tip. Pipe the batter into 2-inch rounds, spaced 1 inch apart, onto the prepared baking sheets. If you like (and I recommend it), garnish the tops of the cookies with slivered almonds, sesame seeds, or shredded coconut, or a mix of these toppings.

5. Bake all the cookies, switching the sheets between the top and bottom racks and rotating front to back once halfway through, until the edges are golden brown, 18 to 20 minutes.

6. Let the cookies set and cool directly on the baking sheets. When they are still warm, they will stick to the parchment paper, but once cooled, they will be easy to remove.

PANDAN, COCONUT, AND CARDAMOM LADOO

Makes
about 22 ladoo

Prep Time
10 minutes

Inactive Time
About 15 minutes

Cook Time
About 11 minutes

Difficulty
★★☆☆☆
(Heating the mixture to the right consistency is slightly challenging.)

2 ½ cups (213 g) desiccated coconut, plus extra for coating

2 tablespoons (28 g) ghee, butter, or olive oil, plus more for shaping

⅓ cup (47 g) chopped pistachios, plus more for garnishing

One 14-ounce (300 g) can sweetened condensed milk

1 tablespoon red miso (gluten-free if that's a concern), or to taste

1 tablespoon pandan extract (with color)

½ teaspoon ground cardamom

¼ teaspoon rose water

Sea salt flakes

Whenever I make extra food or test new recipes, I always share the surplus with my neighbors. One time, after I sent desserts over to my next-door neighbors Shilpa and Rahul, Shilpa returned the favor the next day by sharing her homemade ladoo (or laddu) with us. Ladoo are popular, traditional Indian sweets integral to celebrations and festivities. Shilpa wouldn't share her recipe, as it was her mother-in-law's secret, but she did point me to the Internet, saying how most ladoo are made the same way.

She was right. Most ladoo are spherical and made with a type of flour (like gram, chickpea, or semolina), a sweetener (such as jaggery, syrup, or sugar), and ghee. Recently, condensed milk has become a popular binding ingredient for ladoo, and they're often made like you would make Masala Macaroons (page 204), but without having to use the oven.

I wanted to change things up a bit and present my unique interpretation of ladoo to Shilpa and her family. I worried, however, that these pretty green pandan, coconut, and cardamom balls, slightly floral with rose water, were not "authentic enough" for my neighbors. To my relief and joy, Shilpa and Rahul (and their little one) welcomed my creative twist with open arms.

1. Pulse the desiccated coconut in a food processor or blender for a few seconds until it's a little finer, but not a powder. In a large nonstick pan or heavy saucepan, heat the ghee, butter, or oil over medium heat. Add the desiccated coconut and chopped pistachios. Cook, stirring continuously, until fragrant and lightly roasted, but not browned, about 4 minutes.

RECIPE *continues* →

Ladoo Tip
If you find the mixture too sticky to handle, let it cool a bit more. You can also refrigerate the mixture for 10 to 15 minutes to make shaping easier.

Variations
Use olive oil (instead of ghee) and sweetened condensed coconut milk (instead of dairy condensed milk) to make this recipe vegan.

Substitute the pistachios with any other nut, like slivered almonds.

Storage
Store the ladoo in an airtight container in the refrigerator for up to a week. I like them better when they are cold.

2. Reduce the heat to low and add the condensed milk, still stirring continuously. Mix in the miso, pandan extract, ground cardamom, and rose water until well combined. Continue to mix and stir over low heat, until the mixture thickens and pulls away in a uniform lump from the sides of the pan, about 7 minutes. If you overcook the mixture, the ladoo will be dry. Remove a tiny piece (it'll be hot) and carefully test to see if it can hold its shape. If yes, remove the ladoo dough from the heat and set aside to cool for a few minutes, until it's cool enough to hold and shape with your hands.

3. Line a baking sheet with parchment paper (or you can use plates). Spread about ⅓ cup desiccated coconut in a shallow bowl.

4. Grease your hands with a little ghee, butter, or oil. Portion the dough into walnut-sized pieces, or about a heaping tablespoon each, and shape into smooth, round, and compact balls. Roll each ball in the coconut to thoroughly coat, then press a few pieces of chopped pistachios on top. Sprinkle with some sea salt flakes and arrange on the prepared baking sheet to cool completely. You can also cover and refrigerate until ready for serving.

光酥餅 OLD-FASHIONED CANTONESE SHORTBREAD

Makes
8 large cookies

Prep Time
15 minutes

Inactive Time
30 minutes

Cook Time
About 20 minutes

Difficulty
★★½☆☆
(The texture can be tricky.)

About 2¾ cups (340 g) cake flour

2 tablespoons milk powder or buttermilk powder

2 teaspoons baking powder

Pinch of baker's ammonia

Pinch of kosher salt

1 large egg, beaten

½ cup (125 g) milk

¾ cup plus 1 tablespoon (160 g) granulated sugar

1 tablespoon plus ½ teaspoon (20 g) lard

All-purpose flour, for dusting

Confectioners' sugar, for dusting (optional)

These cookies go by many names: Chinese shortbread, Cantonese shortbread, and Chinese white biscuits. Pronounced gwōng sōu bóng (光酥餅) in Cantonese, they're an old-fashioned and traditional cakey cookie popular across Hong Kong and Guangdong, especially during the early- and mid-1900s. Typically snow white, large, fluffy, and crumbly, they're the perfect snack to pair with afternoon tea (matcha, oolong, or jasmine, preferably). Given these cookies' muddy origins (I've searched extensively and am unable to pinpoint a single inventor or bakery of this treat), I can't help but wonder if they reflect British influence. After all, Hong Kong was a British colony for over 150 years.

The first time these cookies came out of our oven, my mom immediately knew what they were, even though, growing up in Hong Kong, she never got to try them. While they only cost pennies during the mid-1960s, my mother saved up her money for more substantial meals, like instant noodles. When she bit into one of my Cantonese shortbread, she got teary-eyed and said, "So, this is what they taste like. I finally get to eat them, in my seventies."

Note that with each bite, it's intended for the flour to coat your lips. If you feel there's too much flour atop the cookies, feel free to brush it off before eating.

1. In a large mixing bowl, whisk the cake flour, milk or buttermilk powder, baking powder, baker's ammonia, and salt together. Add the egg, milk, granulated sugar, and lard and mix with a spatula until well combined into a wet, sticky but cohesive dough. This dough is meant to be wetter and sticky. Cover and chill in the refrigerator for 30 minutes.

2. About 20 minutes before baking, adjust two racks to the upper- and lower-middle positions of the oven. Preheat the oven to 300°F. Line two baking sheets with parchment paper.

RECIPE *continues* →

Cookie Tip
You can substitute baking soda for the baker's ammonia, but for the most nostalgic and traditional smell, texture, and taste of these cookies, try to find baker's ammonia. Don't be tempted to add a lot more flour to the dough when it's sticky; it's meant to be wetter, but still easy to work with.

Storage
Store the cookies in an airtight container at room temperature for up to 2 days.

3. Place the dough on a lightly floured work surface and dust with all-purpose flour. Knead for about 30 seconds. If the dough is too sticky to work with, dust your hands and the dough with more flour, but not too much, as the shortbread will be too dry. Divide into two equal portions. Working with one portion, roll the dough into a log and divide into four equal portions, each 71 to 75 grams. Roll each portion into a smooth ball and transfer to one prepared baking sheet, spacing them about 3 inches apart. Repeat with the remaining portion of dough to make four more dough balls and transfer to the second baking sheet.

4. Use your palm to gently press down on each dough ball, flattening it to approximately ½ inch thick. Dust the tops with all-purpose flour to achieve a snow-white finish. Lightly pat the tops with your hand to help the flour stick to the cookies. Bake all the cookies, switching the sheets between top and bottom racks and rotating front to back once halfway through, until the tops crack and the bottoms of the cookies begin to brown, about 20 minutes.

5. Allow the cookies to set and cool on the baking sheets. If you like, dust the tops with confectioners' sugar.

肚臍餅 BELLY BUTTON BISCUITS

Makes a couple dozen mini cookies	*Inactive Time* A few hours to overnight	*Difficulty* ★★★★☆ (Whipping egg whites into meringue takes practice, and quite a bit of assembly and patience is required.)
Prep Time 25 minutes	*Cook Time* 27 minutes plus drying time	

For the shortbread cookies

½ cup |1 stick (113 g) unsalted butter, softened

⅔ cup (80 g) confectioners' sugar

2 large egg yolks

1 teaspoon red miso

1 ½ cups plus 2 tablespoons (195 g) cake flour, sifted

Pinch of kosher salt

For the meringue icing

2 large egg whites

¼ teaspoon cream of tartar

6 tablespoons (75 grams) granulated sugar

Food coloring of choice (like pink, yellow, and green; ube and pandan extracts with color can also be used)

Growing up, I fondly recall sharing with my younger sister Evelyn what we called belly button biscuits (肚臍餅) (tóuh chìh béng) in Cantonese, known to many as iced gem biscuits (花佔餅) (fā jim béng). These delightful treats, originally from Britain, feature a small round cookie topped with a bright and colorful hard icing. The treat gained significant popularity in parts of Asia, particularly in Hong Kong, Singapore, and Malaysia, where they are cherished as a nostalgic snack. They made their way to Asian supermarkets in the States, where my mother would buy jars for Evelyn and me.

One could argue there's no wrong way to eat belly button biscuits, but the truly right way, at least according to the 10-year-old me, is to split the hard icing from the base cookie and enjoy the two separately. That cheeky child would also tell you to just eat the icing. Ironically, these days, I find the icing a little too sweet and hard for my taste, so I've opted to top the cookies with a meringue "icing" instead. While this means extra work and you'll have to wait to enjoy the cookies, the light, airy, meringue icing is worth it. And plus, it won't break adult teeth.

1. **Make the shortbread cookies.** Using a stand mixer fitted with the paddle attachment (or in a mixing bowl with a hand mixer, whisk, or spatula), cream the butter and confectioners' sugar until well combined. Add the egg yolks and miso and mix until incorporated. Add the cake flour and salt and mix on low speed just until a shortbread dough forms. Cover and refrigerate for 1 hour to overnight.

2. About 20 minutes before baking, adjust a rack to the middle position and preheat the oven to 300°F. Line a baking sheet with parchment paper.

3. Use a ½-teaspoon measuring spoon to scoop some dough and roll into a ball. If desired, flatten the ball slightly and use the tines of a fork to imprint marks around the edges, for a cute aesthetic. Repeat to make about 25 cookies and evenly

RECIPE *continues* →

Cookie Tips
Whipping the meringue to stiff, glossy peaks will ensure the meringue icing has a perfect texture and stability for piping.

You can bake the meringue and the cookies separately, then stick them together with a dollop of jam, honey, or sweetened condensed milk.

Storage
Store the belly button biscuits in an airtight container at room temperature for up to 4 days.

space them on the prepared baking sheet. Bake the cookies for 12 minutes. Set the cookies aside to cool. Reduce the oven temperature to 200°F.

4. **Make the meringue icing.** Meanwhile, using a stand mixer fitted with the whisk attachment, beat the egg whites and cream of tartar on high speed until white and frothy, about 2 minutes. Add the granulated sugar in increments and whisk on high speed until stiff, glossy peaks form, 6 to 8 minutes.

5. Split the meringue into three or four equal portions and transfer each portion you want colored to separate bowls. You can leave one portion white (uncolored). Add a few drops of a different food coloring of choice to each bowl and use a rubber spatula to gently mix to combine. Transfer the meringue to a piping bag fitted with a star tip.

6. Pipe a dollop of meringue, each resembling a "star-shaped ice gem," onto each cooled cookie. If you have extra meringue, pipe directly on the baking sheet to make meringue cookies.

7. Bake the cookies for 15 minutes, then turn off the oven. Leave the cookies inside the oven with the door closed to dry out the meringue for about 1 hour or overnight, until the meringue is dry and no longer sticky. Remove from the oven and enjoy.

SRI LANKAN "ROCK" SUGAR COOKIES (Gnanakatha) WITH POPPING CANDY

Makes
24 to 26 cookies

Prep Time:
15 minutes

Cook Time:
16 to 18 minutes, plus a few minutes to melt the white chocolate

Difficulty:
★★★☆☆
(This cookie is relatively simple to bake, but there's some dough kneading and decorating at the end with melted white chocolate that requires you to move fast.)

- 1 ⅔ cups (200 g) all-purpose flour
- 1 teaspoon baking powder
- 1 teaspoon ground Ceylon cinnamon
- Pinch of ground anise (optional)
- ½ cup (113 g) margarine, softened
- ½ cup (100 g) granulated sugar
- 1 tablespoon red miso
- 1 large egg
- Milk, if needed

For dipping and topping the cookies

- ¼ cup (36 g) demerara, coarse, or decorating sugar, plus more as needed, placed in a shallow bowl
- About 2 ounces (57 g) white chocolate, chopped
- 1 teaspoon neutral oil or coconut oil
- 1 to 2 (0.33-ounce) packets of popping candy (your favorite flavor)
- Sea salt flakes

Sri Lankan sugar or rock cookies, known as gnanakatha, are the inspiration behind these cookies. Gnanakatha are the result of Portuguese colonization of Sri Lanka, possibly drawing inspiration from the Portuguese sand cookies called areias de Cascais. At the core, gnanakatha are butter cookies, and thanks to a layer of sugar on top, usually sweet. You can likely find them in bakeries and cafes in Sri Lanka.

My addition of popping candy (Philip's favorite) to top the cookies brings a modern and fun twist. My recipe is an interpretation, and by no means a traditional gnanakatha you'd find in Sri Lanka. Still, you can enjoy these teatime treats with a bold cup of tea, like a good Ceylon or black tea, just like the Sri Lankans do.

1. Adjust two racks to the upper- and lower-middle positions of the oven. Preheat the oven to 350°F. Line two baking sheets with parchment paper.

2. Whisk the flour, baking powder, cinnamon, and anise, if using, together in a medium bowl and set aside.

3. Using a stand mixer fitted with the paddle attachment (or in a mixing bowl with a hand mixer, whisk, or spatula), cream the margarine, granulated sugar, and miso until light and fluffy. Add the egg and mix until incorporated. Add the flour mixture and mix on low speed just until a dough forms. If the dough is too crumbly or dry, mix in a little milk, about a teaspoon at a time, until the dough is cohesive and no longer crumbly. Turn the

RECIPE *continues* →

dough out onto a lightly floured work surface and knead until smooth, about 1 minute.

4. Portion the dough into about 25 walnut-sized pieces and roll each into a smooth ball. Flatten each with your palms to about ½ inch thick. Dip one side of each dough round into the bowl of demerara sugar; you only want to coat the top side of the cookie with sugar. Place the rounds on the prepared baking sheets, sugar-side up and spaced 2 inches apart.

5. Bake all the cookies, switching the sheets between top and bottom racks and rotating front to back once halfway through, until the edges are golden brown and set, 16 to 18 minutes. Remove from the oven and after a few minutes, transfer to a wire rack to cool completely.

6. Meanwhile, melt the white chocolate with the oil in the microwave in a small heatproof bowl in 30-second bursts, stirring between each burst, until smooth and creamy. Holding one edge of a cookie, dip the opposite side into the melted chocolate, so only half of the cookie is coated with the white chocolate, and immediately sprinkle with popping candy. Top with sea salt flakes. Melted white chocolate cools and sets fast, so don't delay in decorating the cookies with it. Place the cookies back on the wire rack or parchment paper to allow the chocolate to set completely. Alternatively, you can drizzle the melted chocolate over the cookies, then top with the popping candy and sea salt.

Variation
If you have access to arak (or arrak), a popular spirit in Sri Lanka, add a teaspoon or so to the dough when you mix in the egg. It has notes like those found in rum and whiskey, plus a burst of anise flavor.

Substitution
You can substitute salted butter for the margarine one-to-one; however, you'll find Sri Lankan bakers use margarine more (especially a brand called Astra) to make gnanakatha.

Storage
Store the cookies in an airtight container at room temperature for up to 5 days.

MIDDLE EASTERN SHORTBREAD (Ghraybeh)

Makes	*Prep Time:*	*Cook Time:*	*Difficulty:*
34 to 36 cookies	About 15 minutes *Inactive Time:* 30 minutes	About 12 minutes	★★½☆☆ (Creating the perfect indent for the jam takes practice.)

⅔ cup (150 g) ghee, cold

1 teaspoon rose water or orange blossom water (optional)

⅔ cup (80 g) confectioners' sugar

2 cups (240 g) all-purpose flour

½ teaspoon ground cardamom

Pinch of kosher salt

About ⅓ cup yuzu marmalade, for topping

Pistachios, for topping

Edible rose petals, for topping (optional)

In the past, the Silk Road touched areas that are now Afghanistan, Iraq, Iran, and Syria, so it's fitting to include ghraybeh (or ghoraybeh), a Middle Eastern shortbread, in this chapter. Ghraybeh is usually made with a maximum of three to five ingredients, and you'll commonly see the shortbread as treats and gifts during holidays like Eid in Palestine and Christmas in Lebanon. I decided not to stray too far from traditional ghraybeh recipes, as the simple shortbread cookies are delicious on their own. But I did add a tiny, personalized touch: a baby bed of yuzu marmalade topped with a pistachio, one of my favorite nuts of all time.

1. Using a stand mixer fitted with the paddle attachment (or in a large bowl with a rubber spatula), cream the ghee until light and fluffy. Scrape down the sides and bottom of the bowl with a rubber spatula. If you like, stir in rose or orange blossom water. Add the confectioners' sugar and mix until well incorporated. Add the flour, cardamom, and salt and mix on low speed. The dough will appear dry at first, but will come together. Cover and chill in the refrigerator for 30 minutes.

2. While the dough is chilling, adjust two racks to the upper- and lower-middle positions of the oven. Preheat the oven to 350°F. Line two baking sheets with parchment paper.

3. The dough should now be easy to shape into a smooth ball that doesn't stick to your fingers. Scoop 1 tablespoon (15 to 16 grams) dough for each cookie and shape into a smooth ball, making about 35 balls and placing them 1 inch apart on the prepared baking sheets. Use your thumb to make an imprint in the top center of each dough ball. Fill each indent with about 1 teaspoon of yuzu marmalade. If you like a more jammy cookie, form a well in the dough ball so you can fill it with more marmalade, as pictured.

RECIPE *continues* →

4. Bake all the cookies, switching the sheets between top and bottom racks and rotating front to back once halfway through, until the edges are set, about 12 minutes.

5. Let the cookies rest on the baking sheet for a few minutes before transferring to a wire rack to cool completely. Top the shortbread with more yuzu marmalade, then press a pistachio into the jammy tops of each cookie. If you like, garnish with edible rose petals. These shortbread cookies are rich and buttery, so enjoy with hot tea or strong coffee.

Cookie Tip
Trusting that the dough will be manageable after chilling may be difficult for some. Don't dump in more flour, even if tempted!

Variations
For the yuzu marmalade, you can substitute your favorite jam, or try using Korean citron. Instead of the cardamom, try nutmeg, cinnamon, or five spice powder.

Storage
Store the shortbread in an airtight container at room temperature for up to 1 week.

VIETNAMESE CHEWY SESAME CANDY (Kẹo Mè Xửng)

Makes 24 to 36 candy squares	*Inactive Time* 4 hours to overnight	*Difficulty* ★★★★☆ (Be patient—it'll take you 20 to 25 minutes to heat up the sugar mixture.)
Prep Time 15 minutes	*Cook Time* About 30 minutes	

- 1 tablespoon sesame oil
- ⅔ cup (93 g) toasted white sesame seeds
- ⅓ cup (47 g) toasted black sesame seeds
- 1 cup (240 g) water
- ¼ cup (38 g) tapioca starch
- 1 cup (322 g) light corn syrup
- 1 ⅓ cups (200 g) unpacked light brown sugar
- 2 tablespoons unsalted butter
- 2 tablespoons grated fresh ginger
- 1 tablespoon lemon juice
- 1 tablespoon red miso
- 1 teaspoon ground Vietnamese cinnamon (optional)
- 1 cup (140 g) roasted, unsalted skinless peanuts
- 1 cup (140 g) roasted, unsalted cashews, chopped

Candied nuts, brittles, and chewy sesame candies like this one are very popular across Asia and among Asian diasporas, with variations including walnuts, cashews, and pumpkin seeds. Hence, I grew up eating a lot of these treats, especially around Lunar New Year, as I mentioned in my Lace Cookies with Miso Caramel and Sesame recipe (page 61). As these treats are chewy, like nutty caramel, I had always enjoyed them like they were cookies, rather than candy. I tend to savor small bites at a time rather than popping the whole thing in my mouth like I would a confection.

Chewy sesame candy is so popular in Vietnam that they have a version named after Huế, the country's former imperial capital. Tourists visiting the city would always bring home the crispy, sweet, nutty, and chewy candy that is rich in toasty sesame flavor, just like the ones you'll be making here.

1. Crumple, then uncrumple a large sheet of parchment paper and use to line a 9-inch square cake pan with some overhang. Smooth and press down the parchment paper with your hands. Brush the parchment paper with the sesame oil.

2. Mix the white and black sesame seeds together in a medium bowl. Sprinkle half of the sesame seeds evenly over the prepared baking pan. Set the pan aside, along with the remaining sesame seed mixture.

3. In a heavy saucepan, mix the water and tapioca starch together until the starch dissolves. Place over medium heat and stir in the corn syrup, brown sugar, butter, ginger, lemon juice, miso, and Vietnamese cinnamon, if using. Keep stirring every few minutes, even after the sugar dissolves, and cook for about 20 minutes, until the mixture is amber-colored, thick, and a candy or digital thermometer registers between 240°F and

RECIPE *continues* →

Cookie Tips

The simplest way to toast the sesame seeds or nuts is in a frying pan or skillet over medium-low heat until aromatic, shiny, and golden, a few minutes. The seeds, being smaller, will toast up quicker than the nuts. You can also buy all the ingredients pre-toasted.

You'll need a candy or digital thermometer handy to ensure you get the sugar to the right temperature and texture. Sugar also loves to crystallize when we try to caramelize it; the acidity in the lemon juice and the corn syrup, an invert sugar, will help to prevent crystallization.

Storage

Store the candy, separately wrapped in plastic wrap or parchment paper, in an airtight container at room temperature for up to 1 week.

245°F (the soft ball stage: a bit of the hot syrup dropped into cold water will turn into a pliable ball). Immediately reduce the heat to low and quickly stir in the peanuts and cashews with a rubber spatula or wooden spoon. The sugar will be very hot and can burn you immediately, so exercise caution.

4. Carefully and quickly transfer the mixture to the prepared baking pan, pressing it down into an even layer with the wooden spoon or spatula. Sprinkle the remaining sesame seeds over the candy. It's best to use a greased fondant smoother to compact, flatten, and smooth out the candy further, though a wooden spoon works too.

5. Cover and refrigerate for at least 4 hours (up to 24 hours if you prefer firmer candy), before cutting with a sharp, oiled knife into 24 to 36 equal squares. When set, the inside should remain quite soft and chewy, like a chewy caramel. The candy should not stick to your teeth.

THAI SHORTBREAD COOKIES (Khanom Kleeb Lamduan)

Makes
15 to 16 cookies

Prep Time
50 minutes

Inactive Time
30 minutes

Cook Time
About 11 minutes

Difficulty
(Fine motor skills and assembly required, plus getting the dough to the right consistency can be difficult.)

¾ cup (90 g) cake flour

¼ cup (30 g) all-purpose flour

½ cup (60 g) confectioners' sugar

1 teaspoon ground cardamom (optional, but recommended)

1½ teaspoons red miso

1 teaspoon rose water or orange blossom water, or to taste

About ½ cup (109 g) neutral oil, divided, plus more as needed

3 different food coloring gels (optional)

1 tian op (optional)

Cookie Tip
If you come across a tian op, omit the cardamom and rose water or orange blossom water. After the cookies have cooled down, place them in a shallow bowl or dish with the tian op in the middle. Light the candle (be careful as it burns quickly) and after a few seconds, cover the bowl with a lid or plate. Set aside for about 30 minutes to let the cookies absorb the candle's scent.

Variation
Brush the cookies with egg wash and top with sesame seeds before baking.

Storage
Store the cookies in an airtight container at room temperature for up to 5 days.

Sometimes, you come across a cookie that feels magical and these Thai flower shortbread cookies are the perfect example for me. During one of my first physical therapy jobs, a patient's wife gifted me these colorful cookies to thank me for taking care of her husband. To this day, I remember the fragrant scent of the cookies and their beautiful flower shape. This design isn't purely for aesthetics; it's intentionally crafted to mimic the lamduan, or white cheesewood flower, that's prevalent throughout Southeast Asia and, interestingly, recognized as the national flower of Cambodia. (Although this has been a source of contention between Thailand and Cambodia.)

After baking the cookies, you'd traditionally let them absorb the fragrance of a Thai-scented culinary candle, or tian op. They're usually sold in Asian-specialty supermarkets, and I bought mine online for an upcharge. But if you can't find them, fret not, as the rose water or orange blossom water in the cookies, plus the touch of cardamom, work together to make up for the floral scent.

1. Line a baking sheet with parchment paper.

2. Whisk the cake flour, all-purpose flour, confectioners' sugar, and cardamom, if using, together in a medium bowl. Add the miso and rose water or orange blossom water. Add ¼ cup of the neutral oil and mix with your clean fingertips or a fork. Slowly add a little more of the oil and mix until it resembles crumbly wet sand. Take a small portion of dough and compact it between your palms. If it holds its shape, it's ready. If it crumbles and falls apart, mix in a little more oil, about a teaspoon at a time. (It's likely you will need all ½ cup oil and a little more, about 2 tablespoons.) You want a dough that can hold its shape but isn't too oily. Shape the dough into a smooth ball. You will need to compact and squeeze the dough for it to hold its shape.

RECIPE *continues* →

Light the tian op to infuse the cookies with a smoky scent.

3. If using the food coloring, divide the dough into three equal portions. Working one at a time, color each portion evenly with a different food coloring gel (two or three drops of coloring should suffice), kneading to distribute the color thoroughly. If not using the food coloring, skip this step.

4. Working one at a time, make about 15 dough balls about 1 inch in diameter. Cut one ball into quarters to form four wedges. Roll one of the wedges into a small ball. The three remaining wedges will serve as the petals of one flower cookie, while the small ball will be the center. Using a knife, gently cut a Y-shape indentation on the top of the small ball of dough. Repeat to make flower petals and centers with the remaining dough.

5. Transfer three petal wedges to the prepared baking sheet. (These can be different color wedges, or wedges of the same color; it's up to you.) Gently press the tips of the wedges together to form a Y-shaped flower. Place a small ball of dough on top, directly centered on the flower. Repeat until all the dough is used, making about 15 flowers. Since these cookies aren't supposed to spread, a little spacing between each is enough. Transfer the sheet to the refrigerator to chill for 30 minutes.

6. Preheat the oven to 350°F with a rack in the center. Bake the cookies until they are starting to lightly brown, but just on the bottom, and are completely set, about 11 minutes. Let the cookies cool on the baking sheet. Enjoy with hot black or green tea.

◂
(top) Cut each ball into quarters.
(center) Bring three wedges together.
(bottom) Cut a Y-shape into the middle ball.

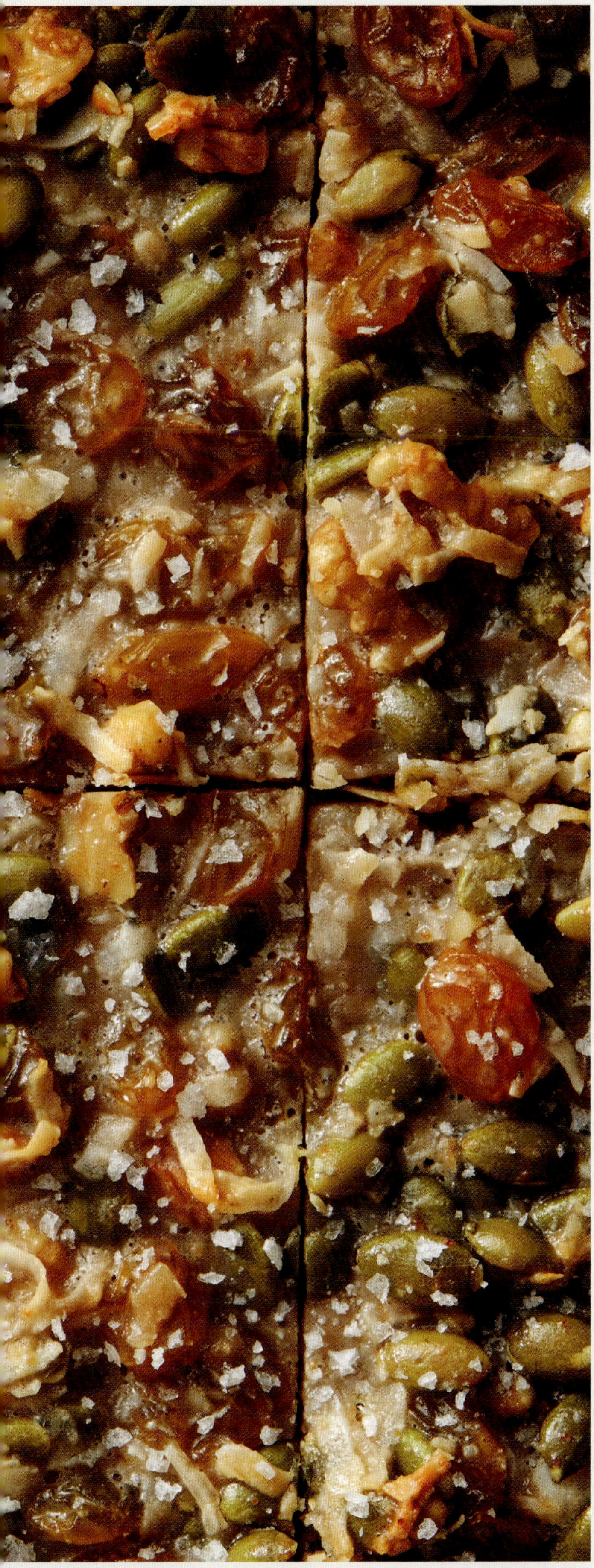

III

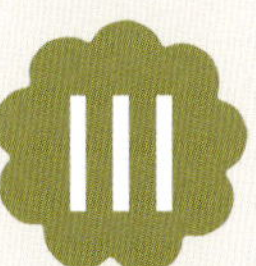

BROWNIES, BLONDIES, AND BARS (PLUS ONE BISCOTTI)

Delicious brownies, blondies, bars, and biscotti, all with subtly Asian twists

Growing up, the rich, overly sweet squares of brownies, blondies, and bars had never been my go-to treats (I've always loved a good crunchy biscotti dipped in hot coffee, however!). As an adult baker, I love experimenting and couldn't wait to reinvent these classic treats to suit my palate. How could I make a blondie less sweet and brownies more nuanced in flavor? Most importantly, what subtly Asian twist could I incorporate?

Playing with ube, pandan, black sesame, and miso, I had so much joy developing the recipes for this chapter, drawing from different cultures across Asia. I've dedicated the Ube Halaya Brownies (page 130) to my two favorite Filipinos, Jake and Philip. In sunlight, these brownies, packed with ube's vanilla and floral notes, gleam purple. Two other treats worth mentioning really nurture my inner child: the Black Sesame and Brown Butter Rice Krispies Treats (page 136) and my Dreams of Montreal Nanaimo Bars (page 166). I remember my mother making Rice Krispies Treats and she would always follow the instructions on the back of the cereal box to a T; my version, laden with nutty black sesame, never fails to impress her these days. As for the Nanaimo bars, I adapted them from the official recipe from the City of Nanaimo (adding pandan), and they always remind me of the ones my grandfather ZeZe would treat me to in Montreal during my childhood summers spent there.

Finally, I only have one biscotti recipe here, Sharon's Sakura and Strawberry Biscotti (page 163). Biscotti recipes are not simple, and kudos to my bestie Sharon for developing a beautiful pink one that tastes like spring, so don't skip it!

FUDGY BROWNIES WITH DALGONA COFFEE

Makes
9 brownies (or more if you slice them smaller)

Prep Time
15 minutes

Cook Time
About 35 minutes

Difficulty
★★★☆☆
(Most folks have experience making brownies already, but here, you're whipping instant coffee into a foamy cream, so that adds to the difficulty.)

Dalgona coffee, also known as whipped coffee, became a global phenomenon in early 2020 after South Korean actor Jung Il-woo introduced it on a TV show, naming it after the popular South Korean street toffee candy its flavor resembles. To make dalgona coffee, you vigorously whip equal parts instant coffee, sugar, and hot water until fluffy, then spoon it over hot or cold milk. Just so you know, it's meant to be bitter and very sweet, thus diluted in milk or water. Here, we spoon the whipped dalgona over delicious coffee-flavored fudgy brownies. Fair warning: Try not to eat these before you sleep because you'll get quite caffeinated from consuming just one. Unless you're like me, who can drink five cups of coffee a day and sleep just fine. Other things keep me up at night. (Pictured on page 127.)

For the brownies

- ½ cup plus 2 tablespoons (75 g) all-purpose flour
- ¼ cup (21 g) unsweetened Dutch-processed cocoa powder, sifted
- ½ teaspoon baking powder
- 6 ounces (170 g) semisweet chocolate, chopped
- ½ cup | 1 stick (113 g) unsalted butter, cubed
- 1 cup (200 g) granulated sugar
- ¼ cup (38 g) unpacked brown sugar
- 3 large eggs
- 1 tablespoon instant coffee powder mixed thoroughly with 2 tablespoons hot water
- 1 teaspoon red miso
- 1 teaspoon hazelnut extract (optional)

For the dalgona coffee topping

- ¼ cup (24 g) instant coffee
- ¼ cup (50 g) granulated sugar
- ¼ cup (60 g) hot water

For garnishing the brownies

- Chopped roasted hazelnuts
- Sea salt flakes

1. Adjust a rack to the middle position and preheat the oven to 350°F. Crumple, then uncrumple a large sheet of parchment paper and use it to line a 9-inch square cake pan with some overhang. Smooth and press down the parchment paper with your hands.

2. **Make the brownies.** Whisk the flour, cocoa powder, and baking powder together in a medium bowl and set aside.

3. Melt the chocolate and butter in the top of a double boiler over simmering water. Or melt in a large bowl in 20-second bursts in a microwave. Stir the melted mixture until smooth and homogenous. Mix in the sugars, eggs, instant coffee mixture, miso, and hazelnut extract, if using. It's okay if the mixture looks oily and gritty at this point.

4. Add the flour mixture to the wet ingredients and mix with a flexible spatula or whisk until just combined.

Brownie Tip
Mix any leftover dalgona coffee topping with cold or hot milk to enjoy as coffee.

Variation
To make gluten-free brownies, substitute the all-purpose flour with an equivalent amount of gluten-free baking flour.

Storage
Store unfrosted brownies in an airtight container at room temperature for up to 2 days.

5. Transfer the batter to the prepared baking pan. Be sure to spread the brownie mixture evenly, covering every corner of the dish. Bake until a bamboo skewer or toothpick inserted in the middle comes out clean or with brownie crumbs (not wet batter), the brownies are set, and the top is shiny and a little cracked, about 35 minutes. Cool completely on a wire rack.

6. **Make the dalgona coffee topping.** While the brownies are cooling, in a mixing bowl using a hand mixer or a whisk, vigorously whisk the instant coffee, sugar, and hot water until the mixture is thick and creamy and holds stiff peaks, a few minutes. (This can also be done in a stand mixer fitted with the whisk attachment or in a food processor.)

7. Slice the cooled brownies into nine equal pieces. Frost the tops with the dalgona coffee topping, using an offset spatula or a piping bag. Garnish the brownies with chopped roasted hazelnuts or sea salt flakes, or both.

UBE HALAYA BROWNIES

Makes	*Prep Time*	*Cook Time*	*Difficulty*
9 to 12 brownies	15 minutes	About 35 minutes	★★★☆☆ (You have to brown butter, but it's relatively easy afterward.)

½ cup | 1 stick (113 g) unsalted butter, cubed

4 ounces (113 g) high-quality white chocolate, chopped

¾ cup (112 g) unpacked light brown sugar

¼ cup (50 g) granulated sugar

½ cup (60 g) cake flour

2 ½ tablespoons (24 g) tapioca starch

½ teaspoon baking powder

⅓ cup (80 g) ube halaya

2 large eggs

1 tablespoon ube extract (with color)

1 tablespoon Japanese whisky or bourbon, plus more for brushing over the brownies

1 tablespoon red miso

⅓ cup (28 g) sweetened or unsweetened shredded coconut, plus more for topping

Sea salt flakes, for garnish

The boys in my family, Jake and Philip, love brownies. Since they're Filipino, I dedicated a special brownie recipe to them, incorporating heirloom produce from the Philippines: ube. These ube brownies are rich, fudgy, and beautifully purple, thanks to the addition of ube halaya and ube extract. Each bite is sweet and nutty, with a hint of umami from the miso. For an added touch of sophistication, brush the top of the still-hot brownies with Japanese whisky or bourbon. These brownies are my tribute to our third-culture household. Using ube to create a new version of one of my boys' favorite Western desserts is a delightful reminder of their roots.

1. Adjust a rack to the middle position and preheat the oven to 350°F. Crumple, then uncrumple a large sheet of parchment paper and use it to line an 8-inch square cake pan with some overhang. Smooth and press down the parchment paper with your hands.

2. To make the brown butter, melt the butter in a saucepan over medium heat, whisking continuously, until the butter foams, the foam subsides, the butter is golden, and brown (not black) bits form on the bottom, at least 5 minutes. You're looking for a nutty aroma, not a burnt smell. Remove from the heat and transfer the brown butter to a large heatproof bowl. Stir in the chopped white chocolate until fully melted. Add the sugars and mix until incorporated. Set aside.

3. Whisk the cake flour, tapioca starch, and baking powder together in a medium bowl.

4. To the chocolate mixture, add the ube halaya, eggs, ube extract, Japanese whisky or bourbon, and miso and mix until fully combined. Add the flour mixture and mix until incorporated and no white flour trails remain. Fold the coconut into the batter. Transfer the batter to the prepared baking pan and level the top with an offset spatula. Top with more coconut if desired.

RECIPE *continues* →

Brownie Tip
I've found that the Butterfly brand of ube extract yields the most vibrant purple.

Variation
Not everyone likes to bake with alcohol, or likes the flavor, so feel free to omit the booze.

Storage
Store the brownies in an airtight container at room temperature for up to 3 days.

5. Bake until the top is set and cracked and a toothpick or bamboo skewer inserted into the middle comes out clean, about 35 minutes.

6. Liberally brush the top with Japanese whisky or bourbon while the brownies are still hot. Garnish with sea salt flakes. The brownies can cool in the pan for up to 10 minutes, then transfer to a wire rack to cool completely. Once cooled, slice into nine to twelve equal brownies. Feel free to cut them smaller, but you and your loved ones probably want these generously sized.

REFRESHING YUZU MERINGUE SQUARES

Makes
16 squares

Prep Time
20 minutes

Cook Time
45 to 50 minutes for the crust and filling; 5 minutes for the meringue

Difficulty
★★★★☆
(The recipe itself is simple but there are many steps involved, including making a crust from scratch, blind baking it, then making the filling, and finally a meringue using a double boiler and a broiler.)

For the crust

1 cup (120 g) all-purpose flour

2 tablespoons plus 2 teaspoons (20 g) confectioners' sugar

5 ½ tablespoons (78 g) unsalted butter, cold

1 tablespoon red miso

1 tablespoon grated lemon zest

1 tablespoon yuzu juice

For the yuzu filling

4 large egg yolks

1 large egg

1 cup (200 g) granulated sugar

½ cup (120 g) yuzu juice

1 tablespoon red miso

½ cup (75 g) glutinous rice flour

2 tablespoons (19 g) cornstarch

2 tablespoons (12 g) grated lemon zest

For the meringue

2 large egg whites

2 tablespoons (25 g) granulated sugar

¼ teaspoon cream of tartar or 1 teaspoon lemon juice

I feel everything tastes better with a squeeze of lemon juice or other acidity. One of my favorite desserts, tangy lemon squares, gets an update here with yuzu, a floral and highly aromatic Japanese citrus fruit that has grapefruit and mandarin notes. It's nearly impossible to buy fresh yuzu in the States since it's illegal to import them from Japan. (But some farmers in California do grow fresh yuzu.) You should, however, be able to find yuzu juice. It does tend to be pricey, but I think it's worth having in your refrigerator because yuzu juice can brighten not just your desserts, but salads, marinades, and soups as well.

1. Adjust a rack to the middle position and preheat the oven to 350°F. Line a 9-inch square cake pan with aluminum foil. Smooth and press down the aluminum foil with your hands.

2. **Make the crust.** Whisk the flour and confectioners' sugar together in a mixing bowl. Using a fork, your clean fingers, or a bench knife, cut in the cold butter, miso, lemon zest, and yuzu juice until pea-sized crumbs form. Press the mixture evenly into the prepared baking pan. Use a fork and poke holes evenly across the surface of the crust. Blind bake (e.g., bake without any filling) until golden brown, about 20 minutes. Set aside to cool.

3. **Make the yuzu filling.** Using a stand mixer fitted with the paddle attachment (or in a large bowl with a hand mixer, whisk, or spatula), beat the egg yolks, egg, granulated sugar, yuzu juice, and miso until smooth. Mix in the glutinous rice flour, cornstarch, and lemon zest.

4. Pour the filling into the crust and bake until the filling is set and a bamboo skewer or toothpick inserted in the middle comes out clean, 25 to 30 minutes. Cool on a wire rack.

RECIPE *continues* →

Variations

To make these gluten-free, substitute 1:1 gluten-free flour for the all-purpose flour.

The yuzu squares also taste amazing on their own, so you can skip the meringue if you're short on time. Just give them a dusting of confectioners' sugar when they're completely cooled.

Storage

Store the squares in refrigerator, covered, for up to 1 week.

5. **Make the meringue.** Whisk the egg whites, granulated sugar, and cream of tartar or lemon juice in the top of a double boiler over simmering water. Lower the heat to medium and whisk continuously until all the sugar dissolves and the mixture is hot, about 135°F, 3 minutes. Be sure to wear an oven mitt to hold the bowl if needed. Remove the bowl from the saucepan and turn off the heat. By hand using a hand mixer or whisk, or in the bowl of a stand mixer fitted with a whisk attachment on medium-high, whisk the mixture until stiff, glossy peaks form, a few minutes. Use a spatula or offset spatula to spread the meringue over the yuzu squares in a swirling pattern.

6. Broil the squares on high on the uppermost rack of the oven, until the meringue is evenly toasted and golden brown, not blackened, up to 2 minutes. Alternatively, use a kitchen blowtorch to brown the meringue. Cover and refrigerate for at least one hour. To serve, cut into 16 equal squares.

BLACK SESAME AND BROWN BUTTER RICE KRISPIES TREATS

Makes
12 to 16 Rice Krispies Treats

Prep Time
10 minutes

Inactive Time
30 minutes

Cook Time
15 minutes

Difficulty
★★☆☆☆
(Cleaning the marshmallow off the pot or saucepan is the most challenging part for me.)

- 6 tablespoons (85 g) unsalted butter
- One 12-ounce (340 g) bag mini marshmallows
- ¼ cup (36 g) black sesame seeds
- 2 ½ tablespoons (38 g) black sesame paste
- 1 teaspoon red miso
- 6 cups (160 g) Rice Krispies cereal
- ⅓ cup (about 4 g) freeze-dried strawberry slices or haw flakes (optional)

Growing up, I ate my fair share of Rice Krispies Treats because they were one of the few Western sweets my mom made over and over again. Maybe it was because they were so easy to make and helped her feel a little closer to the typical mothers we saw on American sitcoms and primetime TV. Or maybe she just liked their chewiness. But for whatever reason, my mom never gave her Rice Krispies Treats an Asian spin. She always followed the recipe directions on the cereal box to a T.

Decades later, I make these black sesame brown butter Rice Krispies Treats with my mother in mind. She loves black sesame desserts, especially sweet black sesame soup, or 芝麻糊. As a child, I remember her telling me how black sesame would keep our Chinese hair black and long. We both have short hair peppered with gray now, but we still have a thing for desserts that sport a lovely shade of gray or black.

1. Crumple, then uncrumple a large sheet of parchment paper and use it to line a 9-inch square cake pan with some overhang. Smooth and press down the parchment paper with your hands. Alternatively, generously grease the baking dish with butter or toasted sesame oil.

2. To make the brown butter, melt the butter in a heavy saucepan or pot over medium heat while whisking continuously until the butter foams, the foam subsides, the butter is golden, and brown (not black) bits form on the bottom, at least 5 minutes. You're looking for a nutty aroma and not a burnt smell. Reduce the heat to low and add the marshmallows. Stir until the marshmallows have melted into one thick fluff, like foamy, melty mozzarella cheese, a few minutes. There should be

RECIPE *continues* →

Rice Krispies Treat Tips
Use an 8-inch square cake pan if you want taller Rice Krispies Treats.

If you want to add a pop of vibrant color here, freeze-dried strawberries or haw flakes should not be optional.

Storage
Store the Rice Krispies Treats at room temperature in an airtight container for up to 3 days.

no lumps of marshmallow. Add the black sesame seeds, black sesame paste, and miso and mix to combine. Turn off the heat and dump in the cereal, about 2 cups at a time, while stirring; if you like, add the freeze-dried strawberries or haw flakes as well. Stir and mix with a spatula or wooden spoon until all the ingredients are thoroughly coated with gray-black melted marshmallows.

3. Transfer the mixture to the prepared pan and flatten into a leveled square. I find it easier to do this with a layer of parchment paper on top and pressing down with a fondant smoother. You can also use a greased spatula or your clean hands when the mixture is cool enough to touch.

4. Cover and let it rest on the counter at room temperature for about 30 minutes to let the mixture set. Then, use a sharp knife to cut into 12 to 16 equal pieces.

YAKI IMO BARS WITH MISO-HONEY CARAMEL

Makes
12 to 16 bars

Prep Time
15 minutes

Cook Time
About 55 minutes for the sweet potatoes; 60 to 70 minutes for the bars; 5 minutes for the caramel

Difficulty
★★★☆☆
(The most difficult part is making the caramel sauce. The caramel sauce is also the most delicious. Then, the rest is easy-peasy, especially with a food processor or blender.)

Across East Asia and in Asian diasporas, you'll find night markets and street food stalls freshly roasting or baking sweet potatoes, especially during the wintertime. I believe the most beloved and popular type of sweet potato is the Japanese sweet potato, or satsumaimo, with a purplish-red skin and tender creamy white to yellow flesh that reminds one of chestnuts. Super delicious and buttery, satsumaimo is the perfect ingredient to add to baked goodies like bread and cookies.

These chewy, slightly gooey bars are inspired by yaki imo, or baked Japanese sweet potato. As a dessert, the bars are light and not-too-sweet, but perfectly balanced by a sweet and rich miso-honey caramel. Top with some sesame seeds and you have a comforting and satisfying sweet that might just transport you to the wintry night markets of South Korea, Taiwan, or Japan.

- 2 medium satsumaimo (about 400 g)
- 1 cup plus 2 tablespoons (280 g) coconut milk or plain plant-based milk
- ½ cup (75 g) packed light brown sugar
- 1 large egg
- 1 tablespoon red miso
- 2 cups (300 g) glutinous rice flour
- 1 teaspoon baking powder

For the miso-honey caramel

- 3 tablespoons (42 g) unsalted butter
- ⅓ cup (113 g) honey
- 1 teaspoon red miso

For optional toppings

- Sesame seeds
- Sweetened or unsweetened shredded coconut
- Sea salt flakes

1. Adjust a rack to the middle position and preheat the oven to 425°F. Line a baking sheet with parchment paper.

2. Wash the sweet potatoes and keep them wet. Transfer them to the prepared baking sheet. (There's no need to poke holes into the sweet potatoes.) Roast, flipping the potatoes upside down midway through, until the skins are slightly blistered and caramelized, about 55 minutes. Set aside to cool. Lower the oven temperature to 350°F.

3. Crumple, then uncrumple a large sheet of parchment paper and use it to line an 8-inch square cake pan with some overhang. Smooth and press down the parchment paper with your hands.

4. In the bowl of a blender, combine the coconut or plant-based milk, brown sugar, egg, miso, glutinous rice flour, and baking powder. Peel and cut up the roasted sweet potatoes and add to

RECIPE *continues* →

Bar Tips
I suggest roasting a bunch of sweet potatoes ahead of time and reserving two for this recipe since they take so long to roast in the oven. I love sweet potato "freezies." After roasting sweet potatoes, freeze them until rock-solid. Before enjoying, thaw on the counter for about 10 minutes and enjoy them cold, like vegan custard. If I want them warmed, I reheat them in the microwave for a quick snack.

Substitutions
Instead of honey, you can use agave syrup or maple syrup. Instead of the satsumaimo, you can use any other sweet potato, but not canned sweet potatoes.

Storage
Store the bars in an airtight container at room temperature for up to 3 days.

the blender bowl. Blend on medium to high speed until smooth, scraping down the sides of the bowl as needed with a rubber spatula. This batter should be runny and flow like thick lava, not thin and watery. If there are clumps and lumps remaining, blend again.

5. Transfer the batter to the prepared baking pan. Bake until the top shows cracks, the edges start to brown, and a bamboo skewer or toothpick inserted into the center comes out damp but clean, 60 to 70 minutes.

6. Remove the bars from the oven and let set in the dish for a few minutes before lifting the parchment paper to transfer the bars to a wire rack to cool completely.

7. **Make the miso-honey caramel.** While the bars are cooling, cook the butter in a saucepan over medium heat while whisking continuously, until the butter foams, the foam subsides, the butter is golden, and brown (not black) bits form on the bottom, at least 5 minutes. You're looking for a nutty aroma and not a burnt smell. Lower the heat to medium-low and add the honey and miso. Keep stirring with a spatula or whisk until the mixture bubbles and foams. The mixture should resemble a thick syrup. Remove from the heat. Once cooled, this mixture turns caramel-like and will thicken a bit more.

8. Slice the bars into 12 to 16 equal pieces. When ready to serve, drizzle the caramel sauce over the bars. Then, if you like, top with any or a mix of the optional toppings.

MODERN FOOD FOR THE GODS (Filipino Bars)

Makes
12 to 16 bars

Prep Time
10 minutes

Cook Time
About 35 minutes

Difficulty
★★★☆☆
(If you melt the butter instead of browning it, the difficulty goes down to ★★☆☆☆.)

- ½ cup | 1 stick (113 g) unsalted butter, cubed
- 1 cup (145 g) lightly packed light brown sugar
- 1¼ cups (150 g) all-purpose flour
- ¼ cup (38 g) glutinous rice flour
- 1 teaspoon baking powder
- ¼ teaspoon baking soda
- 2 large eggs
- 1 tablespoon red miso
- 1 tablespoon Japanese whisky (optional)
- ½ cup (60 g) dried cranberries
- ½ cup (60 g) roasted shelled pistachios
- ⅓ cup (65 g) semisweet chocolate chips
- About 3 tablespoons (60 g) store-bought or homemade ube halaya, mixed with 1 tablespoon ube extract (with color)
- Confectioners' sugar, for dusting (optional)

Food for the Gods is the Filipino take on butterscotch bars, usually made with pitted dates and walnuts. It's a decadent dessert. Growing up, Jake recalls his mom, Lilanie, making them in Bacolod and Jersey City, especially during Christmastime, though they were never his favorite. The reason? She would load them up with raisins and Jake has this lifelong hate for raisins–don't ask–so I never cook or bake with any raisins at home. He also hates chicken nuggets, but that's another story. After some deliberation, I decided to try developing a recipe inspired by Food for the Gods for this book. Instead of the typical walnuts, I subbed in pistachios. Instead of pitted dates (or raisins a la Lilanie), I used dried cranberries. I added a bit of chocolate too, to whet the palate. Finally, I made them purple with ube extract. Hence, they are called Modern Food for the Gods, still inspired by the popular, traditional Filipino bars, but with my own spin. And finally, Jake approved!

1. Adjust a rack to the middle position and preheat the oven to 350°F. Crumple, then uncrumple a large sheet of parchment paper and use it to line an 8-inch square cake pan with some overhang. Smooth and press down the parchment paper with your hands.

2. To make the brown butter, cook the butter in a saucepan over medium heat while whisking continuously, until the butter foams, the foam subsides, the butter is golden, and brown (not black) bits form on the bottom, at least 5 minutes. You're looking for a nutty aroma and not a burnt smell. Add the brown sugar and mix until dissolved. Remove from the heat and set aside to cool, or chill in the freezer for a few minutes for faster cooling.

3. Whisk the all-purpose flour, glutinous rice flour, baking powder, and baking soda together in a medium bowl. Set aside.

RECIPE *continues* →

Variation
To make traditional Food for the Gods, omit the pistachios and dried cranberries and use ½ cup chopped walnuts and ½ cup chopped pitted dates instead. Also omit the ube extract, halaya, and chocolate chips.

Storage
Store the bars in an airtight container at room temperature for up to 3 days.

4. To the cooled brown butter, add the eggs, miso, and Japanese whisky, if using, and mix with a rubber spatula until fully incorporated. Add the flour mixture and mix until homogenous. Fold in the dried cranberries, pistachios, and chocolate chips. Transfer the batter to the prepared baking pan and level the top with a rubber spatula or offset spatula. Dollop the ube halaya mixture evenly spaced apart over the top of the batter. Use a knife or the end of a spoon to swirl the ube halaya through the batter, creating a makeshift marbled effect. Bake until set and a bamboo skewer or toothpick inserted in the middle comes out clean, about 35 minutes.

5. Transfer to a wire rack to cool completely. Slice into 12 to 16 equal bars with a sharp knife. If you like, dust the tops with confectioners' sugar.

MATCHA AND CARDAMOM BROWN BUTTER BLONDIES

Makes	*Prep Time*	*Cook Time*	*Difficulty*
9 to 12 blondies	20 minutes	About 36 minutes	★★★☆☆ (Browning butter takes practice.)

½ cup | 1 stick (113 g) unsalted butter

1 cup (120 g) cake flour

1 teaspoon baking powder

1 tablespoon culinary-grade matcha, plus more for dusting

1 teaspoon ground cardamom

1 heaping teaspoon red miso

¾ cup (113 g) packed light brown sugar

¼ cup (50 g) granulated sugar

2 large eggs

2 tablespoons (30 g) heavy cream

½ cup (60 g) pistachios, chopped

⅓ cup (57 g) white chocolate chips

Confectioners' sugar, for dusting (optional)

Can I tell you a secret? I've never been a fan of blondies. The ones I've tried in the past have been tooth-achingly sweet or a little too dry or just made me crave a brownie instead. Despite all that, I couldn't write a whole section on brownies and bars without including at least one or two knockout blondie recipes! And this blondie, layered with flavors and generous in inclusions, does not disappoint. You get a hint of cardamom contrasting matcha's grassy, umami, and slightly bitter notes. (For this reason, you commonly find cardamom added to matcha lattes.) As a result, the combination of spice and tea makes this chewy, nutty, and buttery treat even more flavorful and warm, like a cozy blanket or a comforting embrace with each bite. Thanks to this recipe, I can safely say I'm now a fan of blondies!

1. Adjust a rack to the middle position and preheat the oven to 350°F. Crumple, then uncrumple a large sheet of parchment paper and use it to line an 8-inch square cake pan with some overhang. Smooth and press down the parchment paper with your hands.

2. To make the brown butter, cook the butter in a saucepan over medium heat while whisking continuously, until the butter foams, the foam subsides, the butter is golden, and brown (not black) bits form on the bottom, at least 5 minutes. You're looking for a nutty aroma and not a burnt smell. Set aside to cool or chill in the freezer for a few minutes for faster cooling.

3. Whisk the cake flour, baking powder, matcha, and cardamom together in a medium bowl. Set aside.

4. Pour the brown butter into the bowl of a stand mixer fitted with the paddle attachment. Add the miso and sugars and mix on medium speed until well combined. If the mixture is too hot,

RECIPE *continues* →

Blondie Tips
You can mix the batter by hand with a whisk and spatula or using a hand mixer. Just note that blondie batters, like brownie ones, tend to be thick and require more effort to hand mix.

Substitutions
Not a fan of pistachios? Use any other nut or omit them.

Storage
Store the blondies in an airtight container at room temperature for up to 3 days.

wait a few minutes before adding the eggs and cream. Mix on medium speed until the mixture is paler in color, about 2 minutes. Add the flour mixture and mix on low speed until just combined. Don't overmix the batter. Using a spatula, fold in the pistachios and white chocolate chips.

5. Transfer the batter to the prepared pan and use a rubber or offset spatula to level and smooth the top of the batter. Bake, rotating the baking dish once halfway through baking, until a bamboo skewer or toothpick inserted into the center comes out clean, the blondie has set, and the top has lightly browned, about 36 minutes.

6. Cool completely on a wire rack. Slice into 9 to 12 equal blondies and dust with matcha powder or confectioners' sugar, if desired.

RED VELVET BROWNIES WITH DOUBANJIANG

Makes	*Prep Time*	*Cook Time*	*Difficulty*
9 brownies	15 minutes	About 50 minutes	(Melting chocolate may take a little practice.)

- 1 cup (150 g) glutinous rice flour
- ¼ cup (20 g) unsweetened Dutch-processed cocoa powder
- About 2 tablespoons (15 g) red beetroot powder
- ½ teaspoon baking powder
- 8 ounces (225 g) high-quality semisweet chocolate, chopped and divided
- ½ cup | 1 stick (113 g) unsalted butter, cubed
- 1 cup (200 g) granulated sugar
- 2 large eggs
- 2 teaspoons doubanjiang, or to taste
- ½ cup (120 g) whole milk or plain plant-based milk
- A few drops of red food coloring gel (optional, for added color)
- Paprika or chili powder, for dusting (optional)

Every Valentine's Day, I've made Jake brownies. One year, I wanted them red and spicy, so they'd be different from all the pure chocolate brownies I had gifted him before. I looked in my pantry and saw a big packet of doubanjiang, the Chinese fermented chili bean paste. Of course, a light bulb appeared above my head, and I knew immediately I had to somehow incorporate doubanjiang into brownies. This condiment is full of heat, salinity, umami, and complexity.

A few drops of red food coloring gel make the fudgy brownies reddish, matching the touch of spiciness from the doubanjiang. There's also a subtle pop of umami that coats your tongue. Depending on your spice tolerance, feel free to adjust the amount of doubanjiang. Give this spicy twist on the classic brownie a try for Valentine's Day or any other special occasion, and maybe you'll make it a new tradition, just like I did!

1. Adjust a rack to the middle position and preheat the oven to 350°F. Crumple, then uncrumple a large sheet of parchment paper and use it to line an 8-inch square cake pan with some overhang. Smooth and press down the parchment paper with your hands.

2. Whisk the glutinous rice flour, cocoa powder, beet powder, and baking powder together in a medium bowl. Set aside.

3. In a large bowl, melt one-half of the chocolate and the butter using a double boiler, or in the microwave in 20-second bursts. Stir the melted chocolate mixture until smooth and homogenous, then mix in the sugar, eggs, and doubanjiang. It's okay if the mixture looks oily and gritty at this point.

4. Add the glutinous flour mixture and mix to combine with a flexible spatula or whisk. Stir in the milk and red food coloring

RECIPE *continues* →

gel, if using, and mix until a thick, smooth, cohesive, and glossy batter forms. Fold in the remaining chopped chocolate.

5. Transfer the batter to the prepared baking pan and spread evenly with an offset spatula to cover every corner of the pan. Bake until a bamboo skewer or toothpick inserted in the middle comes out clean, the brownies are set, and the top is shiny and a little cracked, about 50 minutes.

6. Cool completely in the pan on a wire rack. Slice into nine equal brownies and, if desired, dust with paprika or chili powder for a pop of vibrancy and heat.

Brownie Tips

Made with glutinous rice flour (which, in fact, does not have gluten), you'd think these are fully gluten-free brownies; however, please check labels, as most doubanjiang is not gluten-free.

Substitution

You can use chocolate chips instead of chopping up a bar of baking chocolate.

Storage

Store the brownies in an airtight container at room temperature for up to 3 days. They do get chewier the next day.

CALAMANSI CHEESECAKE BARS WITH PASSIONFRUIT CURD

Makes
9 cheesecake bars

Prep Time
15 minutes

Inactive Time
4 hours to overnight

Cook Time
About 40 minutes

Difficulty
★★★☆☆
(You do need to make a crust first and then a cheesecake batter; and patience is needed—the hardest part!—as the cheesecake chills and sets.)

For the crust

- 2 cups (240 g) graham cracker crumbs
- ½ cup | 1 stick (113 g) unsalted butter, melted
- 2 teaspoons grated lemon zest
- 1 teaspoon calamansi juice
- 1 teaspoon red miso

For the cheesecake batter

- Two 8-ounce (450 g) packages cream cheese, softened
- ⅓ cup (80 g) Greek yogurt
- 2 tablespoons (30 g) calamansi juice
- 1 teaspoon red miso
- ¾ cup (150 g) granulated sugar
- 2 tablespoons (16 g) cornstarch
- 3 large eggs
- ½ cup (120 g) passionfruit curd

For the optional garnishes

- Whipped cream
- Thin lemon slices or candied lemon slices
- Grated lemon zest
- Confectioners' sugar

To me, cheesecake should always be a little tarty. While my go-to ingredient to add tang to cheesecakes has always been lemon, I've recently found myself gravitating to calamansi, the highly tart, aromatic, and floral citrus fruit from the Philippines. Once you taste calamansi, it leaves an impression with a punchy flavor that differentiates it from other citrus fruits. Because calamansi hits so differently, these cheesecake bars are all the more unforgettable. Paired with passionfruit, you get a sublime combo with double the tang. Bring the bars to a potluck, pass them out to your friends at the gym, or showcase them at a baby shower. When folks ask for the recipe, be sure to point them here.

1. Adjust a rack to the middle position and preheat the oven to 350°F. Crumple, then uncrumple a large sheet of parchment paper and use it to line a 9-inch square cake pan with some overhang. Smooth and press down the parchment paper with your hands.

2. **Make the crust.** Using a rubber spatula, mix all the crust ingredients together until combined and resembling wet sand. Transfer to the prepared baking pan and press evenly onto the bottom. You want a single, level layer, so use your clean hands, the bottom of a measuring cup, or the back of a spoon as needed. Bake until the edges start to brown, 10 minutes. Set aside to cool.

3. **Make the cheesecake batter.** Using a stand mixer fitted with the paddle attachment (or in a large bowl with a hand mixer, whisk, or spatula), mix the cream cheese, yogurt, calamansi juice, miso, sugar, and cornstarch together until well combined and smooth. Scrape down the sides and bottom of the bowl

RECIPE *continues* →

Bar Tip
You'll be using store-bought calamansi juice, not freshly squeezed, because it's rather difficult to source fresh calamansi in the West.

Substitution
If you can't find passionfruit curd online at Amazon, try Walmart or Williams-Sonoma, or you can substitute it with lemon curd or pineapple curd (or any fruity jam, really).

Storage
Store the bars in an airtight container in the refrigerator for up to 5 days.

as needed, then mix in the eggs, one at a time, until well incorporated.

4. Pour the cheesecake batter into the prepared graham cracker crust. Gently drop dollops of the passionfruit curd over the batter and use a butter knife, chopsticks, or offset spatula to swirl the batter into a beautiful pattern. Reduce the oven temperature to 330°F. Bake until the sides are set while the center remains wobbly (but not wet), just like how a perfect cheesecake would be, 30 to 40 minutes. Cool at room temperature, then cover and refrigerate for 4 hours, or overnight.

5. When ready to serve, slice into nine equal squares. Top the bars with any of the optional toppings. For example, add a dollop of whipped cream, then top with a lemon slice or candied lemon, some lemon zest, and a dusting of confectioners' sugar. Or keep it simple.

CRAZY RICH BILLIONAIRE'S SHORTBREAD

Makes
24 to 36 bars

Prep Time
25 minutes

Inactive Time
30 minutes

Cook Time
About 60 minutes in total

Difficulty
★★★★☆
(There are many steps involved, so plan accordingly.)

When the groundbreaking movie *Crazy Rich Asians* premiered in 2018, it became the first Hollywood film in twenty-five years to feature a predominantly Asian cast, mostly portrayed in a positive light rather than through stereotypes. As an homage to the movie, which became a source of pride for the Asian diasporas, I created a shortbread fit for a billionaire, but with comforting, warm, and familiar flavors anyone can enjoy.

A jade green buttery pandan shortbread forms a base that is topped with a layer of decadent coconut caramel studded with curried peanuts, followed by chocolate ganache and finally, a layer of fresh raspberries. Of course, for the billionaires (or those who dream of being billionaires, LOL), you can dress up the raspberries with flecks of edible gold foil.

For the curried peanuts

- 2 tablespoons (30 g) neutral oil
- 1 tablespoon curry powder
- 1 teaspoon soy sauce
- 1 teaspoon brown sugar
- Dash of MSG
- 1¼ cups (180 g) skinless shelled peanuts

For the shortbread crust

- 1 cup | 2 sticks (226 g) unsalted butter, cubed and at room temperature
- ½ cup (72 g) packed light brown sugar
- 1 tablespoon red miso
- 1 large egg
- 1 tablespoon pandan extract (with color)
- 2 cups (240 g) all-purpose flour
- ⅓ cup (40 g) sweetened shredded coconut

For the caramel filling

- One 14-ounce can sweetened condensed milk or sweetened condensed coconut milk
- 1 cup (145 g) unpacked light brown sugar
- ½ cup (156 g) light corn syrup
- ⅓ cup (80 g) coconut milk
- 1 tablespoon red miso
- 1 tablespoon Japanese whisky or bourbon

1. **Make the curried peanuts.** Heat a wok or frying pan over medium-high heat. Once the wok or pan is hot enough and releases smoke, add the oil. Add the curry powder, soy sauce, brown sugar, and MSG and stir to form a paste. Once aromatic, about 2 minutes, toss in the peanuts. Cook the peanuts, stirring to coat with the curry paste, until toasty, fragrant, and releasing oil, a few minutes. Remove from the heat and set aside in a bowl to cool.

2. Adjust a rack to the middle position and preheat the oven to 350°F. Crumple, then uncrumple a large sheet of parchment paper and use it to line a 9 by 13-inch baking dish with some overhang. Smooth and press down the parchment paper with your hands.

3. **Make the shortbread crust.** Using a stand mixer fitted with the paddle attachment (or in a mixing bowl with a hand mixer, whisk, or spatula), cream the butter, brown sugar, and miso until well combined. Add the egg and pandan extract and mix until incorporated. Add the flour and coconut and mix on low speed

RECIPE AND INGREDIENTS *continues* →

For the chocolate ganache

Two 4-ounce (225 g) bars semisweet chocolate, finely chopped

⅓ cup (80 g) coconut cream

1 teaspoon neutral oil

For the topping

Sea salt flakes

Fresh raspberries (optional)

Edible gold foil (optional)

Cookie Tip
If time is not on your side, skip the curried peanuts, or make them the day before.

Variation
If you feel the shortbread is too rich for you, omit the chocolate ganache layer and the raspberries. It'll still be very delicious, like a Payday-inspired dessert.

Storage
In an airtight container, the bars can stay in the refrigerator for up to 5 days.

just until a shortbread dough forms. Press the dough into an even layer in the prepared baking dish. Bake until golden, 20 to 25 minutes. Transfer to a wire rack to cool.

4. **Make the caramel filling.** While the shortbread is baking, combine the caramel filling ingredients in a saucepan and whisk continuously over medium heat. The caramel is ready when the mixture darkens into a rich amber color, thickens, and pulls aways from the sides of the saucepan as you stir it, about 8 minutes. (A candy or digital thermometer should register 235°F to 240°F, and if you run a spoon through the caramel, it leaves a clear trail that closes slowly.) Avoid overcooking, as the caramel will taste burnt.

5. Mix the curried peanuts into the caramel and then immediately pour the caramel over the baked shortbread. Smooth the caramel with an offset spatula into a flat, even layer. Refrigerate for at least 30 minutes to allow the caramel to set.

6. **Make the chocolate ganache.** After the caramel is set, combine all the chocolate ganache ingredients in a medium microwave-safe bowl. Microwave in 30-second bursts, stirring with a rubber spatula after each burst, until completely melted and smooth, up to 2 minutes.

7. Pour the chocolate ganache over the set caramel and smooth the chocolate into an even layer. Garnish with sea salt flakes. If you like, top with raspberries, stem end down. Decorate either the raspberries or the chocolate with edible gold foil or flakes, if desired.

8. Cover and refrigerate the shortbread for 20 minutes. Then use a sharp knife to slice the shortbread in 24 to 36 equal bars.

HALO-HALO INSPIRED CEREAL TREATS

Makes
9 to 12 treats

Prep Time
15 minutes

Inactive Time
30 minutes

Cook Time
About 15 minutes

Difficulty
★★★☆☆
(Other than browning the butter and melting marshmallows, you're dumping in the ingredients and mixing things together.)

4 tablespoons (56 g) salted butter, cubed

One 12-ounce (340 g) bag of mini marshmallows

1 tablespoon red miso

2 teaspoons ube extract (with color), or to taste and color

⅓ cup (80 g) macapuno strings, drained and chopped

One 7-ounce (about 210 g) can sweetened or unsweetened adzuki (red) beans, drained (optional)

5 cups (125 g) cornflakes

2 cups (50 g) pinipig, toasted

⅓ cup (40 g) banana or plantain chips, chopped

⅓ cup (50 g) dried mango or dried jackfruit, diced

For the optional toppings

Milk powder

Sweetened condensed milk

Fruity Pebbles cereal

This is the epitome of a third-culture kid creation. At first glance, it'll probably remind you of Rice Krispies Treats, which we associate with Western culture; however, puffed rice treats are actually very popular across Asia. For instance, the Philippines has ampaw (or ampao), a sweet, puffed rice cake. China has sachima (or saqima), one of my favorite snacks growing up, made with deep-fried egg-dough strands bound together by syrup and honey.

Growing up eating so many Rice Krispies Treats and sachima, I just had to include a cereal treat in this book. To challenge myself, of course it had to be halo-halo inspired. Jake introduced me to the Filipino cold dessert, akin to shaved ice with a multitude of add-ins, over a decade ago in a Filipino restaurant in Jersey City. Since then, halo-halo has been one of my favorite desserts. It comes with so many fun and delicious ingredients and is so colorful that any adult eating it briefly becomes a child again.

1. Crumple, then uncrumple a large sheet of parchment paper and use it to line a 9-inch square cake pan with some overhang. Smooth and press down the parchment paper with your hands.

2. To make the brown butter, cook the butter in a large saucepan or frying pan over medium heat while whisking continuously, until the butter foams, the foam subsides, the butter is golden, and brown (not black) bits form on the bottom, at least 5 minutes. You're looking for a nutty aroma and not a burnt smell.

3. Dump in all the marshmallows and reduce the heat to medium-low. Stir until the marshmallows have melted into one thick fluff, like foamy, melty mozzarella cheese, a few minutes. Stir in the miso and ube extract until fully incorporated. Mix in the drained macapuno (mutant coconut meat) strings and adzuki beans, if using, and remove from the heat.

RECIPE *continues* →

Cereal treat tips
For added flavor, I recommend browning the butter, but to save time, you can just melt it before adding the marshmallows.

Substitutions
Pinipig (pounded young sticky rice or sweet rice flakes) can be found online, in Filipino grocery stories, and in Asian supermarkets. If you can't find pinipig, swap it out with puffed rice cereal, like Rice Krispies.

Storage
Store the treats in an airtight container at room temperature for up to 3 days.

4. Working quickly now, add the cornflakes, toasted pinipig, banana or plantain chips, and dried mango or jackfruit. Stir and mix with a spatula or wooden spoon (or both if you find that helpful), until all the ingredients are thoroughly coated with melted marshmallows.

5. Transfer the mixture to the prepared pan and flatten into a level square. I find it easier to do this with a piece of parchment paper on top and pressing down with a fondant smoother. You can also use a greased spatula or your hands if the mixture is cool enough to touch. Cover and let it rest on the counter at room temperature for about 30 minutes to let the mixture set.

6. Use a sharp knife to cut into 9 to 12 equal pieces (or as small or big as you like). If desired, dust with milk powder or drizzle with sweetened condensed milk. Finally, if you like, sprinkle Fruity Pebbles cereal on top for more pops of color.

EIGHT TREASURE MAGIC BARS

Makes
24 bars

Prep Time
10 minutes

Inactive Time
2 hours to overnight

Cook Time
About 25 minutes

Difficulty
★★☆☆☆
(The most difficult part is making the crust. Then, the one-bowl filling comes together easily and quickly.)

- 1⅔ cups (200 g) store-bought graham cracker crumbs
- ⅔ cup (30 g) toasted pinipig or puffed rice cereal
- 1 teaspoon ground Vietnamese cinnamon
- ½ cup |1 stick (113 g) unsalted butter, melted
- 1 cup toasted (130 g) pumpkin seeds
- ½ cup (60 g) chopped walnuts
- 1 cup (150 g) golden raisins
- 1 cup (about 80 g) shredded coconut (sweetened or unsweetened)
- One 14-ounce (397 g) can sweetened condensed milk
- ⅓ cup (80 g) red bean paste (sweetened or unsweetened)
- 1 tablespoon red miso
- Sea salt flakes, for garnish

As a chaotic kitchen wizard (someone who thrives on pushing boundaries when developing new recipes), one of my party tricks is reinventing classic Asian and American dishes. One of my favorite Asian desserts is eight treasure rice, or Chinese rice pudding (baat bóu faahn or 八宝飯). Over a bed of sweet sticky rice, you find eight "treasures"–eight different ingredients such as lotus seeds, red beans, fruits, and nuts. Since magic bars often come with seven ingredients forming "seven layers," I thought, why not reimagine eight treasure rice as an Asian magic bar? (Magic bars, also called Hello Dolly bars, by the way, are American cookie bars made with usually seven different ingredients, all "magically" glued together with sweetened condensed milk.)

Please note, all the ingredients I've chosen for these magic bars should serve only as a guide for you. Embrace your inner chaotic kitchen wizard.

1. Adjust a rack to the middle position and preheat the oven to 350°F. Crumple, then uncrumple a large sheet of parchment paper and use it to line a 9 by 13-inch baking dish with some overhang. Smooth and press down the parchment paper with your hands.

2. Whisk the graham cracker crumbs, pinipig, and cinnamon together in a large bowl. Add the melted butter (you may not need all of it) and mix with a fork until the crumbs are moist. Test a small portion with your hand. Squeeze it together and if it holds, it's ready. Transfer to the prepared baking dish and press to flatten into an even, compact layer.

3. Combine the pumpkin seeds, walnuts, raisins, and shredded coconut in the same large bowl and toss everything together with a rubber spatula. Add the sweetened condensed milk, red bean paste, and miso and stir until most of the dry ingredients

RECIPE *continues* →

Bar Tips
You'll need to refrigerate the bars for at least 2 hours before enjoying them, so plan accordingly.

Substitutions
Swap out the nuts and dried fruits I listed for your favorite nuts and dried fruits. Or swap out one of the nuts for steamed lotus seeds. If you don't have red bean paste, substitute your favorite nut butter.

Storage
Store the bars in an airtight container at room temperature for up to 2 days.

are coated with the wet ingredients. Spread the mixture evenly over the graham cracker crust.

4. Bake until the edges are golden brown and begin to pull away from the baking dish, about 25 minutes. Let the bars cool completely in the baking dish. Once cooled, cover and refrigerate for at least 2 hours or overnight. The bars will be chewy and firm.

5. When ready to serve, slice into 24 equal pieces and top with sea salt flakes.

SHARON'S SAKURA AND STRAWBERRY BISCOTTI

Makes
32 to 35 biscotti, about ¼ inch thick (or depending how thick you cut them)

Prep Time
About 30 minutes

Inactive Time
About 35 minutes

Cook Time
45 to 55 minutes

Difficulty
★★★★☆
(The most technical parts are shaping the dough for baking and slicing evenly, so use a ruler and a serrated knife for best clean cuts.)

About 1 cup (150 g) frozen strawberries

1½ cups (180 g) all-purpose flour

1 teaspoon baking powder

5 tablespoons (70 g) unsalted butter, softened

6 to 8 salted sakura blossoms, finely minced

½ cup plus 1 tablespoon (120 g) granulated sugar

1 large egg

¼ teaspoon freeze-dried sakura powder or 1 teaspoon rose water

Red food coloring gel (optional)

About ¼ cup (20 g) sliced almonds

For decorating the biscotti

Melted white or dark chocolate (optional)

Freeze-dried strawberries (optional)

Biscotti Tips
Slicing the dough evenly is easier if you use a ruler. Add more sakura powder if you want a more intense flavor, up to ½ to 1 teaspoon.

Substitutions
For the sakura powder, you can substitute freeze-dried strawberry powder. For the salted sakura blossoms, try using pickled ume plums or pickled plums.

Storage
Store the biscotti in an airtight container at room temperature for up to 1 week.

This recipe is one of two exclusive ones my dear friend and avid baker, Sharon Hsu (@sparklecakerie on Instagram), developed for this book. Sharon noted how biscotti are not usually a colorful type of cookie, so she was excited to develop a recipe for biscotti that would mimic the beautiful pink blooms of sakura (or cherry blossom) season and also be the cutest addition to teatime or a spring picnic.

Her pretty pink cherry blossom biscotti are crunchy with subtle savory floral notes thanks to the addition of sakura powder and salted sakura blossoms. You also get fruity notes from roasted strawberries. Sharon hopes you get all the warm and fuzzy feelings you experience during springtime when baking these cookies.

1. Adjust a rack to the middle position and preheat the oven to 375°F. Line a baking sheet with parchment paper.

2. Place the frozen strawberries on the prepared baking sheet and roast until tender and red juices seep out and get a little caramelized, about 15 minutes. Remove from the oven and set aside to cool. Do not turn off the oven.

3. Whisk the flour and baking powder together in a medium bowl. Mix the butter, salted sakura blossoms, sugar, egg, sakura powder, and a few drops of food coloring gel, if using, together until fully combined. Add the flour mixture and mix until no dry flour spots remain. Fold in the roasted strawberries and sliced almonds. The dough will be wet and sticky.

4. Lightly flour a work surface. Divide the dough in half and shape each into a rectangular log about 10 inches by 2½ inches by ½ inch. To make the dough more manageable, work with lightly wet fingers. Transfer the logs to a parchment-lined baking sheet, giving each about 3 inches of space.

RECIPE *continues* →

5. Bake at 375°F for about 25 minutes. Remove the baking sheet from the oven and let the logs cool for 5 minutes. Lower the oven temperature to 350°F. Transfer the logs to a cutting board.

6. Wearing an oven mitt on your non-dominant hand, hold a serrated or electric knife with your dominant hand and slice each log, on the diagonal, into even pieces about ¼ to ¾ inch thick. Some of the biscotti may break off, and that's okay.

7. Return the biscotti to the prepared baking sheet, cut sides down, spacing them evenly about ½ inch apart. Bake for 10 minutes. Use tongs to carefully flip each biscotti over and continue baking, rotating the pan halfway through, until crispy, crunchy, and dry, another 8 to 10 minutes.

8. Transfer the biscotti to a wire rack to cool completely. If you like, drizzle melted white or dark chocolate over the biscotti and top with freeze-dried strawberries.

(top) Cut the biscotti on a diagonal.
(bottom) Place cut biscotti back on baking sheet.

DREAMS OF MONTREAL NANAIMO BARS

Makes
16 to 25 bars

Prep Time
15 minutes

Inactive Time
2 hours to overnight

Cook Time
A few minutes to melt the ingredients

Difficulty
★★☆☆☆
(There's some assembly required.)

For the bottom crust layer

½ cup (113 g) unsalted butter, cubed

⅓ cup (100 g) sweetened condensed milk

5 tablespoons (30 g) unsweetened Dutch-processed cocoa powder

1 tablespoon red miso

1 ¾ cups (175 g) store-bought graham cracker crumbs

1 cup (85 g) unsweetened shredded coconut

½ cup (60 g) finely chopped almonds or walnuts

¼ cup (36 g) toasted white sesame seeds

For the middle custard layer

½ cup (113 g) unsalted butter, softened

1 ½ cups (170 g) confectioners' sugar

About 3 tablespoons (40 g) heavy cream

2 tablespoons (18 g) custard powder

1 tablespoon red miso

1 tablespoon pandan extract (with color)

For the top chocolate layer

One 4-ounce bar (113 g) semisweet chocolate, chopped

2 tablespoons (30 g) olive oil

Sea salt flakes, for garnish

I won't sugarcoat this: I grew up in a rough part of Brooklyn, in Coney Island, nearly twenty blocks from the amusement park. Growing up, during most parts of the year, I dreamed about Montreal, where I spent many of my childhood summers. There, Ah Ma took me swimming, ice skating indoors, and for dim sum, and ZeZe, my grandfather, sometimes took me to have a snack at Al Van Houtte, a cafe near their apartment complex, where we'd have carrot cakes or Nanaimo bars. I love the fact that they're a Canadian invention. I've always been very proud of the fact that I'm part Canadian. Back in New York, when people told me to "go back to China," I'd shrug it off and say in my head, "I'm actually Canadian." When I didn't feel like I belonged, I knew I had a place to go back to every summer, where no one ever told me I didn't belong and no one physically or verbally attacked me on the streets for no other reason than looking Chinese.

But I digress. A little about the bars: This is a no-bake recipe, so it's perfect for hot days when you don't want to turn on the oven. I adapted the City of Nanaimo's official recipe, sneaking in a few Asian twists. Since these bars are rich, don't cut them too big, and enjoy them with hot tea or coffee, like ZeZe used to.

1. Grease an 8-inch square cake pan.

2. **Make the bottom crust layer.** In a medium heatproof bowl, microwave the butter in 30-second bursts until melted. Stir in the condensed milk, cocoa powder, and miso until combined. Mix in the graham cracker crumbs, shredded coconut, nuts, and sesame seeds. Press the mixture firmly into the prepared baking pan in an even, packed layer.

3. **Make the middle custard layer.** Using a stand mixer fitted with the paddle attachment (or in a large bowl with a hand mixer, whisk, or spatula), cream the middle layer ingredients together until well combined. Spread it over the crust layer evenly, using a rubber spatula. Cover and refrigerate for 1 hour.

Bar Tip
Keeping the bars chilled helps the layers set properly and maintain their shape, and the cold temperature also enhances the texture and flavor of each layer.

Storage
Store the bars in an airtight container in the refrigerator for up to 5 days.

4. **Make the top chocolate layer.** Melt the chocolate along with the olive oil in the top part of a double boiler over simmering water, or in a large bowl in the microwave in 20-second bursts. Stir the melted mixture until smooth and homogenous. Pour over the custard layer. Cover and refrigerate until set, about 1 hour to overnight.

5. Cut into 16 to 25 equal squares. Top with a sprinkle of sea salt flakes and serve.

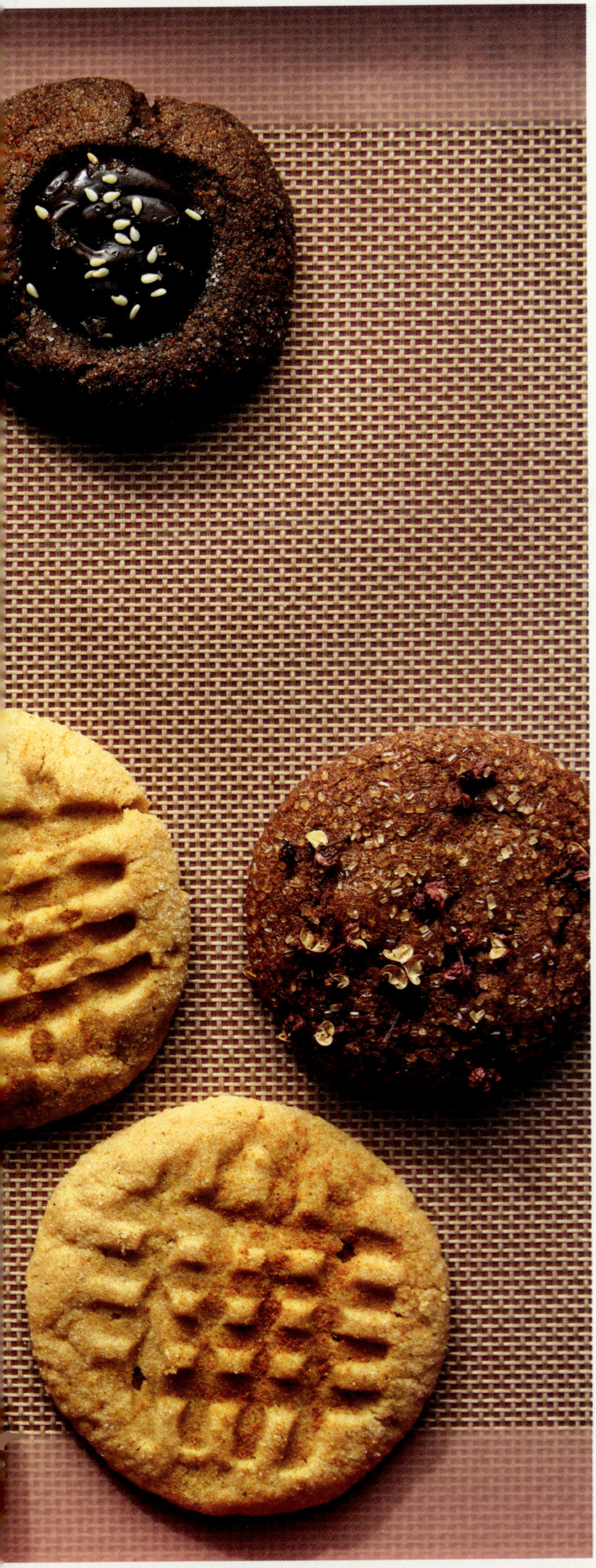

SUGAR AND SPICE AND EVERYTHING NICE

COOKIES WITH A KICK

Spicy and sweet treats featuring lovely Asian spices, hot sauces, and condiments

I don't remember when I tried spicy food for the first time, but for as long as I can remember, we had sriracha, sambal oelek, chili oil, and different spices like cardamom and Vietnamese cinnamon at home. The Vietnamese side of my family loves chilis that burn the tongue. Ah Ma would bite into them raw before eating summer rolls and pho. I was very young when she scolded me for complaining about a pepper being too spicy (tears shot out of my eyes and I thought I couldn't breathe!). ZeZe loved curries, and the spicier the better. Jake always orders the spiciest ramens at our favorite ramen joints. Philip loves sushi and downing globs of wasabi. Something about that burning sensation in the nasal passages just keeps him going back for more. I love sriracha and chili crisp.

So, as you can imagine, it was very natural for me to imagine a cookie tray full of spicy, warm, and tongue-tingling and numbing cookies, one for each member of my family who loves (or loved) food with a kick. Each cookie is like a warm mug of hot cocoa, but spicy. For a cookie that will remind you of laksa noodle bowls from Singapore, you must try my Laksa Cookies (page 201), packed with umami and heat. For something super easy and family-friendly, try my Puppy Chow with a Kick (page 183). It's a no-bake recipe that's perfect for potlucks and parties and will help you use up some of the sriracha in your pantry.

Whether you're a spice novice or a heat-seeking aficionado like me and my family, there's bound to be a spicy cookie here to surprise and tickle your taste buds.

GOCHUJANG AND BERRY JAM CHOCOLATE THUMBPRINTS

Makes
36 thumbprint cookies

Prep Time
15 minutes

Inactive Time
30 minutes

Cook Time
About 5 minutes for the filling; 13 to 15 minutes for the cookies

Difficulty
★★★☆☆
(The cookies may puff a little in the oven and you may need to remake the indents.)

For the cookies

- 1½ cups (180 g) all-purpose flour
- ½ cup (50 g) unsweetened Dutch-processed cocoa powder
- 1 teaspoon cayenne powder, plus more for dusting
- ¼ teaspoon baking powder
- ¼ teaspoon baking soda
- 1 cup (226 g) unsalted butter, softened
- ¾ cup (85 g) confectioners' sugar
- 1 tablespoon red miso
- 1 large egg
- 1 tablespoon Greek yogurt or sour cream
- Milk, if needed
- ¼ cup (50 g) coarse or demerara sugar, placed in a shallow bowl, plus more as needed

For the filling

- ½ cup (120 g) heavy cream
- ¼ cup (80 g) strawberry or raspberry jam
- 1½ tablespoons (22 g) gochujang, or to taste
- 1 cup (170 g) chopped semisweet chocolate or chocolate chips

For optional toppings

- Toasted white sesame seeds
- Sea salt flakes
- Cayenne powder

I am a sucker for any dessert with a generous pat of chocolate in the middle. Make the chocolate spicy, and I might even dance for you. Spicy, melty chocolates remind me of Mexican hot chocolate, especially the delicious cup I enjoyed in Cabo during one of my last trips with my father. Then I get nostalgic for the mugs of hot chocolate Dad ordered for me at the diner in Coney Island. Drinking that hot chocolate, I felt no different from the blond-haired, blue-eyed kids in the booth across from us.

Thinking of my father, I made these cookies on Father's Day of 2024 and gifted them to Jake, the father of my child and an even bigger chocolate lover than me. I also knew Dad was having these in spirit. Since this cookie comes from a place of nostalgia and melancholy, the flavors reflect my feelings on life: It's full of sweetness and richness, but then there's a spicy kick of heat that lingers and burns a little... (Pictured on page 171.)

1. **Make the cookies.** Whisk the flour, cocoa powder, cayenne powder, baking powder, and baking soda together in a medium bowl. Set aside. Using a stand mixer fitted with the paddle attachment (or in a large bowl with a hand mixer, whisk, or spatula), cream the butter, confectioners' sugar, and miso together until light and fluffy. Scrape down the sides and bottom of the bowl. Add the egg and yogurt or sour cream and mix until well incorporated. Add the flour mixture and mix on low speed until just combined. If you find the dough too dry and crumbly, mix in a teaspoon or two of milk. Cover the dough and refrigerate for 30 minutes.

2. About 25 minutes before baking, adjust two racks to the upper- and lower-middle positions of the oven. Preheat the oven to 350°F. Line two baking sheets with parchment paper.

Cookie Tip
If the cookie dough cracks too much when you're making the indents, re-roll into a ball and make the indent again.

Substitution
You can substitute coconut milk for the heavy cream in the filling.

Storage
Store the cookies in an airtight container at room temperature for up to 3 days.

3. Scoop 1 tablespoon of dough, roll into a smooth, shiny ball, and toss in the bowl of sugar to coat evenly. Repeat to make 36 balls, placing them about 1 inch apart on the prepared baking sheets. Using a clean thumb, press down in the center of each dough ball to make a deep, round well. You can also make a heart-shaped well with your thumb by making a V-shaped indentation. Be sure not to punch a hole through the cookies, but keep the well deep as the cookies do puff up and lose some of the indent during baking.

4. Bake all the cookies, switching the sheets between top and bottom racks and rotating front to back once halfway through, until the cookie edges are set and the tops puff and crack, 13 to 15 minutes.

5. If the wells have puffed up, use a little spoon to indent the cookies again. Let the cookies set directly on the baking sheets for a few minutes then transfer to a wire rack to cool completely.

6. **Make the filling.** In a small saucepan, stir the cream, jam, and gochujang over medium heat until bubbles form around the edges. Add the chocolate, remove from the heat, and whisk until smooth.

7. Fill each of the cookies with about a teaspoon of filling. If you like, sprinkle sesame seeds and sea salt flakes over the filling. You can also dust the cookies with a little cayenne powder for more heat and a pop of color. Serve while the filling is still melty, or let the cookies rest at room temperature or chill in the refrigerator until the filling hardens. How you like to enjoy these thumbprint cookies is up to you.

CHILI CRISP CHOCOLATE SKILLET COOKIE

Makes
8 to 12 servings

Prep Time
15 minutes

Cook Time
About 18 minutes

Difficulty
★★☆☆☆
(Honestly, you could just hand mix everything in the skillet and the cookie will still turn out amazing.)

- 1½ cups (180 g) all-purpose flour
- 2 tablespoons (12 g) unsweetened Dutch-processed cocoa powder
- ½ teaspoon baking powder
- ½ teaspoon baking soda
- Pinch of kosher salt
- ½ cup | 1 stick (113 g) unsalted butter, softened
- 1 tablespoon duck fat or bacon fat, plus more for greasing the pan
- ⅔ cup (113 g) unpacked light or dark brown sugar
- ⅓ cup (67 g) granulated sugar
- 1 teaspoon red miso
- 1 large egg
- 1 teaspoon chili crisp (or to taste), plus more for drizzling
- 1½ cups (255 g) chopped dark or semisweet chocolate, divided
- 1 cup (135 g) roasted hazelnuts, chopped
- Sesame seeds, white or black
- A few scoops of your favorite ice cream, but preferably a high-quality vanilla

Craving something sweet with a little heat, but also don't have a lot of time on your hands? Well, this might just be the treat for you. Like all skillet cookies, this may appear like a complicated bake, but is actually not that tricky. First, we quickly mix up a forgiving cookie batter, press it into a skillet with our bare hands, and bake. That's it. Don't have an oven-safe skillet? Use a greased springform pan instead.

The chili crisp in the cookie batter adds a touch of spice and umami that beautifully offsets the subtle sweetness and bitterness of dark chocolate. Please don't skip drizzling chili crisp over the finishing scoop of ice cream. It's a showstopper move that will surely impress party guests. Serve it as cookie slices, or better yet, tell everyone to dive right in with their spoons.

1. Adjust a rack to the middle position and preheat the oven to 350°F. Lightly grease a 9- to 10-inch nonstick ovenproof skillet with duck fat or bacon fat.

2. Whisk the flour, cocoa powder, baking powder, baking soda, and salt together in a medium bowl. Set aside.

3. Using a stand mixer fitted with the paddle attachment (or in a large bowl with a hand mixer, whisk, or spatula), cream the butter, duck fat or bacon fat, sugars, and miso together until light and fluffy, about 1 minute. Scrape down the sides and bottom of the bowl. Add the egg and chili crisp and mix until well incorporated. Add the flour mixture and mix on low speed until just combined. Fold in 1 cup of the chopped chocolate and all the hazelnuts.

RECIPE *continues* →

4. Transfer the cookie dough to the prepared skillet, spreading it evenly and pressing it into the skillet with clean hands. Sprinkle the rest of the chocolate and the sesame seeds all over the top of the cookie. Press the toppings lightly into the dough with clean hands.

5. Bake until set and the edges are browner while the center is still somewhat soft and gooey, about 18 minutes. Let cool directly in the skillet. Slice the cookie, add scoops of ice cream, and drizzle a little chili crisp over the ice cream.

Cookie Tip

You can make the cookie dough in advance and refrigerate it, covered in the skillet, for up to 2 days before baking.

Substitutions

Feel free to use chocolate chips instead of the chopped chocolate. For the duck or bacon fat, you can substitute ghee or unsalted butter.

Storage

Store the cookies in an airtight container at room temperature for up to 3 days.

SPICY GINGER CHAI COOKIES

Makes
about 30 cookies

Prep Time
20 minutes

Inactive Time
30 minutes

Cook Time
About 20 minutes

Difficulty
★★★☆☆
(Mostly because we brown the butter first.)

- ½ cup | 1 stick (113 g) unsalted butter
- 2 cups (240 g) dark rye flour
- 1 tablespoon hojicha powder or black tea powder (optional)
- ½ teaspoon baking soda
- ½ teaspoon baking powder
- 2 teaspoons ground ginger
- 1 teaspoon ground cardamom
- ¼ teaspoon ground black pepper
- 1 cup (200 g) packed light or dark brown sugar
- 1 large egg
- ¼ cup (85 g) blackstrap molasses
- 1 tablespoon lemongrass paste
- 1 tablespoon red miso
- ⅓ cup (53 g) crystallized or candied ginger, chopped finely
- ⅓ cup (67 g) turbinado sugar, placed in a shallow bowl

Growing up, I never made gingerbread or ginger molasses cookies, but since I started baking in 2017, I've developed a fascination with treats that contain ginger. Ginger cookies are found in many Asian cultures, with the Chinese making versions of gingerbread as early as the 10th century. In Korea, there's maejakgwa, a sticky sweet gingery cookie that you fry. Then, there are all the ginger cookies made with jaggery across South Asia. Speaking of South Asia, I have a deep love for spicy chai, so naturally, I wanted to make a cookie that tastes like chai.

These spicy chai cookies pack an extra zingy punch thanks to the ground ginger and candied ginger. Then, there's the rye flour, which amplifies flavors, especially spicy ones. To really bring out chai flavors, I recommend adding hojicha powder or black tea. Chai powder is a good alternative to those tea powders; however, since it already comes with spices, you may want to omit the cardamom and black pepper if you use it.

1. To make the brown butter, cook the butter in a saucepan over medium heat while whisking continuously, until the butter foams, the foam subsides, the butter is golden, and brown (not black) bits form on the bottom, at least 5 minutes. You're looking for a nutty aroma and not a burnt smell. Remove from the heat. Set aside to cool, or chill in the freezer for a few minutes for faster cooling.

2. Whisk the rye flour, hojicha or tea powder, baking soda, baking powder, ground ginger, cardamom, and black pepper together in a medium bowl. Set aside. Pour the cooled butter into the bowl of a stand mixer fitted with the paddle attachment. Add the brown sugar and mix on medium speed until well combined. Add the egg, molasses, lemongrass paste, and miso and mix until thoroughly incorporated. Add the rye

RECIPE *continues* →

Substitutions

If you don't have rye flour, you can substitute about 1¾ cups all-purpose flour.

Swap out the lemongrass paste with about 1 teaspoon grated lemon zest.

Storage

Store the cookies in an airtight container at room temperature for up to 4 days.

flour mixture and mix on low speed until just combined. Using a spatula, fold in the crystallized or candied ginger. Cover and chill the dough for 30 minutes.

3. About 30 minutes before baking, adjust two racks to the upper- and lower-middle positions of the oven. Preheat the oven to 325°F. Line two baking sheets with parchment paper.

4. Scoop a tablespoon of dough, roll into a smooth ball, then roll in the bowl of turbinado sugar to coat. Repeat to make 30 balls, placing them 2 inches apart on the prepared baking sheets.

5. Bake all the cookies, switching the sheets between top and bottom racks and rotating front to back once halfway through, until the cookie edges are set and the tops puff and crack, 13 to 15 minutes. Allow the cookies to cool directly on the baking sheets.

MATCHA AND WASABI DROP COOKIES

Makes
20 to 22 cookies

Prep Time
15 minutes

Inactive Time
30 minutes to overnight

Cook Time
14 to 16 minutes

Difficulty
★★☆☆☆
(You don't need to shape these cookies, and the glaze is easy to make.)

For the cookies

2 cups (240 g) cake flour

1 tablespoon culinary-grade matcha

1 teaspoon baking powder

½ teaspoon baking soda

¾ cup | 1½ sticks (170 g) unsalted butter, softened

¾ cup (150 g) granulated sugar

1 tablespoon red miso

1 large egg

1 tablespoon yuzu juice

1 tablespoon wasabi paste

½ cup (60 g) wasabi peas, whole or crushed

For the glaze

1½ cups (180 g) confectioners' sugar, plus more if needed

1½ tablespoons yuzu juice

1 teaspoon olive oil

1 teaspoon wasabi paste

Pinch of kosher salt

For toppings

Freshly grated lemon zest

Toasted white sesame seeds

Crushed wasabi peas

These drop cookies are dedicated to Subtle Asian Baking member Phyllis Y., who asked if I could include a cookie with a "spicy citrus twist." Wasabi, to me, isn't spicy in the mouth or on the tongue, per se, like chili pepper or gochujang, but it has an unforgettably sharp, shocking pungent kick. And while we usually think of enjoying wasabi with sushi, there are many snacks and sweet treats that include wasabi. One of my favorite snacks growing up was wasabi-flavored peas from Japan, so I had to find a way to incorporate them into a cookie.

Adding wasabi to a cookie is no easy feat because 1) it's hard to find real wasabi and grate it directly from the stem; and 2) wasabi can either be too overpowering or get lost in all the sweetness. Here, I made sure you get a hint of wasabi in both the glaze and the cookie itself. Of course, if you're a wasabi fan, feel free to add more wasabi for an extra kick. Enjoy them with a hot cup of white tea!

1. **Make the cookies.** Whisk the cake flour, matcha, baking powder, and baking soda together in a medium bowl and set aside.

2. Using a stand mixer fitted with the paddle attachment (or in a large bowl with a hand mixer, whisk, or spatula), cream the butter, sugar, and miso together until light and fluffy, about 1 minute. Scrape down the sides and bottom of the bowl. Add the egg, yuzu juice, and wasabi paste and mix until well incorporated. Add the flour mixture and mix on low speed just until a cookie dough forms. Fold in the wasabi peas. Cover the dough and chill in the refrigerator for 30 minutes to overnight.

3. About 30 minutes before baking, adjust two racks to the upper- and lower-middle positions of the oven. Preheat the oven to 350°F. Line two baking sheets with parchment paper.

RECIPE *continues* →

Cookie Tip
The glaze can melt if your cookies are too warm. It's best to glaze cookies after they have cooled completely.

Substitutions
If yuzu juice is hard to find, use lime or lemon juice.

Storage
Store the cookies in an airtight container at room temperature for up to 4 days.

4. Drop 1 heaping tablespoon of the dough onto the prepared baking sheet. Repeat to make about 20 cookies, spacing them 2 inches apart. Since these are drop cookies, they're meant to be rustic and just plopped onto the baking sheet.

5. Bake all the cookies, switching the sheets between top and bottom racks and rotating front to back once halfway through, until the cookie edges and bottoms are golden brown, 14 to 16 minutes.

6. Let the cookies set directly on the baking sheets for a few minutes before transferring to a wire rack to cool completely.

7. **Make the glaze.** Meanwhile, whisk all the glaze ingredients together in a medium bowl until smooth. If the glaze is too runny, add 1 to 2 teaspoons confectioners' sugar. Spoon the glaze over the cooled cookies so the tops are covered generously with glaze. Alternatively, drizzle the glaze over the cookies, or dip the cookies into the glaze.

8. Garnish the cookies with the toppings. You can mix and match, but definitely add crushed wasabi peas to some of the glazed cookies. Serve the cookies with light dessert wine or a light tea, like white tea.

PUPPY CHOW WITH A KICK

Makes
9 to 10 cups puppy chow

Prep Time
15 minutes

Inactive Time
About 20 minutes

Cook Time
About 5 minutes

Difficulty
★☆☆☆☆
(Possibly one of the easiest recipes in this book.)

- 1 cup (170 g) semisweet chocolate chips
- ¾ cup (180 g) creamy nut butter, like peanut, almond, walnut, or cashew butter
- 4 tablespoons (57 g) salted butter
- 2 tablespoons (42 g) honey or maple syrup
- 2 tablespoons sriracha (30 g), or more to taste
- 6 cups (about 180 g) rice Chex cereal or puffed cereal squares
- 3 cups (225 g) Ritz Bits peanut butter sandwich crackers
- About 1½ cups (180 g) confectioners' sugar
- Cayenne powder, for garnish (optional)

Puppy chow (chocolate and peanut butter-covered Chex cereal, dusted with confectioners' sugar) is a snack from the Midwest, created back in the 1950s, but by whom, no one knows exactly. The treat's origin is as muddy as its other name: muddy buddies. Growing up in Brooklyn, I had never heard of or had puppy chow until I was an adult at a work potluck. My coworkers kept going back to grab more of what looked like the kibble my shih-poo Panda enjoys. I tried some and soon, one handful became two, then three, then four. I kept going back for more, popping each chocolatey piece into my mouth like a tiny cookie.

Flash forward to years later when I made puppy chow for the first time. I wanted it different though. Spicy with a pop of red. I reached for the bottle of sriracha in my fridge, a condiment I always squirted over my pho or used to make spicy mayo. In my spicy puppy chow, sriracha punches up the tang and umami while adding a beautiful heat. A dusting of cayenne powder adds a beautiful red color. Who knows, maybe this will become your go-to potluck dish and a favorite in your family, too.

1. Line a baking sheet with parchment paper.

2. Combine the chocolate chips, nut butter, and butter in a large microwave-safe bowl. Microwave in 30-second bursts, stirring with a rubber spatula after each burst, until completely melted and smooth, up to 2 minutes. Stir in the honey or maple syrup and sriracha. Give it a taste. If it's not spicy enough for you, stir in a little more sriracha.

3. Add the cereal and the peanut butter sandwiches, a cup of each at a time, and gently stir with a rubber spatula or wooden spoon to coat with the chocolate mixture. Once thoroughly mixed, set aside to cool for a few minutes.

RECIPE *continues* →

Variation
Instead of using Ritz Bits, use pretzels or Chex Mix.

Substitutions
You can use any brand of puffed square cereal other than Chex. Any mini peanut butter crackers other than Ritz Bits will do as well. And feel free to substitute a cup of your favorite nuts for a cup of the cereal or crackers.

Storage
Store the puppy chow in an airtight container at room temperature for up to 5 days, or up to a week in the refrigerator.

4. Add half of the confectioners' sugar to a large food storage bag, like a gallon-sized zip-top bag. Transfer the chocolate-coated mix to the bag and add the rest of the confectioners' sugar. Seal the bag and shake until well coated.

5. Spread the puppy chow out in an even layer on the prepared baking sheet. Refrigerate, covered, for at least 20 minutes before serving. If you like, dust with some cayenne powder for a pop of color; however, note that cayenne powder can be quite spicy. To serve, transfer the puppy chow to serving or snack bowls.

GINGER SNAPS WITH SICHUAN PEPPERCORNS

Makes
about 18 cookies

Prep Time
About 15 minutes

Inactive Time
30 minutes

Cook Time
About 12 minutes

Difficulty
(Not too difficult, though you will have to roll the cookie dough balls in sugar and press the peppercorns into the tops.)

- 1 cup (120 g) all-purpose flour
- 1 teaspoon baking soda
- 1 tablespoon ground ginger
- ½ teaspoon ground Vietnamese cinnamon
- ½ teaspoon ground cloves
- 1 tablespoon toasted Sichuan peppercorns, crushed with a mortar and pestle, plus more for topping
- ¼ cup plus 1 tablespoon (67 g) neutral oil
- ½ cup (85 g) jaggery
- 2 tablespoons (42 g) unsulfured molasses
- 1 teaspoon red miso
- 1 large egg
- ¼ cup (50 g) granulated sugar or demerara sugar, placed in a shallow bowl, plus more as needed

Ah Ma, my paternal granny, was a spitfire in her prime. She could eat the spiciest peppers without flinching. I remember her chewing on bird's eye chilis like they were the sweetest candy. Early on, she taught me to appreciate the spicy food that is common in Vietnamese cuisine. One time, she yelled at me because I found something a bit too spicy in my bún thịt nướng (Vietnamese grilled pork with rice noodles)! Tears were coming out of my eyes!

My beloved granny was a tough cookie. She was the only baker I knew in my family growing up, but she made mainly cakes and mooncakes, not cookies. But in an alternative universe, I imagined these ginger snaps would be the sort of cookies she'd make on a Sunday morning for her grandchildren. To give them an extra kick on top of the warm spices, we'll be adding toasted Sichuan peppercorns. Ah Ma won't be able to taste these, but I'm sure they're a cookie she'd be proud of, even though they would not have been spicy enough for her.

1. Whisk the flour, baking soda, ground ginger, cinnamon, cloves, and crushed Sichuan peppercorns together in a medium bowl. Set aside.

2. Use a rubber spatula or whisk to mix the oil, jaggery, molasses, miso, and egg in a large bowl until combined. Add the flour mixture and mix until a dough forms and the dry flour trails disappear. Cover the dough and refrigerate for at least 30 minutes.

3. About 30 minutes before baking, adjust two racks to the upper- and lower-middle positions of the oven. Preheat the oven to 375°F. Line two baking sheets with parchment paper.

4. Scoop 1 heaping tablespoon of dough, roll into a smooth ball, and roll in the sugar to coat. Repeat to make 18 balls, placing them 2 inches apart on the prepared baking sheets. Sprinkle

RECIPE *continues* →

Substitutions
Substitute dark brown sugar one-to-one for the jaggery. If Sichuan peppercorns pack too much heat for you, use pink peppercorns, which are more floral than spicy.

Storage
Store the cookies in an airtight container at room temperature for up to 4 days.

some crushed toasted Sichuan peppercorns over the tops of each dough ball and press in lightly with your fingers.

5. Bake all the cookies, switching the sheets between top and bottom racks and rotating front to back once halfway through, until the cookie edges and centers are set, about 12 minutes.

6. Allow the cookies to cool directly on the baking sheets.

SURPRISING PEANUT BUTTER COOKIES

Makes	*Prep Time*	*Cook Time*	*Difficulty*
about 36 cookies	10 minutes *Inactive Time* 30 minutes to overnight	About 12 to 15 minutes	★★½☆☆ (Using curry powder may deter some, but trust the process!)

2 cups (240 g) all-purpose flour

1 ¼ teaspoons Asian curry powder (I use S+B Curry Powder), plus more for dusting the cookies

1 teaspoon baking soda

½ teaspoon baking powder

¼ teaspoon MSG (optional)

½ cup | 1 stick (113 g) unsalted butter, softened

½ cup (113 g) shortening or lard

1 cup (258 g) conventional creamy peanut butter

1 cup (180 g) unpacked light brown sugar

½ cup (100 g) granulated sugar, plus more for rolling the cookies

2 large eggs

1 ½ teaspoons light soy sauce

Peanut butter cookies came into existence around the 1910s and since then they've become one of America's favorite cookies. Easy to whip up and beautifully buttery, they always hit the spot. But let's be honest, the recipe hasn't changed much over the years. Everyone's grandma passes down a similar recipe for peanut butter cookies. Which isn't entirely bad, because why change a good thing? Well, I decided to sneak a little surprise into the classic: curry powder and soy sauce. Whenever I make curry, I like to incorporate peanut butter, which adds creaminess and tempers the heat. And soy sauce always brings a hint of umami and replaces salt for salinity. So, I figured, why not go the other way and curry-fy a peanut-forward treat?

Coming out of the oven, the cookies will give off a strong aroma, but the curry flavor will be subtle and develop more the next day, with an almost je ne sais quoi quality to it.

1. Whisk the flour, curry powder, baking soda, baking powder, and MSG, if using, together in a medium bowl. Set aside.

2. Using a stand mixer fitted with the paddle attachment (or in a large bowl with a hand mixer, whisk, or spatula), cream the butter, shortening or lard, peanut butter, and sugars together until light and fluffy. Scrape down the sides and bottom of the bowl. Mix in the eggs, one at a time, then the soy sauce until well incorporated. Add the flour mixture and mix on low speed just until a cookie dough forms. Cover the dough and refrigerate for 30 minutes to overnight.

3. About 25 minutes before baking, adjust two racks to the upper- and lower-middle positions of the oven. Preheat the oven to 325°F. Line two baking sheets with parchment paper. Add about ¼ cup granulated sugar to a shallow bowl.

RECIPE *continues* →

Cookie Tip
If you use natural peanut butter with a layer of oil on top of the jar, be sure to stir it thoroughly first, and expect a crumblier cookie.

Variation
Top each cookie with a chunk of dark chocolate or a mini Reese's peanut butter cup before baking.

Storage
Store the cookies in an airtight container at room temperature for up to 5 days.

4. Scoop 1 tablespoon of dough, shape into a smooth ball, and roll in the bowl of sugar to coat. Repeat to make 36 balls, placing them 2 inches part on the prepared baking sheets. Use the tines of a fork to flatten and indent crisscross patterns over the tops of each cookie. Alternatively, use a meat mallet to flatten and add a pattern to the cookies. If you like, dust each cookie with a scant amount of curry powder.

5. Bake all the cookies, switching the sheets between top and bottom racks and rotating front to back once halfway through, until the cookies are set while the middles are still quite soft, and the edges are golden brown, about 15 minutes.

6. Let the cookies set directly on the baking sheets for a few minutes, then transfer to a wire rack to cool completely.

SWEET SRIRACHA COOKIES

Makes
about 19 cookies

Prep Time
15 minutes

Inactive Time
About 30 minutes

Cook Time
About 16 minutes

Difficulty
★★★★☆
(The most difficult part is not overmixing when adding the sriracha butter to the cookie dough.)

For the sriracha butter

1 tablespoon unsalted butter, softened

1 tablespoon cream cheese, softened, or 1 tablespoon Greek yogurt

2 tablespoons (28 g) light brown sugar

1½ tablespoons sriracha

1 tablespoon all-purpose flour

Pinch of MSG

A tiny drop of red food coloring gel (optional)

For the cookie dough

7 tablespoons (98 g) unsalted butter, softened

¾ cup (150 g) granulated sugar

¼ cup (45 g) unpacked light brown sugar

1 large egg

1 tablespoon red miso

1 tablespoon Japanese whisky or bourbon

1½ cups (180 g) all-purpose flour

½ teaspoon baking soda

For topping the cookies

Sea salt flakes

When Eric Kim published his viral gochujang caramel cookies in *The New York Times*, the world, including me, fell in love with them. His beautiful cookies motivated me to craft my own sweet and spicy version. I don't have many fond childhood memories of gochujang—unlike Eric, whose grandmother left his family a ten-year-old jar of gochujang. So instead, I chose a spicy condiment that always invokes a sense of home: sriracha. For as long as I can remember, every family home I've visited always had a bottle or two of sriracha. During the sriracha shortage, I kept a bottle for three years. It turned brown, but it still tasted fine.

Don't worry, you're not using ten-year-old sriracha here. To help describe this cookie, imagine if a spicy snickerdoodle and a sassy sugar cookie had a baby. My sweet sriracha cookie, with its pop of heat and umami, thin crispy edges, layers of flavors, and satisfying chew, is that baby. The bit of MSG and the pleasant heat will keep you coming back for more. I had to hide these cookies from myself.

1. **Make the sriracha butter.** Using a rubber spatula, cream the butter, cream cheese or yogurt, and brown sugar together in a small bowl. Mix in the sriracha, flour, and MSG until smooth. If you want the sriracha to show up more vibrantly red post baking, mix in a tiny drop of red food coloring gel. Cover and refrigerate.

2. **Make the cookie dough.** Whisk the butter, sugars, egg, miso, and Japanese whisky or bourbon together in a large mixing bowl by hand. Add the flour and baking soda and mix with a flexible spatula just until no dry flour spots remain and a smooth dough forms. Spread the dough evenly in the bowl.

3. This is an Eric Kim trick: Drop the sriracha butter in spaced-out dollops (three or four of them) onto the dough in the bowl. Using a spoon or butter knife, gently swirl the sriracha butter into the cookie dough in long figure-8s or long ovals. You want ribbons of the sriracha butter. Don't fully incorporate the sriracha butter into the dough, or overmix, as you want to keep

RECIPE *continues* →

Cookie Tips
Keep the cookies in the oven for an extra minute or two if you like them extra crispy. The cookies also toast up nicely the next day in the toaster oven, or baked for a few minutes at 350°F.

Variation
You can omit the Japanese whisky or bourbon to keep the cookie non-alcoholic.

Storage
Store the cookies in an airtight container at room temperature for up to 5 days.

distinct streaks of orange visible. When you use a cookie scoop later, it will further mix the sriracha butter into the cookie dough. Cover the bowl and refrigerate for 30 minutes.

4. About 25 minutes before baking, adjust two racks to the upper- and lower-middle positions of the oven. Preheat the oven to 350°F. Line two baking sheets with parchment paper.

5. Scoop nineteen 2-tablespoon portions of dough and space 2 inches apart on the prepared baking sheets.

6. Bake all the cookies, switching the sheets between top and bottom racks and rotating front to back once halfway through, until the cookies are set and the bottoms and edges are golden, about 16 minutes.

7. Let the cookies cool for 5 minutes directly on the baking sheets, then transfer to a wire rack to cool completely. Sprinkle sea salt flakes over the cookies.

◂ Scooping the swirled cookie dough into balls.

CHOCOLATE MOCHI BARS WITH SAMBAL OELEK

Makes	***Prep Time***	***Cook Time***	***Difficulty***
16 to 24 bars	10 minutes	50 minutes	★☆☆☆☆ (If not using a blender, then hand-mixing the batter increases the difficulty.)

- 1 cup (240 g) milk or plant-based milk
- ⅔ cup (134 g) granulated sugar
- ¼ cup (60 g) maple syrup
- 2 large eggs
- 2 tablespoons neutral oil
- 1 tablespoon sambal oelek
- 1 tablespoon red miso
- 2 cups (300 g) glutinous rice flour
- 2 tablespoons (10 g) unsweetened Dutch-processed cocoa powder
- 1 teaspoon baking powder
- ½ cup (85 g) chopped semisweet chocolate or chocolate chips
- Confectioners' sugar, for dusting
- Gochugaru chili flakes, for dusting (optional)

These might be one of the easiest and tastiest spicy chocolate mochi bars you'll ever make. Whenever I speak or host an event in Seattle, like a charity baking pop-up, I make these mochi treats, cut them up real small, and pass them out as samples. Ninety percent of the people who sample them will buy something from me or support my cause that day. Yes, they're that good. Plus, they are Philip's favorite mochi bars. Whenever they come fresh out of the oven, he's there, faster than our gluttonous poodle mix, Panda (who isn't allowed to eat anything with chocolate).

P.S.: A hot sauce inclusion is a must, and I've tried sriracha and gochujang, but I'm suggesting you jump outside the box a little and mix in sambal oelek, an Indonesian chili paste made from ground fresh chilis. Over time, sambal oelek has gained popularity beyond Indonesia and is now used in various Southeast Asian cuisines, including Malaysian and Thai. In these bars, sambal oelek adds heat, tanginess, and a surprisingly pleasant hint of garlic.

1. Adjust a rack to the middle position and preheat the oven to 350°F. Crumple, then uncrumple a large sheet of parchment paper and use it to line a 9-inch square baking dish with some overhang. Smooth and press down the parchment paper with your hands.

2. In a blender, blend the milk, granulated sugar, maple syrup, eggs, oil, sambal oelek, and miso until smooth. Scrape the sides of the blender as needed to ensure all ingredients are well incorporated. (This can also be done in a stand mixer using the paddle attachment, but you'll need to mix the wet ingredients first.) Add the glutinous rice flour, cocoa powder, and baking powder and blend until the batter is smooth and well combined. Pour the batter into the prepared baking dish.

RECIPE *continues* →

Variations
Along with the chocolate chips, feel free to mix in about ½ cup of your favorite nuts or dried berries, or a combination of both.

Storage
Store the mochi bars in an airtight container at room temperature for up to 3 days.

Sprinkle the chopped chocolate or chocolate chips evenly over the top.

3. Bake until the top is set and puffy, the surface is dry and begins to crack, and a bamboo skewer inserted into the center comes out clean, 50 minutes.

4. Lift the bars out of the baking dish using the parchment paper and transfer to a wire rack to cool completely. Once cooled, slice into 16 to 24 equal bars. Dust the bars with confectioners' sugar and, if desired, a sprinkle of gochugaru chili flakes (possibly your new favorite chili flakes!) for an extra kick.

MAGIC IN THE MIDDLES WITH A KICK

Makes
about 22 cookies

Prep Time
20 minutes

Inactive Time
30 minutes

Cook Time
About 10 minutes

Difficulty
★★★½☆
(There's a lot of assembly.)

For the filling

⅔ cup (160 g) creamy or chunky peanut butter

⅓ cup (43 g) confectioners' sugar

2 tablespoons (30 g) Thai sweet chili sauce

1 teaspoon chili powder

Pinch of kosher salt

For the cookies

1½ cups (180 g) all-purpose flour

¼ cup (30 g) milk powder

1½ tablespoons high-quality culinary-grade matcha

½ teaspoon baking soda

½ cup | 1 stick (113 g) unsalted butter, softened

¾ cup (150 g) packed light brown sugar

¼ cup (50 g) granulated sugar

1 teaspoon red miso

¼ cup (60 g) creamy peanut butter

2 large eggs

For coating the cookies

¼ cup (35 g) toasted sesame seeds

½ cup (100 g) granulated sugar, divided

Sea salt flakes, for garnish (optional)

Magic in the middles, once dubbed "America's most wanted cookies," are usually chocolate cookies with a peanut butter filling. In the past, Keebler had called them Magic Middles and sold them as vanilla or chocolate chip cookies with a chocolatey "magical" middle. I don't remember seeing the commercials because they aired around 1989, when I was still too young to remember much of anything. Then, suddenly, Keebler took them off the market. As this cookie's popularity had resurged recently (I guess because of America's yearning for times past), I took a stab at making them, but with a twist. I included a spicy-hot peanut butter filling, reminiscent of the fiery and delicious peanut sauces found throughout Southeast Asian cuisines, like the sauce you drizzle over satay skewers. It's also the sauce Ah Ma made for us to dip our gỏi cuốn (Vietnamese spring rolls) into.

Then, there's the earthy, slightly bitter notes of matcha in the cookie that complement the rich creaminess of peanut butter remarkably well. I'm surprised I have not seen this combo before. There's always a first!

1. Adjust two racks to the upper- and lower-middle positions of the oven. Preheat the oven to 350°F. Line two baking sheets with parchment paper.

2. **Make the filling.** Line two plates with parchment paper. Using a stand mixer fitted with the paddle attachment (or in a mixing bowl with a hand mixer, whisk, or spatula), cream the peanut butter, confectioners' sugar, chili sauce, chili powder, and salt until well combined. Scoop a heaping teaspoon portion and drop onto a prepared plate, then repeat to make about 22 equal portions. With lightly floured hands, roll each into a ball. Chill, uncovered, in the freezer for 15 minutes.

3. **Make the cookies.** Meanwhile, whisk the flour, milk powder, matcha, and baking soda together in a medium bowl. Set aside.

RECIPE *continues* →

Variation
To make chocolate magic in the middles, omit the milk powder, matcha, and 2 tablespoons of the flour from the cookie dough and add ½ cup unsweetened Dutch-processed cocoa powder.

Storage
Store the cookies in an airtight container at room temperature for up to 3 days.

4. Using a stand mixer fitted with the paddle attachment (or in a mixing bowl with a hand mixer, whisk, or spatula), cream the butter, sugars, and miso until well combined. Add the peanut butter and eggs and mix until incorporated. Add the flour mixture and mix on low speed just until a cookie dough forms. Cover and chill the dough in the refrigerator for 15 minutes.

5. **Make the coating.** Combine the sesame seeds and ¼ cup of the granulated sugar in a shallow bowl and whisk together. Place the remaining ¼ cup granulated sugar in a separate shallow bowl.

6. **Assemble the cookies:** Scoop 1 tablespoon dough and roll into a ball. Flatten into a disc and add a portion of filling to the middle. Wrap the dough entirely around the filling and roll again to shape into a smooth ball. Roll in the bowl of sesame seeds and sugar and then in the bowl of sugar to coat thoroughly. Repeat to make 22 balls, placing them 2 inches apart on the prepared baking sheets. Flatten each ball slightly with the bottom of a glass coated in granulated sugar, just before the edges begin to crack.

7. Bake all the cookies, switching the sheets between top and bottom racks and rotating front to back once halfway through, until the cookies are set and the centers are soft and puffy, 9 to 10 minutes.

8. Let the cookies set on the baking sheets for a few minutes. If you like, sprinkle sea salt flakes over the still-warm cookies. Transfer to a wire rack to cool completely. These cookies are best when the centers are warm and gooey.

LAKSA COOKIES

Makes
24 to 36 cookies, depending on the size of your cookie cutter

Prep Time
30 minutes

Inactive Time
60 minutes

Cook Time
24 to 30 minutes

Difficulty
★★★☆☆
(A bit of everything involved, from chopping ingredients, to chilling the dough, to cutting out cookies. The dough is a little delicate.)

- 1⅓ cups (170 g) all-purpose flour
- 1 tablespoon cornstarch
- ½ teaspoon baker's ammonia or baking soda
- ½ teaspoon baking powder
- ½ cup | 1 stick (113 g) unsalted butter, softened
- ½ cup (60 g) confectioners' sugar
- ½ teaspoon red miso
- 2 to 3 tablespoons (30 to 45 g) store-bought laksa paste, to taste
- 1 teaspoon lime juice, or to taste
- 1 teaspoon coconut extract
- About ⅓ cup (50 g) dried shrimp, finely minced (optional)
- 2 tablespoons (10 g) finely minced laksa leaves or curry leaves (optional), plus more for garnishing
- 1 large egg, beaten, for egg wash
- Toasted white sesame seeds, for topping

There are few things I enjoy more than eating a hot bowl of spicy, umami-rich laksa noodle soup. Making laksa one day, I thought, why not capture all these incredible flavors in a cookie? This concept might seem unconventional at first. I mean, dried shrimp, curry leaves, laksa, and lime in a cookie? Well, I don't want to gatekeep a good savory cookie. And besides, this is not a newly invented cookie: Laksa cookies are popular across Asia, often sold and gifted during Lunar New Year. Some variations include curry powder, while others, spicier than mine, feature lots of chili flakes.

So, if you're a fan of daring flavor combinations and the iconic taste of laksa, your reward will be a delightful gateway to the vibrant hawker centers of Singapore: each bite warm and buttery with a surprising punch of flavor.

1. Whisk the flour, cornstarch, baker's ammonia or baking soda, and baking powder together in a medium bowl. Set aside.

2. Using a stand mixer fitted with the paddle attachment (or in a large bowl with a hand mixer, whisk, or spatula), cream the butter, confectioners' sugar, and miso together until light and fluffy. Scrape down the sides and bottom of the bowl. Add the laksa paste, lime juice, and coconut extract and mix until well incorporated. Add the flour mixture and mix on low speed just until a cookie dough forms. If you like, fold in the dried shrimp and laksa leaves.

3. With a lightly floured rolling pin on a lightly floured surface or large sheet of parchment paper, roll out the dough to ¼-inch thickness (about as thick as a chopstick), approximately 14 by 12 inches. Refrigerate, covered, for 60 minutes.

4. About 25 minutes before baking, adjust a rack to the middle position and preheat the oven to 350°F. Line two baking sheets with parchment paper.

RECIPE *continues* →

LAKSA COOKIES, *continued*

Cookie Tip
Rather than rolling out the dough and using a cookie cutter to cut out shapes, you can make drop cookies by either spooning and dropping the dough onto the baking sheet or shaping the dough into even balls before baking.

Substitution
If you can't find laksa leaves, you can swap them out for Thai basil or Vietnamese mint leaves.

Storage
Store the cookies in an airtight container at room temperature for up to 5 days.

5. Use a 2-inch circle, fluted circle, or heart-shaped cookie cutter to cut out shapes from the dough. Gather the scraps, re-roll, and continue cutting until all the dough is used. Carefully place the cookies on the prepared baking sheet, spacing them 1 inch apart.

6. Brush all the tops with the egg wash and sprinkle with sesame seeds. Bake, one sheet at a time (while the other sheet chills in the fridge), until the bottoms and edges of the cookies are golden brown, 12 to 15 minutes.

7. Let the cookies set on the baking sheet for a few minutes, then transfer to a wire rack to cool completely. Garnish with minced laksa leaves.

MASALA MACAROONS

Makes
about
30 macaroons

Prep Time
About
10 minutes

Cook Time
16 to 18 minutes

Difficulty
★☆☆☆☆
(Not eating them all before they set will be challenging!)

- One 14-ounce (396 g) can sweetened condensed milk
- 1 ripe small banana, mashed
- 1 teaspoon red miso
- One 14-ounce (396 g) bag shredded coconut (I prefer unsweetened, but you can also use sweetened)
- 2 teaspoons garam masala
- ½ teaspoon ground cardamom
- ½ teaspoon ground ginger
- About ⅓ cup (60 g) semisweet chocolate chips, plus more as needed
- 1 teaspoon neutral oil
- Sea salt flakes, for garnish
- Sprinkles, for garnish (optional)

People often confuse macaroons with macarons, which is a pet peeve of mine. Even though they have very similar names, they are very distinct cookies. While both are usually made with whipped egg whites, macaroons are dense and chewy coconut-based treats, whereas macarons are delicate, meringue-based French confections. Here, we won't be using egg whites to bind the ingredients together because let's face it, I'm lazy, and whenever I can skip whipping up egg whites, it's a win for me. A mashed banana helps bind the macaroon batter just fine.

Ever since I was a kid, I've been a fan of macaroons and don't mind their usual sweetness. However, admittedly, they can be quite one-note in flavor and sometimes so sweet that your teeth hurt. Adding warm spices like garam masala, cardamom, and ginger really elevates these cookies. Then, round them out by dipping the bottoms in chocolate and drizzling some on top, finishing with a crown of sea salt flakes. Voilà, you have delicious, elevated macaroons perfect for snacking and impressing friends.

1. Adjust two racks to the upper- and lower-middle positions of the oven. Preheat the oven to 350°F. Line two baking sheets with parchment paper.

2. In a large mixing bowl, mix the condensed milk, mashed banana, and miso until combined. Add the shredded coconut, garam masala, cardamom, and ginger and mix until well combined and the dough can hold itself together.

3. Scoop heaping tablespoons of batter for each macaroon and place on the prepared baking sheet. Keep their rounded mound shapes and give each about 1 inch of space.

4. Bake all the macaroons, switching the sheets between top and bottom racks and rotating front to back once halfway

RECIPE *continues* →

MASALA MACAROONS, *continued*

Macaroon Tip
Macaroons taste chewier and delicious after chilling overnight in the refrigerator.

Variation
To make these vegan, use vegan coconut condensed milk and vegan chocolate.

Storage
Store the macaroons in an airtight container in the refrigerator for up to 2 weeks or at room temperature for up to 1 week.

through, until the edges are crispy and golden brown and the tops are lightly toasted, 16 to 18 minutes.

5. Let the macaroons set on the baking sheets for 5 minutes before transferring to a wire rack to cool completely.

6. While the macaroons are cooling, combine the chocolate chips and oil in a medium heatproof bowl and microwave in 30-second bursts, stirring after each interval, until the chocolate is melted and smooth.

7. Dip the bottoms of the cooled macaroons into the melted chocolate. Place them back on the parchment-lined baking sheets to set. Drizzle additional melted chocolate on top of each macaroon. Before the chocolate sets completely, sprinkle a few flakes of sea salt on top of each macaroon. If you like, for the kiddos in your life or those who wish to nurture their inner child, decorate the macaroons with sprinkles.

KIMCHI SCONES

Makes	*Prep Time*	*Cook Time*	*Difficulty*
16 scones	20 minutes *Inactive Time* About 30 minutes	20 to 25 minutes	★★★☆☆ (You need to be gentle with this dough.)

A few years ago, Jake, Philip, my parents, and I went on a cruise that hosted a daily teatime event where we enjoyed British tea and scones. I do believe that was the first time I had scones, or maybe that was the first time scones registered in the mental bakery compartment of my brain. Since then, I've made probably a few hundred scones over the years, from nutty and sweet to chaotic savory—like a hot pot version slathered in a "it-has-a-little-of-everything" sauce you might concoct at a hot pot restaurant. This kimchi scone is a little less chaotic than my hot pot one, and a new favorite of mine, with each bite being layered with flavors thanks to the tang and crunch of stir-fried kimchi, the mild grassy zing of scallions, and the richness of cheese and butter. If you're a teatime and scones traditionalist, you can pair these savory bites with clotted cream. Or stick with my gochujang honey glaze, a sauce you can repurpose for fried chicken and Korean-style dinner dishes.

For the scones

Neutral oil, for greasing

1 cup kimchi (240 g), drained and finely chopped

2 cups (240 g) bread flour

¾ cup (90 g) cake flour

3 tablespoons (38 g) granulated sugar

1 teaspoon baking powder

¼ teaspoon kosher salt

¼ teaspoon ground black pepper

¼ teaspoon MSG (optional)

⅔ cup (65 g) shredded Parmesan or cheddar cheese

¼ cup (25 g) chopped scallions (both white and green parts)

½ cup | 1 stick (113 g) unsalted butter, very cold

2 large eggs

1 ½ tablespoons gochujang

1 tablespoon kimchi juice

½ cup milk or plant-based milk

1 large egg, beaten, for egg wash

Toasted white sesame seeds

For the gochujang honey glaze

2 tablespoons (42 g) honey

2 tablespoons (40 g) gochujang

2 tablespoons (24 g) light brown sugar

2 teaspoons warm water, plus more as needed

1 teaspoon soy sauce

For optional toppings

Finely minced chives or scallions

Toasted white sesame seeds

1. **Make the scones:** Lightly grease a pan or wok with oil and heat over medium-high heat. Add the kimchi and stir-fry until aromatic and lightly browned on both sides, a few minutes. Transfer to a plate and set aside to cool.

2. Line a baking sheet with parchment paper.

3. Whisk the bread flour, cake flour, sugar, baking powder, salt, pepper, and MSG, if using, together in a large mixing bowl. Add the cooled kimchi, Parmesan or cheddar, and scallions and stir until just combined and still scraggly. Add the butter and chop it into the dry ingredients, using a pastry cutter or fork. Alternatively, use your clean hands to rub or smear the butter into the flour between your fingers. Either way, work in the butter until pea-sized pieces of flour-coated butter remain.

4. Gently mix in the eggs, gochujang, kimchi juice, and milk until a shaggy, crumbly dough forms. Turn it out on the prepared baking sheet. Pat it gently into a rough rectangle about 1 inch thick. Fold it in half. Give the dough a quarter turn and pat it

RECIPE *continues* →

Scone Tip
Scone dough is meant to be lightly handled, so don't overmix.

Variations
Use chives instead of scallions. Feel free to omit the glaze if short on time.

Storage
Store unglazed scones in an airtight container at room temperature for up to 3 days or refrigerate for up to 5 days. Reheat in the oven or toaster before serving for best texture.

down again into a rectangle and fold it in half again. Repeat this pat and fold one more time.

5. Divide the dough into two equal portions. Shape each portion into a round disc about 1 inch thick. Using a sharp knife or pastry cutter, cut one disc into eight equal wedges, like slicing a pizza pie. Repeat with the second portion of dough. Cover and chill in the freezer for 30 minutes.

6. About 30 minutes before baking, adjust a rack to the middle position and preheat the oven to 400°F.

7. Brush the tops of the scones with the egg wash, then top with sesame seeds. Bake for 10 minutes and reduce the heat to 350°F. Bake until golden brown, another 10 to 15 minutes.

8. **Make the glaze.** Meanwhile, whisk all the glaze ingredients together in a small bowl until smooth.

9. While the scones are hot, brush the tops or drizzle with the glaze. Let the scones cool directly on the baking sheet. If you like, top the glaze with minced scallions or chives or toasted sesame seeds, or a mix of both.

◂ Brush scones with gochujang honey glaze.

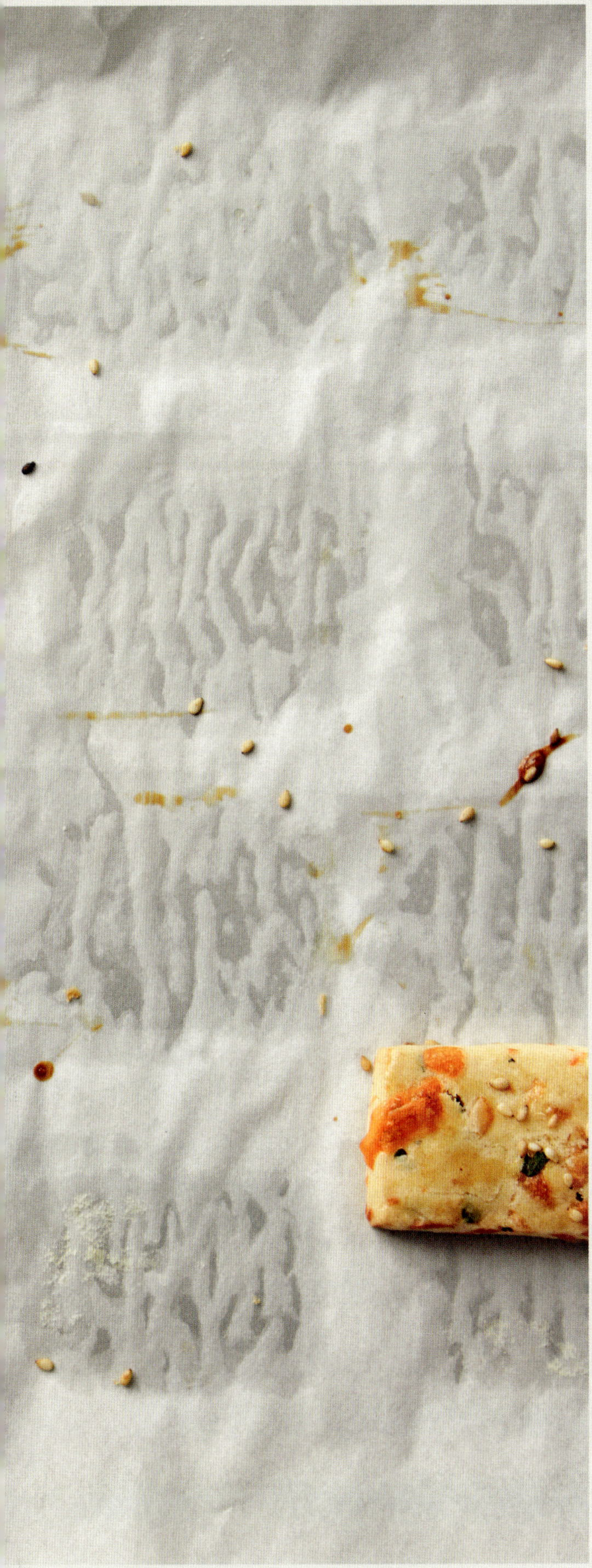

V

UMAMI UNLEASHED

Not-too-sweet cookies packed with umami and savory notes

I've always found joy in the interplay between sweet and savory flavors, especially when it comes to desserts and cookies. So, if you're like me, you're in for a treat (or several) with this chapter. Unlike Western cookies, where sometimes you only get a pop of savory here and there with a sprinkling of sea salt flakes, you'll see that with most of my cookies, I like to balance the sweetness not with salt, but with miso. In this chapter, we'll be using more savory components commonly used across East and Southeast Asia, including salted duck egg yolk, soy sauce, furu (fermented bean curd), and fish sauce.

To whet your palate, try my Instant Ramen Cookies (page 214), where you'll use the savory seasoning packets and crunchy ramen bits to add flavor and texture to a fun cookie. Another Asian noodle-inspired cookie is Pho Cookies (page 234), a warm, delectable treat that feels like a comforting bowl of pho made by a Vietnamese auntie, thanks to all the spices, inclusion of fish sauce, and a refreshing lime glaze. Fish sauce makes another appearance in my boozy and delicious Bourbon and Fish Sauce Cookies (page 246). The Peppery and Cheesy Cilantro Cookies (page 240) are chock-full of umami and not too sweet. It's also one of my mother's favorite recipes because whenever I make these cookies, she tells me not to share them with my neighbors, even when there's extra. And I always make extra cookies. And if you're looking for a gluten-free buttery cookie, look no further than the Indonesian Cheese Sago Cookies (Sagu Keju) on page 249. These melt in the mouth and burst with cheese and salted duck egg yolk.

INSTANT RAMEN COOKIES

Makes	*Prep Time*	*Difficulty*
about 18 cookies	15 minutes	★★½☆☆ (It's not too complicated, and loads of cathartic fun when you're smashing up packages of noodles.)
	Cook Time 10 to 12 minutes	

- 1 cup (120 g) all-purpose flour
- ½ cup (60 g) cake flour
- ¼ cup (36 g) toasted white sesame seeds
- ½ teaspoon baking soda
- ½ teaspoon baking powder
- ½ cup | 1 stick (113 g) unsalted butter, softened
- ⅓ cup (67 g) packed light brown sugar
- ⅓ cup (67 g) granulated sugar
- 1 cup (240 g) peanut butter (chunky or smooth)
- 1 large egg
- 1 heaping teaspoon red miso or 2 teaspoons soy sauce
- Two 3-ounce packets (about 170 g total) instant ramen (Nissin, Indomie, NongShim...), crushed into tiny pea-sized pieces, seasoned with about ¾ of the dry seasoning packets (reserving some to sprinkle over the cookie dough balls), and divided

Is it really that farfetched to add instant ramen, a beloved staple worldwide, to a cookie? After all, we've seen cookies with pretzels and chips, so why not crunchy instant ramen? Instant ramen noodles are precooked and fried, so you can actually eat them straight out of their packaging. I used to do this as a child, and busy college students snack on crunchy instant ramen all the time.

This cookie is a fun one to make with kiddos, as they can help crush the instant ramen. To do so, keep the ramen in its packaging bag and smash it with a food mallet or rolling pin. (Just be careful because the bag may break during this process.) Or the kids can just whack the package directly against a counter (but transfer the ramen to a sturdier bag first). Then, be sure to add the dry seasoning it comes with and shake, shake, shake. If you're wondering what ramen flavor to try, start with a standard one like soy sauce, vegetable, or chicken, then experiment with the spicier or bolder flavors.

Now, why is this cookie made with peanut butter? In ramen and instant noodle broth, peanut butter adds subtle sweetness and a creamy, nutty flavor that balances the savory taste of ramen. It's no wonder the classic combination works so beautifully in cookie form. (Pictured on page 213.)

1. Adjust two racks to the upper- and lower-middle positions of the oven. Preheat the oven to 350°F. Line two baking sheets with parchment paper.

2. Whisk the all-purpose flour, cake flour, toasted sesame seeds, baking soda, and baking powder together in a medium bowl. Set aside.

3. Using a stand mixer fitted with the paddle attachment (or in a large bowl with a hand mixer, whisk, or spatula), cream the butter and sugars together until light and fluffy. Add the peanut butter, egg, and miso or soy sauce and mix until well incorporated. Scrape down the sides and bottom of the bowl. Add the flour mixture and mix on low speed just until a cookie dough forms. Fold in half of the crushed and seasoned ramen. Transfer the remaining crushed ramen to a shallow bowl.

Cookie Tip
You can make the dough ahead of time and refrigerate it, covered, overnight.

Substitution
In case of peanut allergies, substitute almond butter or tahini for the peanut butter.

Storage
Store the cookies in an airtight container at room temperature for up to 4 days.

4. Scoop about 2 tablespoons dough and roll into a smooth ball. Press into the bowl of crushed ramen pieces to coat thoroughly. Repeat to make and coat about 18 balls, placing them 2 inches apart on the prepared baking sheets. Slightly flatten each ball with your palm. Sprinkle a little of the remaining dry seasoning from the ramen packaging over the cookies.

5. Bake all the cookies, switching the sheets between top and bottom racks and rotating front to back once halfway through, until the cookies are set and the centers are soft but not gooey, 10 to 12 minutes.

6. Allow the cookies to cool completely on the baking sheets.

FUDGY SOY SAUCE-CHOCOLATE CHIP COOKIES

Makes
about 12 cookies

Prep Time
15 minutes

Inactive Time
At least 1 hour to overnight

Cook Time
About 18 minutes

Difficulty
★★☆☆☆
(If you've made chocolate chip cookies before, this one won't stump you.)

- 1 cup (120 g) all-purpose flour
- ¼ cup (30 g) cake flour
- ½ teaspoon baking powder
- ¼ teaspoon MSG
- ½ cup | 1 stick (113 g) unsalted butter, softened
- About 2 tablespoons (25 g) brown sugar
- About ⅔ cup (130 g) granulated sugar
- 1 large egg
- 1 to 2 tablespoons light soy sauce, to taste
- 1½ cups (255 g) semisweet chocolate chips
- Sesame seeds, for garnish (optional)

Adding soy sauce to chocolate chip cookies may sound a bit out there. I mean, even my younger self would question this move. But hear me out: Soy sauce and MSG bring an incredible umami richness and balancing depth to the cookies. You have the familiar chocolatey goodness and sweetness, plus a pop of intriguing savoriness. The flavor doesn't overpower; instead, it'll tantalize your taste buds and may leave you wanting more.

So, if you're someone who loves to push the boundaries in the kitchen, or if you're just curious about how these flavors work together, I encourage you to give this recipe a try. Who knows, the cookies might just become your new baking staple, a delightful surprise to share with loved ones.

1. Whisk the all-purpose flour, cake flour, baking powder, and MSG together in a medium bowl. Set aside.

2. Using a stand mixer fitted with the paddle attachment (or in a large bowl with a hand mixer, whisk, or spatula), cream the butter and sugars together until light and fluffy. Add the egg and soy sauce and mix until well incorporated. Scrape down the sides and bottom of the bowl. Add the flour mixture and mix on low speed just until a cookie dough forms. Fold in the chocolate chips. Cover the dough with plastic wrap and refrigerate for at least 1 hour, or overnight.

3. About 25 minutes before baking, adjust two racks to the upper- and lower-middle positions of the oven. Preheat the oven to 350°F. Line two baking sheets with parchment paper.

4. Scoop about 2 tablespoons of dough (28 to 30 grams) and shape roughly into a ball. Repeat to make 12 balls, placing them 2 inches apart on the prepared baking sheets.

RECIPE *continues* →

Cookie Tip
Feel free to make slightly smaller cookies, using about 1 tablespoon of dough per cookie instead of 2. Reduce the baking time to 12 to 15 minutes.

Substitution
Instead of chocolate chips, chop up two 4-ounce bars of semisweet chocolate.

Storage
Store the cookies in an airtight container at room temperature for up to 4 days.

5. Bake all the cookies, switching the sheets between top and bottom racks and rotating front to back once halfway through, until the cookie edges begin to brown, about 18 minutes.

6. If you like, sprinkle sesame seeds over the cookies. Let the cookies set for a few minutes on the baking sheets. Enjoy these cookies warm for maximum fudginess.

CHINESE SAUSAGE (Lap Cheong) COOKIES

Makes
18 to 20 cookies

Prep Time
20 minutes

Inactive Time
About 70 minutes

Cook Time
About 15 minutes

Difficulty
★★★★☆
(Browning the butter takes a bit of practice to get right.)

- 1 cup | 2 sticks (226 g) unsalted butter
- 1 cup (200 g) packed dark brown sugar
- ¼ cup (50 g) granulated sugar
- About 2 links lap cheong, sliced into thin coins (my favorite brand is Orchard Sausages)
- 2 cups (240 g) all-purpose flour
- ½ cup (60 g) cake flour
- 1 teaspoon baking soda
- 1 teaspoon five spice powder (optional, but recommended)
- 1 tablespoon sour cream or Greek yogurt
- 2 large eggs
- 1 tablespoon red miso
- 1 ½ cups (255 g) semisweet or dark chocolate chips
- Sesame seeds, for garnish (optional)
- Flaky sea salt, for topping (optional)

Just as pork floss, salted duck egg yolk, and scallions have found their place in Asian baked goodies, and bacon has found its place in Western baked goodies, lap cheong (dried Chinese sausage) should be utilized in the same way. Resembling thin salami when uncooked, lap cheong is a delightful mix of floral, salty, and sweet, making it a versatile ingredient that offers a unique floral note and sweetness not commonly found in Western sausages. On its own, it pairs beautifully with simple staples like white rice or noodles, enhancing those dishes with its distinct flavor. It also balances well with other ingredients in savory fillings.

Now, we're taking it a step further by incorporating it into a layered brown butter cookie. Imagine the surprise and delight when friends and family taste a cookie that combines the caramel richness of brown butter with the sweet-savory allure of lap cheong.

1. To make the brown butter, cook the butter in a saucepan over medium heat while whisking continuously, until the butter foams, the foam subsides, the butter is golden, and brown (not black) bits form on the bottom, at least 5 minutes. You're looking for a nutty aroma and not a burnt smell. Remove from the heat and transfer to a large heatproof bowl. Add the sugars and mix until they dissolve. Set aside to cool or chill in the freezer for a few minutes for faster cooling.

2. In a skillet or frying pan, pan-fry the lap cheong over medium heat until lightly browned all over, 3 to 5 minutes. Transfer to a paper towel–lined plate to cool.

3. Whisk the flours, baking soda, and five spice powder, if using, together in a medium bowl. Set aside.

4. To the butter mixture, add the sour cream or yogurt, eggs, and miso, and mix until well combined. Add the flour

RECIPE *continues* →

Cookie Tip
If you're a pro at pan-banging cookies (the technique of lifting and dropping a baking sheet during baking to create rippled edges and a chewy, gooey center in cookies), you can channel your inner Sarah Kieffer (of *The Vanilla Bean Blog* fame!) and pan-bang these while they're in the oven.

Substitutions
Unlike other cookies here, where you can swap out the five spice powder for another warm spice of your choice, I highly recommend including it in these cookies, as five spice complements and amplifies the nuanced flavors of lap cheong.

Storage
Store the cookies in an airtight container at room temperature for up to 4 days.

mixture and stir with a rubber spatula or wooden spoon until homogenous. Fold in the lap cheong and chocolate chips.

5. Line two baking sheets with parchment paper. Scoop about 3 tablespoons of the dough and roll into a ball. Repeat to make about 18 balls, placing them 2 inches apart on the prepared baking sheets. Chill in the refrigerator for 1 hour.

6. About 25 minutes before baking, adjust two racks to the upper- and lower-middle positions of the oven. Preheat the oven to 350°F.

7. Bake all the cookies, switching the sheets between top and bottom racks and rotating front to back once halfway through, until the edges turn golden, about 15 minutes. Remove the cookies from the oven. If you like, sprinkle with sesame seeds and sea salt, then let the cookies set on the baking sheet for at least 5 minutes. Transfer to a wire rack to cool. Note these cookies are best served warm to enjoy the gooey chocolate and hot lap cheong.

SHARON'S SALTED EGG YOLK AND CORNFLAKE COOKIES

Makes
12 cookies

Prep Time
About
35 minutes

Cook Time
15 to 17 minutes

Difficulty
★★☆☆☆
(Dehydrating canned corn kernels and browning butter are involved.)

- 1 8-ounce can (216 g) corn kernels, drained thoroughly
- ½ cup | 1 stick (113 g) unsalted butter, cold or room temperature
- 1 ¾ cups (210 g) all-purpose flour
- 2 tablespoons (15 g) freeze-dried corn powder or corn meal
- ½ teaspoon baking soda
- ½ teaspoon kosher salt
- ¾ cup (160 g) granulated sugar
- 2 large eggs
- 2 cooked salted duck egg yolks (about 30 g), mashed with a fork into small chunks
- 1 ½ cups (45 g) cornflakes, crushed to pea-sized and placed in a shallow bowl

This is the second exclusive recipe my dear friend and avid baker Sharon Hsu developed for *108 Asian Cookies.* Whenever her Taiwanese mother-in-law comes back from visiting Taiwan, she brings back little pastries for Sharon to try, such as egg yolk pastry, which is sweet and salty. Thinking of Taiwanese pastries inspired Sharon to create this beginner-friendly recipe that doesn't require a mixer. Her intention behind this recipe is to help elevate our baking skills. Browning the butter and dehydrating the corn kernels are essential steps to unlock the cookie's ultimate flavor and texture, and these extra steps are certainly worth it. The centers of the cookies are designed to be cakey-soft, with contrasting bites of chewiness from the dried corn and crunchiness from the crushed cornflakes. The rich, salty umami flavor of the salted egg yolk crumbles contrasts with the light sweetness of the cookies. As a teatime snack, Sharon shared these with her mother-in-law, who approved of them, deeming them "not too sweet," just like the popular treats she brings back from Taiwan.

1. Adjust two racks to the upper- and lower-middle positions of the oven. Preheat the oven to 350°F. Line two baking sheets with parchment paper.

2. Spread the corn kernels evenly on one of the baking sheets. Bake the corn kernels on the lower-middle rack, stirring once about halfway through baking, until most of the water has evaporated, about 20 minutes. Set aside to cool. Keep the oven turned on.

3. While the corn kernels are in the oven, make the brown butter. Cook the butter in a saucepan over medium heat while whisking continuously, until the butter foams, the foam subsides, the butter is golden, and brown (not black) bits form on the

RECIPE *continues* →

Storage
These cookies are best eaten the same day they're baked, as the cornflakes lose crispness overnight. So Sharon recommends eating or sharing all the cookies the day they're made.

bottom, at least 5 minutes. You're looking for a nutty aroma and not a burnt smell. Remove from the heat and set aside to cool, with the butter still in the saucepan. Or cool in the freezer for a few minutes for faster cooling.

4. Whisk the all-purpose flour, corn powder or corn meal, baking soda, and salt together in a large bowl. Set aside. Add the sugar and eggs to the saucepan with the butter and whisk until combined. Pour the butter mixture into the large bowl with the flour mixture. Using a spatula, fold together until just combined, then fold in the corn kernels and salted egg yolks. Stop folding once everything is fully incorporated and no dry flour spots remain.

5. Line the baking sheet used to roast the corn kernels with fresh parchment paper.

6. Scoop 3 tablespoons of dough (about 60 grams) and shape into a ball. Roll in the crushed cornflakes until evenly coated. Repeat to form and coat 12 balls, placing them 3 inches apart on the two prepared baking sheets.

7. Bake all the cookies, switching the sheets between top and bottom racks and rotating front to back once halfway through, until the edges and tops begin to brown and the centers are set, 15 to 17 minutes. Let the cookies set and cool directly on the baking sheets.

CHEESY CHIVE BISCUITS WITH FERMENTED TOFU

Makes
6 biscuits

Prep Time
22 minutes

Inactive Time
20 minutes

Cook Time
About 22 minutes

Difficulty
★★★½☆
(If you've never made scones or biscuits before, this will be a new experience. The dough, with pea-sized pieces of butter, may throw you off but trust the process.)

I don't remember how old I was when my mom bought a glass jar of furu from an Asian supermarket in NYC's Chinatown. She told me that, back in Hong Kong, this fermented tofu was her stand-in for cheese because real cheese wasn't readily available (or affordable to her). Growing up there, Western foods fascinated her but were inaccessible. She told me how people in Hong Kong and China would spread furu over toast for breakfast or as a midnight snack. "Our version of cheese, or Chinese cheese," she would jokingly say, and I'd feel a little sad about it. But these days, I proudly use furu as a seasoning for fried rice and as a component in marinades. Here, furu is added to cheesy chive biscuits to enhance all the umami and savory flavors. In fact, I think it could be a stand-in for miso in many of my baking recipes.

Please note that we're only making six tall biscuits here, so consider doubling the ingredients to make a dozen if delicious biscuits like these tend to go fast in your household.

For the biscuits

- 1½ cups (180 g) all-purpose flour, plus more for dusting the work surface
- 2 tablespoons (25 g) granulated sugar
- 1 tablespoon baking powder
- Pinch of MSG (optional)
- 4 tablespoons (57 g) unsalted butter, cold, cut into cubes
- 1 tablespoon furu (fermented tofu), the tofu only, no liquid
- 1½ cups (170 g) shredded cheese, like sharp cheddar or Parmesan, or a mix
- ¼ cup (15 g) minced fresh chives
- ¼ cup (30 g) toasted white sesame seeds
- ¾ cup plus 2 tablespoons (210 g) cold buttermilk, plus extra for brushing the biscuits

For the furu butter

- 2 tablespoons (28 g) unsalted butter, cubed and softened
- 1½ tablespoons (30 g) honey
- 1 teaspoon furu, the tofu only, no liquid
- Pinch of white pepper
- Pinch of MSG

1. Adjust a rack to the middle position and preheat the oven to 375°F. Crumple, then uncrumple a large sheet of parchment paper and use it to line a 9-inch square cake pan with some overhang. Smooth and press down the parchment paper with your hands.

2. **Make the biscuits.** Whisk the flour, sugar, baking powder, and MSG, if using, together in a large mixing bowl. Add the cold butter and furu. Cut the butter and furu into the flour mixture by rubbing and smearing the butter and furu into the flour between your fingers in each hand, until pea-sized pieces of flour-coated butter remain. Alternatively, you can use a fork or a bench scraper to cut the butter into the flour mixture.

RECIPE *continues* →

Biscuit Tip
Freezing the biscuits before baking them keeps the butter cold. As the cold butter melts in the oven, it creates tiny pockets of steam that lift the dough, helping the biscuits rise and leading to their appealing flakiness.

Substitution
Swap out the chives for scallions. You can also substitute any other sharp cheese for the cheddar or Parmesan.

Storage
Store the biscuits in an airtight container at room temperature for up to 1 day; afterward, refrigerate for up to 1 week or freeze indefinitely.

3. Add the cheese, chives, and sesame seeds and toss them with your hands until evenly distributed. Slowly stir in all the buttermilk, then stop mixing once a cohesive dough forms. The dough should be a little tacky and craggy but still workable.

4. Lightly flour your work surface. Place the dough on the floured area and roll into a rectangle about ¾ inch thick and about 8 by 10 inches. Fold into thirds like a letter and roll out again, this time to a uniform thickness of 1 ½ inches. Using a 2 ½-inch biscuit or cookie cutter, cut the dough into three to four equal rounds. Cut straight down without twisting the cutter. Gather the scraps, re-roll the dough as needed, and continue cutting until all dough is used and you have a total of six rounds. Transfer the rounds to the prepared baking pan. Chill the rounds, uncovered, in the freezer for 20 minutes.

5. Brush the tops of the biscuits with buttermilk. (For more color, you could instead brush the biscuits with a beaten egg.) Space the biscuits close together (touching), as the proximity will help them rise in oven.

6. Bake the biscuits until puffy, cooked through, and golden brown, about 22 minutes. Let the biscuits cool directly in the baking pan, or transfer to a wire rack to cool completely.

7. **Make the furu butter.** While the biscuits are still in the oven, whisk all the furu butter ingredients together in a small bowl until smooth. If the butter remains lumpy, you can microwave the mixture for about 10 seconds and then whisk it until smooth.

8. To serve, slice a warm biscuit in half crosswise, so the two halves can sandwich a generous layer of sweet and salty furu butter.

MIXED NUTS MOONCAKE, BUT AS KITCHEN SINK COOKIES

Makes
22 to 24 large cookies

Prep Time
About 30 minutes

Inactive Time
About 30 minutes

Cook Time
About 12 minutes

Difficulty
★★★★☆
(This is not a difficult cookie, per se, but there are many steps involved, including dry-roasting the nuts, pan-frying the ham, and making the browned butter.)

1 cup | 2 sticks (226 g) unsalted butter, softened

2 ⅓ cups (280 g) all-purpose flour

½ teaspoon baking soda

½ teaspoon baking powder

½ teaspoon five spice powder

2 tablespoons (40 g) golden syrup or honey

2 tablespoons (30 g) Shaoxing or other rice wine

1 tablespoon red miso

½ cup (75 g) finely chopped Chinese, Italian, Spanish, or American dry-cured ham

⅓ cup (40 g) walnuts or pecans, chopped

⅓ cup (50 g) whole almonds

¼ cup (30 g) pumpkin seeds

¼ cup (35 g) sunflower seeds

⅓ cup (35 g) slivered almonds

¼ cup (35 g) sesame seeds

¾ cup (150 g) packed light brown sugar

½ cup (100 g) granulated sugar

2 large eggs

⅓ cup (45 g) dried currants or cranberries

⅓ cup (50 g) chopped candied winter melon (optional)

I love the "anything goes" concept of kitchen sink cookies: just dump anything you can find in your kitchen—other than your sink—into the mixer bowl and voilà! Cookies! I immediately thought of ńgh yàhn yuht béng (五仁月餅) or mixed nuts mooncake during the development of this recipe. It is a Cantonese-style mooncake that people either love or not. For all my life, I've been in the *love them* boat. Each toothsome bite hits your taste buds with contrasting flavors: toasty nuts, savory and smoky ham, sweet dried fruits, and the unmistakable warmth from five spice powder. I took everything I love about the mooncakes and incorporated them into this savory-sweet kitchen sink cookie. Feel free to change up your mix-ins. And who knows, maybe during Mid-Autumn Festival, you'll seek out mixed nuts mooncakes.

1. To make the brown butter, cook the butter in a heavy saucepan or pot over medium heat, whisking continuously, until the butter foams, the foam subsides, the butter is golden, and brown (not black) bits form on the bottom, at least 5 minutes. You're looking for a nutty aroma and not a burnt smell. Remove from the heat and set aside to cool. You can chill it in the freezer for a few minutes for faster cooling, but don't forget that it's there.

2. Whisk the flour, baking soda, baking powder, and five spice together in a medium bowl. Set aside. Mix the golden syrup or honey, Shaoxing or rice wine, and miso together in a large bowl. Set aside.

3. In a heavy saucepan or frying pan over medium heat, pan-fry the ham until fragrant and lightly browned all over. Reduce the heat to medium-low. With the ham still in the pan, add the walnuts or pecans and the whole almonds and dry-roast for 2 minutes over medium heat. Then add the pumpkin seeds,

RECIPE *continues* →

Cookie Tip
Skip browning the butter if you're pressed for time, but it will add more flavor to the cookies.

Variations
Replace my suggested nuts and dried fruit with your favorites. Swap out the ham for Chinese sausage.

Storage
Store the cookies in an airtight container at room temperature for up to 3 days.

sunflower seeds, and slivered almonds and dry-roast for another minute. Finally, add the sesame seeds and dry-roast until aromatic and toasted, an additional minute. Be sure to stir all the nuts from time to time with a wooden spoon or rubber spatula. Transfer the nuts and ham to the bowl with the syrup or honey mixture. Mix everything together and set aside.

4. Pour the cooled brown butter into the bowl of a stand mixer fitted with the paddle attachment. Add the brown and granulated sugars and mix on medium speed until well combined. Add the eggs, but if the butter is still too hot, first wait a few minutes. Mix on medium speed until the mixture is paler in color, about 2 minutes. Add the flour mixture and mix on low speed until just combined. Mix in the nut and seed mixture and, using a spatula, fold in the dried currants or cranberries and the candied winter melon, if using. Cover the dough and chill in the refrigerator for 30 minutes.

5. About 30 minutes before baking, adjust two racks to the upper- and lower-middle positions of the oven. Preheat the oven to 350°F. Line two baking sheets with parchment paper.

6. Scoop 3 tablespoons of dough and shape into a ball. Repeat to make about 23 cookies, placing them about 2 inches apart on the prepared baking sheets.

7. Bake all the cookies, switching the sheets between top and bottom racks and rotating front to back once halfway through, until the edges are golden brown, about 12 minutes. Let the cookies set on the baking sheets for a few minutes before transferring to a wire rack to cool completely.

TAHINI-DOENJANG COOKIES

Makes	*Prep Time*	*Cook Time*	*Difficulty*
about 22 cookies	18 minutes *Inactive Time* Overnight	About 19 minutes	★★☆☆☆ (Making cookies with tahini is like working with peanut butter.)

Try saying this cookie's name three times really fast! Initially, I wanted these to be savory-sweet miso and walnut butter cookies, but when I was developing the recipe, I only had about a spoonful of walnut butter in the pantry. A bottle of tahini, however, right next to the walnut butter jar, was new and full. Then when I reached for the miso in the fridge, I mistakenly grabbed the doenjang (Korean fermented soybean paste) instead. The resulting crispy and chewy cookies are rich in umami, and now I feel my mistake was just meant to be.

For the cookies

About 1 ¾ cups (225 g) all-purpose flour

½ teaspoon baking soda

½ teaspoon baking powder

¼ teaspoon nutmeg

Pinch of MSG (optional)

½ cup | 1 stick (113 g) unsalted butter, softened

1 cup (200 g) packed light brown sugar

⅓ cup (67 g) granulated sugar

2 large eggs

⅓ cup plus 1 tablespoon (100 g) smooth tahini (roasted or unroasted)

1 tablespoon doenjang

1 tablespoon bourbon

8 ounces dark chocolate, chopped into chunks

For coating the dough balls

¼ cup (35 g) toasted white sesame seeds, placed in a shallow bowl

¼ cup (50 g) demerara or granulated sugar, plus more as needed, placed in a shallow bowl

For garnishing the cookies

Sea salt flakes (optional)

1. **Make the cookies.** Whisk the flour, baking soda, baking powder, nutmeg, and MSG, if using, together in a medium bowl. Set aside.

2. Using a stand mixer fitted with the paddle attachment (or in a large bowl with a hand mixer, whisk, or spatula), cream the butter and sugars together until light and fluffy. Scrape down the sides and bottom of the bowl. Add the eggs, tahini, doenjang, and bourbon and mix until well incorporated. Add the flour mixture and mix on low speed just until a cookie dough forms. Fold in the chocolate chunks. Cover the dough with plastic wrap and refrigerate overnight.

3. About 30 minutes before baking, adjust two racks to the upper- and lower-middle positions of the oven. Preheat the oven to 350°F. Line two baking sheets with parchment paper.

4. **Form, coat, and bake the cookies.** Scoop 2 tablespoons of dough, shape into a ball, and roll in the bowl of sesame seeds, then in the sugar, until thoroughly coated. Repeat to form and coat 22 balls, placing them 2 inches apart on the prepared baking sheets.

5. Bake all the cookies, switching the sheets between top and bottom racks and rotating front to back once halfway through, until the top and edges start to crisp and the middles puff up

RECIPE *continues* →

TAHINI-DOENJANG COOKIES, *continued*

Cookie Tips
I added bourbon and nutmeg to this cookie to balance the strong flavors of the tahini and doenjang. People often mistakenly think doenjang and miso are interchangeable, but doenjang is chunkier, bolder, and punchier than miso, so a little goes a long way!

Variation
For more sweetness, use white chocolate instead of dark.

Storage
Store the cookies in an airtight container at room temperature for up to 3 days.

a little, about 17 minutes. If the cookies are too puffy for your liking, wear oven mitts, and press the cookies down gently with a rubber spatula.

6. Allow the cookies to cool on the baking sheets for a few minutes, then transfer to a wire rack to cool completely. If you like, sprinkle sea salt flakes over the cookies.

PHO COOKIES

Makes	*Prep Time*	*Cook Time*	*Difficulty*
about 24 cookies	20 minutes *Inactive Time* 15 minutes	9 to 12 minutes	★★☆☆☆ (This recipe is relatively straightforward.)

- 2 cups (240 g) all-purpose flour
- 1 cup (120 g) cake flour
- ½ teaspoon baking soda
- ½ teaspoon baking powder
- ½ teaspoon ground cinnamon
- ½ teaspoon ground cardamom
- ¼ teaspoon ground coriander
- ¼ teaspoon MSG
- 1 cup | 2 sticks (226 g) unsalted butter, softened
- ¾ cup (150 g) packed light brown sugar
- 2 large eggs
- 1 teaspoon fish sauce
- 1 cup (120 g) confectioners' sugar
- 1½ tablespoons fresh lime juice
- 1 tablespoon grated lime zest
- Finely minced mint or Thai basil leaves, for garnish (optional)

I'm not going to lie: This recipe kept me up at night. After I developed the instant ramen cookie (page 214), I knew I had to turn pho, my favorite Vietnamese noodle soup dish, into a cookie as well. But I was seriously racking my brains on this one. Pho broth usually includes more than a handful of spices, including star anise, black cardamom, cinnamon, fennel, coriander, and cloves. There's often a beef or other meaty component, not to mention the rock sugar, ginger, and fish sauce. I experimented and added everything to my first pho cookie dough, and the results were a bit off-putting, to say the least!

So, I toned the cookie down a bit and selected just a few key aromatic spices to incorporate, walked back the fish sauce, and sweetened the glaze. Now I know this is still not a conventional cookie, but with each bite, I hope all of its *pho-nomenal* flavors surprise and delight you—in a pleasant way, like you're eating a warm bowl of pho.

1. Adjust two racks to the upper- and lower-middle positions of the oven. Preheat the oven to 375°F. Line two baking sheets with parchment paper.

2. Whisk the all-purpose flour, cake flour, baking soda, baking powder, cinnamon, cardamom, coriander, and MSG together in a medium bowl. Set aside.

3. Using a stand mixer fitted with the paddle attachment (or in a large bowl with a hand mixer, whisk, or spatula), cream the butter and brown sugar together until light and fluffy. Scrape down the sides and bottom of the bowl. Add the eggs and fish sauce and mix until well incorporated. Add the flour mixture and mix on low speed just until a cookie dough forms.

4. Scoop a heaping tablespoon of dough and shape into a ball. Repeat with the remaining dough to make 24 balls, placing them 1 inch apart on the prepared baking sheets. Flatten each ball slightly with your hands. Chill in the freezer, uncovered, for 15 minutes.

RECIPE *continues* →

PHO COOKIES, *continued*

Cookie Tip
The cookie dough can be made ahead of time and stored in an airtight container in the refrigerator for up to 4 days before baking.

Storage
Store the cookies in an airtight container at room temperature for up to 3 days.

5. Bake all the cookies, switching the sheets between top and bottom racks and rotating front to back once halfway through, until the tops and edges start to crack and the cookies puff up a little, 9 to 12 minutes. Let the cookies cool completely on the baking sheets.

6. Mix the confectioners' sugar, lime juice, and lime zest together in a medium bowl until smooth and all the sugar has dissolved. Feel free to either drizzle the glaze over the cookies or dip the tops of the cookies into the glaze. If you like, garnish the glazed cookies with minced Thai basil or mint leaves.

MAPLE CHAR SIU COOKIES

Makes about 9 large cookies *Prep Time* 15 minutes	*Inactive Time* 30 minutes *Cook Time* 24 minutes	*Difficulty* ★★★½ (Quite a bit of steps are involved, but overall it's not a difficult cookie to put together!)

For the cookies

2 ½ cups (300 g) all-purpose flour

About ⅔ cup (85 g) cake flour

⅓ cup (40 g) toasted white sesame seeds

¼ teaspoon baking soda

¼ teaspoon cream of tartar

¼ teaspoon five spice powder

½ cup | 1 stick (113 g) unsalted butter, softened

6 tablespoons (88 g) neutral oil, such as vegetable or canola

½ cup plus 1 tablespoon (120 g) granulated sugar, plus more for shaping the cookies

½ cup (60 g) confectioners' sugar

1 teaspoon red miso

1 large egg

1 tablespoon maple syrup

For the maple char siu glaze

3 tablespoons (42 g) unsalted butter

½ cup (50 g) finely minced char siu

3 tablespoons (45 g) maple syrup

⅓ cup (40 g) confectioners' sugar

For the frosting

4 tablespoons (57 g) unsalted butter, softened

1 cup (120 g) confectioners' sugar, divided

1 tablespoon heavy cream

1 tablespoon maple syrup

As a Canadian, I would be committing a crime if I didn't include a maple cookie in this book. This is also one of the cookies I wish I could have presented to my late father. One of my favorite core memories from childhood is of eating buttered toast with char siu (Chinese barbecue pork) when we didn't have access to our kitchen because the floorboards were being redone in our Coney Island home. With only our toaster available, char siu sandwiches with a lot of unsalted butter were what we all ate for lunch and dinner for almost a week, but they were craveable and delicious every time. These cookies are a creamy, decadent, and sweet nod to that sandwich, evoking memories of my father and my relatively happy childhood. So the next time you visit a Chinatown or Chinese supermarket, be sure to stock up on some char siu, which you can keep refrigerated for a few days or frozen for months.

1. **Make the cookies.** Whisk the flours, sesame seeds, baking soda, cream of tartar, and five spice powder together in a medium bowl. Set aside. Using a stand mixer fitted with the paddle attachment (or in a large bowl with a hand mixer, whisk, or spatula), cream the butter, oil, sugars, and miso together until light and fluffy. Scrape down the sides and bottom of the bowl. Add the egg and maple syrup and mix until well incorporated. Again, scrape the bowl as needed. Add the flour mixture and mix on low speed just until a dough forms. Cover and chill the dough in the refrigerator for 30 minutes to overnight.

2. About 25 minutes before baking, adjust a rack to the middle position and preheat the oven to 350°F. Line two baking sheets with parchment paper.

3. Scoop about nine 3.2-ounce (90 g) portions of dough and place 3 inches apart on the prepared baking sheets. Use the bottom of a glass or cup coated with granulated sugar to press down on each dough ball until the cookie edges begin to crack.

RECIPE *continues* →

Storage
Store the cookies in an airtight container at room temperature for up to 2 days, or up to 5 days in the refrigerator.

4. Bake, one sheet at a time (while the other sheet chills in the fridge), until the edges are set, about 12 minutes. (These are meant to be paler sugar cookies.) Let the cookies set on the baking sheet for a few minutes before transferring to a wire rack to cool completely.

5. **Make the maple char siu glaze.** Add the butter to a saucepan and cook over medium heat. Once the butter browns, 1 to 2 minutes, add the minced char siu and fry over medium heat until browned all over. With a slotted spoon, remove just the browned char siu and transfer to a small bowl. Add the maple syrup to the pan and cook until the syrup bubbles and thickens slightly, a few minutes. Remove the pan from the heat and stir in the confectioners' sugar. Once the sugar dissolves completely and the mixture is smooth, stir in the char siu. Allow the glaze to cool completely. Once cooled, the glaze will thicken more but should still be pourable and easy to drizzle.

6. **Make the frosting.** In a stand mixer fitted with the paddle attachment, mix the butter on high speed until fluffy, about 3 minutes. Scrape the bowl as needed. Add half of the confectioners' sugar and mix on medium speed until incorporated. Add the remaining confectioners' sugar and mix until incorporated as well. Add the cream and maple syrup and mix just until the frosting is spreadable. (Note that you will have just enough frosting for nine cookies so if you like more frosting, make double the amount.)

7. **Frost and decorate the cookies.** Working one at a time, spread frosting over each cookie. Add a spoonful of completely cooled maple char siu glaze onto the middle of the frosting. You can also drizzle the glaze over the cookies.

PEPPERY AND CHEESY CILANTRO COOKIES

Makes	*Prep Time*	*Cook Time*	*Difficulty*
About 5 dozen mini cookies	25 minutes *Inactive Time* About 60 minutes	About 20 minutes	★★★☆☆ (There is effort involved in shaping the dough.)

2 ¾ cups (324 g) cake flour
1 teaspoon ground black pepper
½ teaspoon MSG
¼ teaspoon baking soda
¼ teaspoon white pepper
⅔ cup | 1 ⅓ sticks (150 g) unsalted butter, softened
⅔ cup (75 g) confectioners' sugar
1 teaspoon red miso
1 large egg plus 1 large egg yolk
1 cup (125 g) shredded mozzarella cheese
½ cup (50 g) grated Parmesan cheese
¼ cup (4 g) chopped fresh cilantro
1 large egg, beaten, for egg wash

For the optional toppings

Black or white sesame seeds
Chopped fresh cilantro
Chili crisp

The inspiration for these cookies came from two sources: the unforgettable cheesy, peppery cookies I discovered on a recent trip to Tokyo (but ironically, forgot the brand), and the East Asian culinary trend of incorporating unexpected ingredients like cilantro into a wide array of dishes, including cakes, breads, ice cream wraps (in Taiwan), and, now, cookies. This trend, often driven by a desire to surprise and delight and start a new food trend with unusual flavor combinations, has seen the rise of creations like green onion lattes and century egg coffee from China.

My cookies here aren't as wild as loading lattes with chopped scallions, and you might find them your new favorite savory-sweet cookies. Take my mom, for example. The first time I made a batch, I intended to share them with our favorite neighbors, as usual. But with one taste, my mom's instant reaction was a pleased "mmm, not too sweet," followed by the suggestion that we hoard them for ourselves. So, eat these peppery cheesy cilantro cookies alone, like my mom does, or include them on a charcuterie board with other savory and sweet snacks.

1. Whisk the cake flour, black pepper, MSG, baking soda, and white pepper together in a medium bowl. Set aside.

2. Using a stand mixer fitted with the paddle attachment (or in a large bowl with a hand mixer, whisk, or spatula), cream the butter, sugar, and miso together until light and fluffy. Scrape down the sides and bottom of the bowl. Add the egg and egg yolk and mix until well incorporated. Add the flour mixture and mix on low speed just until a cookie dough forms. Fold in the cheeses and cilantro.

3. With a lightly floured rolling pin on a lightly floured surface or large sheet of parchment paper, roll the dough into a rectangle

RECIPE *continues* →

Cookie Tip
Instead of cutting the dough into rectangles, you can cut out shapes with cookie cutters. Be sure to gather the scraps, re-roll, and continue cutting until all the dough is used.

Variations
Not a fan of cilantro? Try other herbs, like scallions, Thai basil, or mint. Also feel free to experiment with different cheeses.

Storage
Store the cookies in an airtight container for up to 3 days.

about 10 by 12 inches, and ⅓ to ½ inch thick. Ragged edges are fine. Refrigerate, covered, for 60 minutes.

4. About 25 minutes before baking, adjust two racks to the upper- and lower-middle positions of the oven. Preheat the oven to 320°F. Line two baking sheets with parchment paper.

5. Use a pizza wheel or sharp knife to trim the dough rectangle's ragged edges, then cut lengthwise into five strips. Cut each strip into ten to twelve crosswise pieces; you'll have 50 to 60 rectangles.

6. Transfer the rectangles carefully to the prepared baking sheets, spacing them close together as the cookies don't spread or expand much. Brush all the tops with the egg wash. If you like, sprinkle on sesame seeds. Bake all the cookies, switching the sheets between top and bottom racks and rotating front to back once halfway through, until the bottoms and edges of the cookies turn golden brown, about 20 minutes.

7. Let the cookies set on the baking sheet for a few minutes, then transfer to a wire rack to cool completely. If you like, garnish with chopped cilantro and drizzles of chili crisp.

MISO PISTACHIO PUDDING COOKIES

Makes	***Prep Time***	***Cook Time***	***Difficulty***
24 to 25 cookies	15 minutes ***Inactive Time*** 30 minutes	15 minutes	★★☆☆☆ (There's little here in the steps to stump you.)

1½ cups (180 g) all-purpose flour

One 3.4-ounce (96 g) box instant pistachio pudding mix (still dry, don't follow the box instructions to prepare it)

3 tablespoons (24 g) ground pistachios or pistachio flour

½ teaspoon baking powder

½ teaspoon baking soda

¾ cup | 1½ sticks (140 g) unsalted butter, room temperature

¾ cup (150 g) unpacked light brown sugar

¼ cup (50 g) granulated sugar

1 tablespoon red miso

1 large egg

About 6 drops green food coloring gel or green pandan extract, for color (you want these to be a light but vibrant green, so adjust to your preference)

⅔ cup (113 g) milk chocolate chips

⅔ cup (90 g) shelled pistachios (salted or unsalted), chopped

¼ cup (30 g) dried cranberries

Sea salt flakes, for garnish (optional)

I have always gravitated toward green desserts like spumoni ice cream and verdant macarons, especially if they have pistachios in them. Pistachios originated in central Asia, Pakistan, and India, where they were first cultivated over 3,000 years ago.

With the addition of both ground and chopped pistachios, these pudding cookies are appealing to me since every bite is generous with nutty, buttery pistachios. A good dollop of miso in the dough adds a pleasant umami. And thanks to the pudding mix, the cookies come out of the oven soft and tender. Maybe it surprises you to add pudding mix to a cookie, but sometime around the 1960s or earlier, Americans became obsessed with incorporating Jell-O pudding mix into their desserts. We always had Jell-O in my childhood home in Coney Island; the strawberry, lime, and pineapple Jell-O and pistachio pudding mix boxes were right at home next to our Asian baking staples like rock sugar, rice flour, and tapioca starch. Today, retro Jell-O desserts like pretzel salads and trifles are making a comeback, so it's definitely a good idea to keep some in your pantry for treats like these.

1. Whisk the flour, pudding mix, ground pistachios or pistachio flour, baking powder, and baking soda together in a medium bowl. Set aside.

2. Using a stand mixer fitted with the paddle attachment (or in a large bowl with a hand mixer, whisk, or spatula), cream the butter, sugars, and miso together until light and fluffy, about 2 minutes. Scrape down the sides and bottom of the bowl. Add the egg and green food coloring or pandan extract and mix until well incorporated. Add the flour mixture and mix on low speed just until a cookie dough forms. Fold in the chocolate chips, pistachios, and dried cranberries until evenly distributed. Cover the dough and refrigerate for 30 minutes.

RECIPE *continues* →

Substitution
If you don't have a food processor to grind the pistachios or don't have access to pistachio flour, omit it and use a total of 1 ⅔ cups all-purpose flour instead.

Variation
Use the cookies to make ice cream sandwiches. I'd recommend pairing them with chocolate, vanilla, strawberry, or caramel ice cream.

Storage
Store the cookies in an airtight container at room temperature for up to 2 or 3 days.

3. About 30 minutes before baking, adjust two racks to the upper- and lower-middle positions of the oven. Preheat the oven to 350°F. Line two baking sheets with parchment paper.

4. Scoop 2 tablespoons of dough and roll into a smooth ball. Repeat to make 24 balls, placing them 2 inches apart on the prepared baking sheets..

5. Bake all the cookies, switching the sheets between top and bottom racks and rotating front to back once halfway through, until the cookie edges begin to brown, about 15 minutes. If you like, sprinkle sea salt flakes over the cookies while they are still hot. Let the cookies set on the baking sheets for a few minutes before transferring to a wire rack to cool completely.

BOURBON AND FISH SAUCE COOKIES

Makes about 24 cookies

Prep Time 15 minutes

Inactive Time About 1 hour

Cook Time About 15 minutes

Difficulty ★★☆☆☆ (Getting used to incorporating fish sauce to cookie dough adds to the challenge.)

- 1 cup | 2 sticks (226 g) unsalted butter
- ⅔ cup (133 g) packed light or dark brown sugar
- ½ cup (100 g) granulated sugar
- 2 ½ cups (300 g) all-purpose flour
- ½ teaspoon baking powder
- ½ teaspoon baking soda
- ½ teaspoon ground Vietnamese cinnamon
- ½ teaspoon nutmeg
- 2 large eggs
- 3 tablespoons (43 g) bourbon
- 1 tablespoon fish sauce, or to taste
- 8 ounces (226 g) semisweet or dark chocolate, chopped
- ⅓ cup (40 g) pecans or walnuts, chopped
- 24 roasted pecan or walnut halves (or a mix of both), for topping
- Sea salt flakes, for garnish (optional)

As a new food journalist in 2024, I wrote a lot about bourbon and unexpectedly found myself a fan of this American spirit, so I started finding ways to sneak it into desserts. During one of my chaotic kitchen episodes, I mixed bourbon with fish sauce and caramel to make a drizzle for my coffee, and it worked beautifully. Both the bourbon and fish sauce have such strong, bold flavors that they actually complement and balance each other out. And when you add it to a warm, brown butter chocolate chip cookie with a good chew? Boy, oh boy, the resulting flavors are purely divine. Merging the cozy warmth of bourbon with the bold umami of fish sauce in a chocolate chip cookie is a flavor journey you didn't know you needed to embark on!

1. To make the brown butter, cook the butter in a saucepan over medium heat, whisking continuously, until the butter foams, the foam subsides, the butter is golden, and brown (not black) bits form on the bottom, at least 5 minutes. You're looking for a nutty aroma and not a burnt smell. Remove from the heat. Add the sugars and mix until dissolved. Transfer to a mixing bowl and set aside to cool, or chill in the freezer for a few minutes for faster cooling.

2. Whisk the flour, baking powder, baking soda, cinnamon, and nutmeg together in a medium bowl. Set aside.

3. To the cooled brown butter mixture, add the eggs, bourbon, and fish sauce and mix with a rubber spatula until fully incorporated. Add the flour mixture and mix until homogenous. Fold in the chopped chocolate and chopped pecans or walnuts. Cover the dough and refrigerate for 1 hour.

RECIPE *continues* →

Cookie Tips
To help the cookies maintain their texture, store them with a slice of bread.

Since this is a Vietnamese-inspired cookie, I implore you to use Vietnamese cinnamon. As for the fish sauce, I recommend using Three Crabs brand, as that's the one I use for all my Vietnamese cooking, from making pho to pork chops. (It's the best because every one of my Vietnamese aunties recommends and uses that brand.)

If the fish sauce is too pungent for you, start by adding 2 teaspoons to the cookie dough and gradually work up to 1 tablespoon.

Substitution
You can substitute chocolate chips for the chopped chocolate.

Storage
Store the cookies in an airtight container at room temperature for 3 to 4 days.

4. About 30 minutes before baking, adjust two racks to the upper- and lower-middle positions of the oven. Preheat the oven to 350°F. Line two baking sheets with parchment paper.

5. Scoop 2 tablespoons of dough and roll into a ball. Repeat to make about 24 balls, placing them 2 inches apart on the prepared baking sheets. Press a walnut or pecan half on top of the center of each dough ball.

6. Bake all the cookies, switching the sheets between top and bottom racks and rotating front to back once halfway through, until the cookies are set and the edges are golden brown, about 15 minutes. Let the cookies cool directly on the baking sheets. If you like, sprinkle sea salt flakes over the still-warm cookies.

INDONESIAN CHEESE SAGO COOKIES (Sagu Keju)

Makes
about 21 cookies

Prep Time
20 minutes

Cook Time
30 to 35 minutes

Difficulty
★★★☆☆
(Piping cookies takes practice.)

- 6 tablespoons (85 g) unsalted butter, softened
- 1 tablespoon lard or margarine
- ⅔ cup (80 g) confectioners' sugar
- 1 large egg yolk
- ½ teaspoon pandan extract (with color)
- 3 tablespoons (45 g) coconut cream
- About 2 cups (240 g) tapioca flour
- 1 teaspoon ground black pepper
- ¼ teaspoon MSG
- ¾ cup (80 g) grated cheese (such as Edam, Parmesan, cheddar, or a mix), plus more for garnishing
- 2 frozen cooked salted duck egg yolks, grated and divided

Sagu keju, also known as sago cheese cookies, are more than they appear. With each bite, they're crunchy, crumbly, cheesy, and melt-in-the-mouth buttery. With a sweet and savory vibe, it's no wonder they're a longstanding Indonesian staple. While people enjoy sagu keju during big celebrations such as Eid al-Fitr, Christmas, and Lunar New Year, they are also perfect for everyday snacking. Traditionally, the cookies call for sago flour, but it's very common for them to be made with tapioca flour. Since I have not been able to find sago flour at my local Asian supermarkets or online, I use tapioca flour here.

The cheese, however, steals the spotlight with these cookies, with Edam cheese, a product of the Netherlands, being a popular inclusion. This shouldn't surprise you, given Indonesia's history as a Dutch colony. I also took the liberty to grate in frozen salted duck egg yolk because you can never have too much umami in a savory-sweet cookie!

1. Adjust a rack to the middle position and preheat the oven to 285°F. Line a baking sheet with parchment paper.

2. Using a stand mixer fitted with the paddle attachment (or in a large bowl with a hand mixer, whisk, or spatula), cream the butter, lard or margarine, and confectioners' sugar together until light and fluffy, about 2 minutes. Scrape down the sides and bottom of the bowl. Add the egg yolk and pandan extract and mix until well incorporated. Add the tapioca flour, black pepper, and MSG and mix on low speed just until a cookie dough forms. Fold in the grated cheese and three-fourths of the grated salted duck yolks until evenly distributed.

3. Transfer the dough to a large piping bag fitted with a large Ateco or Wilton open star tip. Hold the bag vertically about

RECIPE *continues* →

Cookie Tips
Don't have pandan extract? Do what Indonesian bakers traditionally do and dry-roast the tapioca flour for a few minutes in a pan with a few pandan leaves to impart flavor. You can also heat the tapioca flour and pandan leaves in a microwave. Give it a good stir, remove the leaves, and be sure the flour is completely cooled before adding it to the cookie dough.

If you find piping the dough to be tough, it's easier if you use two layers of piping bags and give the dough a good knead inside the bags with your warm hands.

Substitutions
If you don't have lard, you can use a total of 7 tablespoons unsalted butter.

Storage
Store the cookies in an airtight container at room temperature for up to 2 days.

2 inches above the prepared baking sheet and pipe 1½-inch rounds or wreaths 1 inch apart until you use up all the dough; you should make about 21 cookies.

4. Top the cookies with some grated cheese and the crumbles from the remaining salted duck egg yolk. Bake until the cookies are set and the edges are lightly browned, 30 to 35 minutes. Let the cookies set on the baking sheet for a few minutes, then transfer to a wire rack to cool completely.

VI

MODERN ALCHEMY AND DELIGHTFUL FUSIONS

Born from the minds of chaotic kitchen wizards with surprising flavors, fusion food, and twists

This is what I like to call a petit de tout chapter, or a little of everything. Fusing East and West inspirations, the results are treats like my beautifully blue Butterfly Pea Flower Madeleines on page 258. With the nutty and earthy flavors of a Southeast Asian staple, Asian pigeonwings, otherwise known as butterfly pea flower, they look quite magical, like fairy food. Then there's a cookie recipe by a child baker: Dash's Chocolate Chip Cookies with Furikake Chex Mix (page 267). Dash Hsu created this cookie along with his mother, Agnes, who used to own several bakeries in San Francisco. They've incorporated a delicious and popular Hawaiian snack, furikake Chex mix, into the chocolate chunk cookie that used to be one of the bestselling items at Agnes's bakeries.

From Indonesia, my longtime friend and Subtle Asian Baking member, chef, and restaurateur Gunawan Wu sent his recipe for me to adapt: magnificent Ondeh-Ondeh Macarons (page 282), featuring the flavors of ondeh-ondeh, a traditional Indonesian treat.

If you're a fan of boba, don't skip the Bubble Tea Cookies (page 276), a tea-flavored treat topped with a frosting that will remind you of sweet cheese foam and lots of boba pearls. It's a magnificent cookie and I wish we could see boba used more often as a cookie inclusion or topping outside of East Asia.

I end the chapter with a whimsical cookie that's perfect for coffee lovers like me, Coffee Bean Cookies (page 299), where you'll be shaping dough into bite-sized cookies. While I don't know the exact origins of this cookie, they were immensely popular among East Asian bakers, especially during the height of the COVID-19 pandemic.

COOKIES AND CREAM WITH UBE CHEESECAKE COOKIES

Makes
about
20 cookies

Prep Time
15 minutes

Inactive Time
30 minutes

Cook Time
About
15 minutes

Difficulty
★★★½☆
(Multiple steps involved, but otherwise not too difficult.)

1½ cups (180 g) all-purpose flour
½ teaspoon baking powder
½ cup | 1 stick (113 g) unsalted butter, softened
4 ounces (113 g) cream cheese (half an 8-ounce block), softened
¾ cup (150 g) unpacked light brown sugar
¼ cup (50 g) granulated sugar
1 tablespoon red miso
1 large egg
1 tablespoon grated lemon zest
1 tablespoon fresh lemon juice
About 2 teaspoons ube extract (with color)
20 store-bought chocolate cookies and cream sandwich cookies, plus more in case some crack or break
Sesame seeds (black or white), placed in a shallow bowl (optional)
Shredded coconut, placed in a shallow bowl (optional)

This recipe was born when I had a sudden craving for something sweet and couldn't decide between a cookie and cheesecake. Why not have both? This treat is a cookie, first and foremost, being crispy on the outside and compact in form. One bite, however, reveals a soft, creamy center and a crumb that just melts on the tongue, like cheesecake. It's only fitting to open the fusion/alchemy chapter with this recipe, as it sets the tone for what's to come. Everything in this section will be surprising with a twist! Fusion and modern cookie alchemy at their finest.

Here you'll be sandwiching homemade cheesecake cookie dough between store-bought chocolate cookies and cream sandwich cookies, like Oreos. Note these cookies are meant to spread a little, and they should be soft right out of the oven. Resist the urge to pick them up, as they will immediately crumble if you do, and be patient as the cookies set and crisp up at room temperature. (Pictured on page 255.)

1. Line two baking sheets with parchment paper.

2. Whisk the flour and baking powder together in a medium bowl. Set aside.

3. Using a stand mixer fitted with the paddle attachment (or in a large bowl with a hand mixer, whisk, or spatula), cream the butter, cream cheese, sugars, and miso together until light and fluffy. Scrape down the sides and bottom of the bowl. Add the egg, lemon zest and juice, and ube extract and mix until well incorporated. Add the flour mixture and mix on low speed just until a cookie dough forms.

Cookie Tip
Don't skip the lemon zest and juice, as they bring a refreshing flavor and work beautifully with ube. I've always felt cheesecake is no good without tang. (Maybe it's because I grew up in New York City, where all the best cheesecakes, like the ones from Junior's, were tangy.)

Storage
Store the cookies in an airtight container at room temperature for up to 2 days.

4. Working one at a time, gently twist open a sandwich cookie and scrape off the cream layer. (Or, if you like the cream layer, keep it intact.) Scoop about 1 heaping tablespoon of cookie dough and roll into a smooth ball. Place this dough ball between the two halves of the cookie, gently pressing them together to form a sandwich. If you like, thoroughly roll the rims of the cookie in the sesame seeds and/or coconut. Repeat to use up all the cookie dough and assemble about 20 cookies. Place them on the prepared baking sheets at least 2 inches apart to accommodate spreading during baking. Chill, uncovered, in the freezer for 30 minutes.

5. About 25 minutes before baking, adjust two racks to the upper- and lower-middle positions of the oven. Preheat the oven to 350°F.

6. Spritz some water over the tops of every cookie. Bake all the cookies, switching the sheets between top and bottom racks and rotating front to back once halfway through, until the cookie edges begin to brown, about 15 minutes. Let the cookies set and cool directly on the baking sheet.

BUTTERFLY PEA FLOWER MADELEINES

Makes about 12 madeleines	***Inactive Time*** 2 ¼ hours to overnight	***Difficulty*** ★★★★☆ (Don't be discouraged if the madeleines don't come out perfectly the first time you make them.)
Prep Time 15 minutes	***Cook Time*** 10 to 12 minutes	

For the longest time, I was afraid to make madeleines because I thought you'd need to have attended pastry school or learned from French masters to perfect them. They're also finicky: a sign of a successful madeleine is its characteristic hump, which you achieve by baking at a high temperature for just 2 minutes before quickly dropping the temperature. Longer than that and these beauties will burn, and trust me, there's no way to make blackened madeleines taste good, even after you scrape or cut off the char.

While I love a classic lemony madeleine, I wanted these in a stunning shade of blue so they look beautiful, like artisan soaps at first glance. Butterfly pea flower doesn't impart too bold of a taste but adds a bit of floral nuttiness and pretty blue color. And it is a bit magical since it turns from blue to purple with the addition of acidity, like a squirt of lemon juice. It's also a super popular dessert ingredient across Asia, especially Southeast Asia, so I thought it'd be nice to incorporate it into a popular Western dessert.

For the madeleines

- ⅓ cup plus 1 tablespoon (50 g) all-purpose flour, plus more for dusting
- 50 g (½ cup) almond flour, sifted
- 2 teaspoons butterfly pea flower powder
- 1 teaspoon baking powder
- Pinch of kosher salt
- Pinch of ground cardamom
- Pinch of ground nutmeg
- ½ cup | 1 stick (113 g) unsalted butter, cubed, plus more butter for greasing
- 3 large eggs, room temperature
- ⅓ cup (67 g) granulated sugar
- 1 tablespoon grated lemon zest
- 1 teaspoon red miso
- About 12 pieces of any pecan-sized nut, chopped winter melon candy, or candied ginger

For the white chocolate shells

- ⅔ cup (107 g) high-quality chopped white chocolate
- 1 tablespoon salted butter, plus more for greasing
- Pinch of kosher salt
- Blue food coloring gel
- Rose petals or edible gold leaf, for garnish (optional)

1. **Make the madeleines.** Whisk the flour, almond flour, butterfly pea flower powder, baking powder, salt, cardamom, and nutmeg together in a medium bowl. Set aside.

2. To make the brown butter, melt the unsalted butter in a saucepan over medium heat while whisking continuously, until the butter foams, the foam subsides, the butter is golden, and brown (not black) bits form on the bottom, at least 5 minutes. You're looking for a nutty aroma and not a burnt smell. Remove from the heat and transfer the brown butter to a large heatproof bowl. Set aside to cool.

3. Using a stand mixer fitted with the whisk attachment (or in a large bowl with a hand mixer or whisk), beat the eggs, sugar, lemon zest, and miso together until paler in color and thickened, about 8 minutes. Scrape the sides and bottom of the bowl as needed with a flexible spatula. Gradually fold (do not stir or whisk) in the flour mixture until just incorporated. Then gently

RECIPE *continues* →

Cookie Tips
Note that the batter needs to be refrigerated for at least 2 hours. And while you can bake the madeleines with a metal madeleine pan, you should use a silicone one to make the white chocolate shells. If you don't have a 12-cavity silicone madeleine mold, please invest in one for this recipe so the chocolate shells will set smoothly and the madeleines pop right out beautifully. Otherwise, skip making the chocolate shells as they would not be smooth and would stick to metal madeleine molds.

Storage
Madeleines taste best the day they're made, but unused batter can be refrigerated in an airtight container for up to 3 days.

fold in the cooled brown butter by the tablespoonful. (Check the temperature of the brown butter with a digital or candy thermometer first. It should be under 100°F.) The batter is ready when it's no longer lumpy but is smooth and shiny. Cover and refrigerate for 2 hours to overnight, allowing the batter to thicken.

4. About 30 minutes before baking, adjust a rack to the middle position and preheat the oven to 400°F. Grease a 12-cavity scalloped madeleine mold with butter. Lightly dust each cavity with all-purpose flour.

5. Gently spoon or pipe the batter into each cavity, filling each about three-fourths full. Press a nut or winter melon candy or candied ginger into the center of each madeleine. Make sure to cover the add-in with a little more batter if needed.

6. Bake for 2 minutes, then lower the oven temperature to 350°F. Bake until the madeleines have risen, each with a springy hump in the center, and the edges are light golden brown, 8 to 10 minutes.

7. Let the madeleines set in the molds for a few minutes before transferring to a wire rack to cool completely.

8. **Make the white chocolate shells.** With salted butter, lightly grease a 12-cavity *silicone* madeleine mold. Microwave the white chocolate and salted butter in 30-second bursts, stirring with a rubber spatula after each burst, until melted and smooth. Stir in the salt and enough food coloring gel to achieve a light blue, then mix until smooth and incorporated. Line each cavity of the greased silicone mold with a smooth, even, and opaque layer of the white chocolate mixture. Press a cooled madeleine into each chocolate-covered cavity. Let the chocolate set at room temperature or in the refrigerator for at least 15 minutes.

9. Pop the madeleines out of the silicone mold and garnish with rose petals or edible gold leaf, if using. Serve with jasmine, oolong, or green tea.

ROSE'S ONO OISHII COOKIES

Makes	*Prep Time*	*Cook Time*	*Difficulty*
about 19 cookies	20 minutes *Inactive Time* 30 minutes to overnight	22 to 27 minutes	★★★☆☆ (Not too difficult, but multiple steps and assembly are required.)

For the cookies

½ cup (1 stick) plus 1 tablespoon (128 g) unsalted butter, softened

¼ cup (50 g) granulated sugar

¼ cup (55 g) packed light brown sugar

1 ½ tablespoons (22 g) yuzu juice or extract

1 teaspoon yuzu jam

1 teaspoon red miso

1 ⅓ cups (160 g) all-purpose flour

¼ teaspoon baking soda

Pinch of kosher salt

For the jam filling

¼ cup (80 g) passionfruit jelly or jam, seeds removed (for aesthetics)

4 fresh raspberries (for the pink color)

For the soy sauce glaze

⅓ cup (40 g) confectioners' sugar, plus more if needed

1 tablespoon yuzu juice or extract, plus more if needed

2 teaspoons soy sauce

Confectioners' sugar, for dusting

When I did a fundraiser for the Wing Luke Museum in Seattle, I offered up a custom cookie recipe for the auction and Rose Gyotoku generously bid on it. Japanese American, born and raised in Seattle, Rose has many ties to Hawaii and Japan. Lilikoi (or passionfruit) and yuzu are two of her favorite foods, along with soy sauce rice crackers from Japan.

Learning all this, I immediately had a cookie in mind for Rose. It had to be a thumbprint cookie, as the thumbprint bears the mark of the baker, like an artist's signature, and I'm as much of an artist as I am a baker.

Rose reached out and gave me a name for these cookies: "Ono" means pleasing or enjoyable in Hawaiian; "oishii" means delicious in Japanese.

1. **Make the cookies.** Line two baking sheets with parchment paper. Using a stand mixer fitted with the paddle attachment (or in a large bowl with a hand mixer), cream the butter, sugars, yuzu juice or extract, yuzu jam, and miso together until light and fluffy. Scrape down the sides and bottom of the bowl. Add the flour, baking powder, and salt and mix on low speed just until a dough forms.

2. Scoop a tablespoon of dough and roll into a ball. Repeat to make 19 balls, placing them 2 inches apart on the prepared baking sheets. Use your thumb or a rounded teaspoon to make an indentation in the center of each dough ball. Chill the cookies, uncovered, in the refrigerator for 30 minutes.

3. About 25 minutes before baking, adjust a rack in the center and preheat the oven to 350°F.

4. **Make the jam filling.** Mash the jam and raspberries in a small bowl. Add ½ to 1 teaspoon of jam to each of the cookie indentations.

RECIPE *continues* →

Storage
Store the cookies in an airtight container at room temperature for up to 1 day.

5. Bake the cookies, one sheet at a time (while the other sheet chills in the refrigerator), until the bottoms and edges are golden brown, 12 to 14 minutes. Transfer the cookies to a wire rack to cool completely.

6. **Make the soy sauce glaze.** Mix the glaze ingredients together in a small bowl until combined and smooth. If the glaze is too runny, mix in more confectioners' sugar, about a teaspoon at a time. If it's too thick, mix in a little more yuzu juice.

7. Drizzle the glaze over the top of the cookies. Or top the jam centers with glaze. Dust the cookies with confectioners' sugar. Enjoy the cookies with a lighter tea, like white or green.

WHITE RABBIT SUGAR COOKIES

Makes
22 to 24 cookies

Prep Time
20 minutes

Inactive Time
About 70 minutes

Cook Time
About 12 minutes

Difficulty
★★★☆☆
(Multiple steps are involved, but the cookies themselves are straightforward.)

For the cookies

1½ cups (180 g) all-purpose flour
1 tablespoon cornstarch
½ teaspoon baking powder
¼ teaspoon baking soda
½ cup | 1 stick (113 g) unsalted butter, softened
¾ cup (150 g) granulated sugar
1 teaspoon red miso
2 tablespoons (29 g) Greek yogurt
1 medium egg

For the White Rabbit candy filling

¼ cup (60 g) heavy cream
About 10 White Rabbit candies (only remove the candy's outer wrapper), chopped
2 tablespoons (28 g) white chocolate chips or chopped white chocolate
1 tablespoon unsalted butter

Sea salt flakes (optional), for garnish

Since the 1940s, White Rabbit candy, a milk-based treat that originated in Shanghai, has resonated deeply, evoking cherished childhood memories with many across Asia and within Asian diasporas (including me!). I've probably eaten hundreds of these sweet and creamy candies growing up. I always bite off the edible paper wrapper first and let it melt on my tongue. Those wrappers—and the cute rabbit mascot—bring a little magic to these simple sugar cookies.

And now, I'm thrilled to share a slice of my heritage and childhood with you!

1. **Make the cookies.** Whisk the flour, cornstarch, baking powder, and baking soda together in a medium bowl. Set aside.

2. Using a stand mixer fitted with the paddle attachment (or in a large bowl with a hand mixer, whisk, or spatula), cream the butter, sugar, and miso together until light and fluffy, about 1 minute. Scrape down the sides and bottom of the bowl. Add the yogurt and egg and mix until well incorporated. Add the flour mixture and mix on low speed just until a cookie dough forms. Cover the dough and chill in the refrigerator for 1 hour.

3. About 30 minutes before baking, adjust two racks to the upper- and lower-middle positions of the oven. Preheat the oven to 350°F. Line two baking sheets with parchment paper.

4. **Make the White Rabbit candy filling.** Heat the cream in a small saucepan over medium-high heat until it simmers and bubbles form around the edges. Reduce the heat to medium-low and mix in the candies, white chocolate, and butter. Continue mixing until smooth and all the candy and white chocolate have melted, then remove from heat. Refrigerate for 10 minutes.

RECIPE *continues* →

大白兔奶糖
WHITERABBIT

Variations
Omit the Greek yogurt for a crunchier cookie. For a chewier cookie, add 1 tablespoon corn syrup to the dough in step 2, and account for more spreading during baking.

Storage
Store the cookies in an airtight container at room temperature for up to 3 days.

5. Scoop 1 tablespoon of dough and roll into a ball. Repeat to make about 23 balls, placing them on the prepared baking sheets about 2 inches apart. Flatten each ball to about ¼ inch thick with a smooth-bottom glass coated in granulated sugar. Make a heart-shaped or round indentation with your thumb in the center of each cookie. Fill the indentations with as much of the candy filling as you can. Repeat until all the cookies have filled indentations.

6. Bake all the cookies, switching the sheets between top and bottom racks and rotating front to back once halfway through, until the cookie edges begin to brown lightly, about 12 minutes.

7. Let the cookies set on the baking sheets for a few minutes. Transfer to a wire rack to cool completely. Add any remaining White Rabbit candy filling over the cookies' indentations, like a glaze. If you like, top the cookies with flaky sea salt for a pop of salinity.

DASH'S CHOCOLATE CHIP COOKIES WITH FURIKAKE CHEX MIX

Makes
about 17 large cookies

Prep Time
10 minutes for the furikake Chex mix; 10 minutes for the cookies

Inactive Time
20 minutes

Cook Time
55 minutes for the furikake Chex mix; about 15 minutes for the cookies

Difficulty
★★★½☆
(It's easier if you make the furikake Chex mix a day or two before making the cookies, or use store-bought furikake Chex mix.)

Dashiell (Dash) Hsu, known as @dashbakesthegreats on Instagram, is an amazing child baker. I happen to be good friends with his mom, Agnes Hsu, who once owned five bakeries in the San Francisco Bay Area and has a deep love of baking. It's possible Dash's love for baking began in the womb.

When I asked Agnes if she and Dash wanted to contribute a cookie recipe to this book, she immediately thought of her chocolate chunk cookies, one of the bestselling treats in her bakeries. Brainstorming with Dash, mother and son came up with the idea to incorporate umami-ful furikake Chex mix to give the chocolate chunk cookies a fun East-meets-West twist. It's a cookie with a chewy interior, lofty impressions, and crispy edges.

From selling her bakeries and stepping away from baking to nurturing a love for baking in Dash and contributing this joyful recipe, Agnes's (and Dash's!) baking journey has come full circle. Agnes and Dash hope this cookie will inspire you and me to bake with our loved ones and create new memories together.

For the furikake Chex mix

- 2 tablespoons (28 g) unsalted butter
- 2 tablespoons (28 g) neutral oil
- ¼ cup (85 g) light corn syrup
- 1 tablespoon maple syrup
- 2 tablespoons (25 g) granulated sugar
- 2 teaspoons soy sauce
- 3 cups (about 150 g) mini pretzels
- 3 cups (about 105 g) wheat Chex cereal
- About 2 cups (85 g) Honeycomb cereal
- ⅓ cup furikake seasoning, plus more for sprinkling over the cookies

1. **Make the furikake Chex mix.** Adjust a rack to the middle position and preheat the oven to 250°F. Line a large rimmed baking sheet, about 12 by 19 inches or similar size, with parchment paper.

2. Combine the butter, oil, corn syrup, maple syrup, granulated sugar, and soy sauce in a microwave-safe bowl and microwave for 30 seconds. Carefully remove from the microwave and whisk until combined. Keep mixing until the mixture becomes syrupy.

3. Combine the pretzels, Chex cereal, and Honeycomb cereal in the prepared pan and toss with clean hands to evenly distribute

RECIPE AND INGREDIENTS *continues* →

For the cookies

1 ⅔ cups (200 g) all-purpose flour

1 cup plus 1 teaspoon (125 g) bread flour

1 ½ teaspoons baking powder

¾ teaspoon baking soda

1 teaspoon kosher salt

1 cup | 2 sticks (226 g) unsalted butter, melted in the microwave and cooled

1 ¼ cups (255 g) unpacked light brown sugar

¼ cup (50 g) granulated sugar

1 large egg

1 large egg yolk

1 tablespoon maple syrup

1 ¼ cups (200 g) dark chocolate chips

Cookie Tips
Store the furikake Chex mix in an airtight container. Note that you won't be using all of it for the cookies and will have extra for snacking and sharing.

Variations
Try adding different Asian mix-ins to the furikake Chex mix, such as wasabi peas, pieces of instant dry ramen, or sesame sticks. You can also add your favorite nuts to the mix.

Storage
Store the cookies in an airtight container at room temperature for up to 3 days. You can prepare the Chex mix up to 3 days ahead of making the cookies.

all the pieces. Pour the syrupy butter mixture over the pretzels and cereal mixture. Top with the furikake seasoning. Toss everything with two large spoons to evenly distribute all the syrup and furikake.

4. Bake for 20 minutes, rotating the pan halfway. Remove the pan from the oven and toss the pieces with a spoon or wooden spoon, then bake for another 20 minutes, again rotating the pan halfway. Again, remove the pan from the oven and toss the pieces with a spoon or wooden spoon. Return the pan to the oven and bake until the mixture is golden, toasted, and crispy, another 15 minutes. You will know when the mix is ready when it is dry and there is a slight sheen. Set aside to cool; the sheen should harden.

5. **Make the cookies.** Adjust two racks to the upper- and lower-middle positions of the oven. Preheat the oven to 375°F. Line two baking sheets with parchment paper.

6. Whisk the all-purpose flour, bread flour, baking powder, baking soda, and salt in a large bowl. Set aside.

7. Using a stand mixer fitted with the paddle attachment (or in a large bowl with a hand mixer, whisk, or spatula), mix the cooled melted butter, sugars, egg, egg yolk, and maple syrup until thickened into a brown syrupy mixture. Add the flour mixture and mix on low speed just until a dough forms. Fold in the chocolate and 3 cups of the furikake Chex mix. Cover and chill the dough in the refrigerator for 20 minutes.

8. Scoop out about ¼ cup (about 2 ounces) of the dough and roll into a smooth ball. Repeat to make 17 balls, placing them 3 inches apart on the prepared baking sheets. Press pieces of the furikake Chex mix onto the cookies and top with a sprinkle of furikake seasoning.

9. Bake all the cookies, switching the sheets between top and bottom racks and rotating front to back once halfway through, until set and the edges are lightly browned, about 15 minutes. Let the cookies cool on the baking sheets for a few minutes before transferring to a wire rack to cool completely.

BUILD-YOUR-OWN ASIAN FRUIT-PIZZA COOKIE ADVENTURE

Makes
24 to 26 cookies

Prep Time
25 minutes

Inactive Time
30 minutes

Cook Time
12 to 14 minutes

Difficulty
★★★☆☆
(Trying to fit in all your favorite fruits will be a fun challenge. You'll also be dicing and slicing fruits, and assembly required.)

For the cookies

- 2 ½ cups (300 g) all-purpose flour
- ½ teaspoon baking powder
- ½ teaspoon baking soda
- 1 cup | 2 sticks (226 g) unsalted butter, softened
- ⅔ cup (133 g) granulated sugar
- ⅓ cup (67 g) packed light brown sugar
- 1 tablespoon red miso
- 1 large egg
- 1 tablespoon Japanese whisky or bourbon (optional)

For the cream cheese frosting

- One 8-ounce (226 g) block cream cheese, cubed and softened
- 4 tablespoons (57 g) unsalted butter, cubed and softened
- 2 tablespoons (30 g) yuzu or calamansi juice
- 1 teaspoon red miso
- ¾ cup (90 g) confectioners' sugar

For the fruit toppings

- About 1 cup mixed Asian fruits (sliced or cut into small pieces) and berries, plus more as needed

For optional toppings

- Toasted white sesame seeds
- Grated Parmesan cheese

Every time I see a fruit-pizza cookie, a dish that originated in California sometime in the 1960s, I think of the fruit tarts I grew up eating from the Asian bakeries in New York City's Chinatown. Fruit-pizza cookies have gained popularity recently thanks to cookie giants like Crumbl, and I thought it would be fun to include one in this book. Just note that you won't be slicing these cookies like a pizza, as each one is the size of a regular cookie.

Also, when you make these cookies, there's one rule to follow—you must include only fruits from Asia, like dragon fruit, persimmon, mulberries, lychee, kiwi, rambutan, and mango. Visit your local Asian grocery store or supermarket with a friend or kiddo and make it an adventure. No cheating with strawberries or blueberries, okay? P.S.: You get extra points if you use durian.

1. **Make the cookies.** Line two baking sheets with parchment paper.

2. Whisk the flour, baking powder, and baking soda together in a medium bowl. Set aside. Using a stand mixer fitted with the paddle attachment (or in a large bowl with a hand mixer), cream the butter, sugars, and miso together until light and fluffy, about 2 minutes. Scrape down the sides and bottom of the bowl. Add the egg and Japanese whisky or bourbon, if using, and mix until combined. Add the flour mixture and mix on low speed just until a dough forms.

3. Scoop 1 heaping tablespoon of dough and roll into a smooth ball. Repeat to make about 25 balls, placing them on the prepared baking sheets 2 inches apart. Press down on each dough ball with the sugared bottom of a cup or glass until the edges begin to crack and the cookie is about ¼ inch thick. Cover and refrigerate for 30 minutes.

RECIPE *continues* →

Cookie Tip
Cut up the fruits the day before and store them in separate airtight containers in the refrigerator. This also makes the assembly process quicker.

Variation
For added warmth, grate a little fresh ginger and stir into the frosting.

Storage
Frosted cookies without fruits can be refrigerated for up to 4 days in an airtight container. If you anticipate needing to store leftover cookies, don't add the fruit to the frosted cookies you intend to store.

4. About 25 minutes before baking, adjust two racks to the upper- and lower-middle positions of the oven. Preheat the oven to 350°F.

5. Bake all the cookies, switching the sheets between top and bottom racks and rotating front to back once halfway through, until the bottoms and edges are golden brown and set, 12 to 14 minutes. Transfer the cookies to a wire rack to cool completely.

6. **Make the frosting.** While the cookies are cooling, using a stand mixer fitted with the paddle attachment (or in a medium bowl with a hand mixer), beat the cream cheese, butter, yuzu or calamansi juice, and miso together until smooth and creamy. Gradually add the confectioners' sugar, a small portion at a time, and beat until fully incorporated, smooth, and spreadable.

7. Spread an even layer of cream cheese frosting on top of each cooled cookie. Be a little generous with the frosting. Finish by arranging different fruits on top of the frosting. Be as creative as you'd like here. If you like, top the fruits with a sprinkle of sesame seeds and grated Parmesan cheese for a balancing pop of umami.

CANDIED-WALNUT BROWNIE BRITTLE

Makes
30 to 40 pieces of brittle, depending on how you cut or break them

Prep Time
25 minutes

Cook Time
25 minutes for the walnuts; 20 to 25 minutes for the brittle

Difficulty
★★★☆☆
(While these are easy to put together, please do note that multiple steps are involved, including boiling the walnuts to reduce bitterness before roasting them.)

For the candied walnuts

2 cups (240 g) shelled walnuts

¼ cup (50 g) granulated sugar

2 tablespoons (28 g) unsalted butter, softened

1 tablespoon red miso

⅓ cup (40 g) toasted white sesame seeds

For the brownie brittle

½ cup (60 g) all-purpose flour

2 tablespoons (12 g) unsweetened Dutch-processed cocoa powder

½ teaspoon baking soda

Pinch of kosher salt

2 large egg whites

½ cup (100 g) granulated sugar

4 tablespoons (57 g) unsalted butter, melted

1 tablespoon Japanese whisky or bourbon

½ cup (85 g) chocolate chips

Sea salt flakes (optional)

If you've never had brownie brittle before, you're not alone. I only learned about it when my husband and son brought home various versions to try. If you're not familiar, brownie brittles are thin, flat, cookie versions of brownies. After our brownie brittle fest, I wanted to surprise them with a homemade version that included a taste of my childhood: Hong Kong candied walnuts (琥珀核桃). During Lunar New Year in Hong Kong, people would enjoy candied walnuts as a festive treat. You'll also find them at banquets, as a snack, and as the star of one of my favorite dishes, honey walnut shrimp.

Candied nuts along with brittle candy are very popular across Asia and among Asian diasporas, with variations that include ingredients like sesame, pumpkin seeds, and peanuts. I grew up eating a lot of nut brittles, and while they're considered candy, I've always thought of them as an Asian cookie. To my delight, my candied-walnut brownie brittle has become a new favorite in the house. It's a perfect blend of crispy and chewy, especially good on days when you crave the comfort of a brownie but also want a cookie.

1. **Make the candied walnuts.** Adjust a rack to the middle position and preheat the oven to 350°F. Line a baking sheet with parchment paper.

2. Add enough water to a saucepan to cover the walnuts, and bring to a boil over high heat. Reduce the heat to medium-low, add the walnuts, and simmer for 5 minutes. (This will help reduce the walnuts' bitterness.) Drain the walnuts and immediately transfer to a mixing bowl. Add the sugar and mix until dissolved, then add the butter, miso, and sesame seeds and mix until well combined.

3. Transfer the coated walnuts to the prepared baking sheet, spreading them in an even layer. Roast for 10 minutes, then flip the walnuts and rotate the baking sheet. Keep the walnuts in

RECIPE *continues* →

Brittle Tip
To make things easier, candy the walnuts a day or two in advance. You'll probably want to make extra to save for snacking, too.

Storage
Store the candied walnuts in an airtight container at room temperature for up to 5 days, and the brownie brittle for up to 4 days.

a single layer and roast until well toasted and lightly browned, another 15 minutes. Let the walnuts cool directly on the baking sheet.

4. If you're not making the brownie brittle on the same day, store the candied walnuts in an airtight container. If you are making the brittle right away, set the walnuts aside and reduce the oven to 325°F. Line a baking sheet with parchment paper.

5. **Make the brownie brittle.** Whisk the flour, cocoa powder, baking soda, and salt together in a medium bowl and set aside. In another medium bowl, whisk the egg whites until foamy and white. While still whisking, add the sugar, a little at a time, and continue whisking until thickened, shiny, and the mixture forms a ribbon trail in the bowl when you lift the whisk. Don't whisk until soft peaks form. Add the melted butter and Japanese whisky or bourbon and whisk until smooth. With a rubber spatula, fold in the flour mixture until no dry flour spots remain.

6. Transfer the batter to the prepared baking sheet. Use an offset spatula to spread the batter thinly and evenly over the parchment paper, forming a large rectangle. Top evenly with the chocolate chips and candied walnuts. (You don't need to use all of the candied walnuts—just as much as you'd like. Save the rest for snacking or sharing.) Bake the brittle until set and crispy, 20 to 25 minutes.

7. If you want even squares or rectangles, score the top of the brittle with a knife or pizza roller while it is still hot. Otherwise, let the brittle cool completely on the baking sheet, then break into small, rustic pieces. If you like, sprinkle sea salt flakes over the brittle.

BUBBLE TEA COOKIES

Makes	*Prep Time*	*Cook Time*	*Difficulty*
26 to 28 cookies	20 minutes *Inactive Time* 30 minutes	7 to 8 minutes for the brown sugar syrup; 12 to 14 minutes for the cookies	★★★★☆ (While this is not a super difficult recipe per se, there are many moving steps.)

I've been drinking coffee religiously for over twenty years now, and maybe I should stop since it adds to my anxiety and jitteriness. But it's hard to kick a habit, and I've actually been drinking boba tea (or bubble tea) even longer (although it's mainly reserved for weekends and special occasions these days).

Growing up, I had always referred to boba tea as bubble tea, so I've named these cookies Bubble Tea Cookies. The first time I had boba was sometime back in the 1990s, from a bakery in Montreal's Chinatown: an unforgettable iced taro latte bubble tea. So for many years, all I ever wanted was taro milk with boba. These days, however, I like my tea not too sweet, with a lot of tea flavor, like black tea, oolong, or hojicha. I'm also a sucker for brown sugar syrup, so you'll be drizzling that over the bubble tea cookies.

P.S.: Cheese foam is an S-class, elite-level topping for boba tea, so the cookie's frosting is made with salted cream cheese.

For the cookies

- 2 ½ cups (300 g) all-purpose flour
- 2 teaspoons hojicha powder or milk tea powder
- ½ teaspoon baking powder
- ½ teaspoon baking soda
- 1 cup | 2 sticks (226 g) unsalted butter, softened
- ⅔ cup (134 g) granulated sugar
- ⅓ cup (67 g) packed light brown sugar
- 1 tablespoon red miso
- 1 large egg
- ½ cup (85 g) white chocolate chips
- ⅓ cup (50 g) lightly salted roughly chopped macadamia nuts

For the boba and brown sugar syrup

- ½ cup (80 g) store-bought boba pearls
- ¼ cup (55 g) packed dark brown sugar
- 1 to 2 tablespoons water

For the frosting

- One 8-ounce (227 g) block cream cheese, softened
- ½ cup | 1 stick (113 g) unsalted butter, softened
- 2 tablespoons (30 g) heavy cream, plus more as needed
- 1 tablespoon red miso
- Pinch of kosher salt
- 1 cup (120 g) confectioners' sugar, or more to taste

Sea salt flakes, for garnish

1. **Make the cookies.** Line two baking sheets with parchment paper.

2. Whisk the flour, hojicha or milk tea powder, baking powder, and baking soda together in a medium bowl. Set aside. Using a stand mixer fitted with the paddle attachment (or in a large bowl with a hand mixer), cream the butter, sugars, and miso together until light and fluffy. Scrape down the sides and bottom of the bowl. Add the egg and mix until combined. Add the flour mixture and mix on low speed just until a dough forms. Fold in the chocolate chips and chopped macadamia nuts.

3. Scoop a heaping tablespoon of dough and roll into a smooth ball. Repeat to make about 27 balls, placing them on the prepared baking sheets 2 inches apart. Press down on each dough ball with the bottom of a cup or glass coated with granulated sugar until the edges begin to crack. Refrigerate for 30 minutes.

RECIPE *continues* →

Cookie Tip
The frosting can be made a day in advance and refrigerated overnight in an airtight container.

Substitution
In a pinch, you can use caramel sauce or maple syrup instead of making the brown sugar syrup.

Storage
It's best to consume the assembled cookies the day they were made because cooked boba does not store well, but you can store unfrosted cookies in an airtight container at room temperature for up to 5 days.

4. About 25 minutes before baking, adjust two racks to the upper- and lower-middle positions of the oven. Preheat the oven to 350°F.

5. Bake all the cookies, switching the sheets between top and bottom racks and rotating front to back once halfway through, until the bottoms and edges are golden brown and set, 12 to 14 minutes. Transfer the cookies to a wire rack to cool completely.

6. **Make the boba and brown sugar syrup.** Cook the boba pearls according to the packaging's instructions, then set them aside to cool. Cook the dark brown sugar and water in a small saucepan over medium heat until the sugar dissolves and the mixture comes to a boil. Reduce the heat to low and simmer, stirring occasionally, until the syrup is thickened enough to coat the back of a spoon, 7 to 8 minutes. Remove from the heat. Stir the cooked boba into the syrup and set aside to cool.

7. **Make the frosting.** Using a stand mixer fitted with the paddle attachment (or in a medium bowl with a hand mixer), beat the cream cheese, butter, miso, and salt together until smooth and creamy. Gradually add the confectioners' sugar, a small portion at a time, and beat until fully incorporated, smooth, and spreadable. If the frosting is not sweet enough for you, feel free to add more confectioners' sugar, up to ⅓ cup.

8. Pipe or spread frosting on top of each cooled cookie. Try to create a higher border on the edge of the cookie with the frosting so the boba won't slip off. For example, pipe an additional coil of frosting around the edge. Top the frosting with the syrupy boba pearls and crown with sea salt flakes.

MANGO LASSI COOKIES

Makes	*Prep Time*	*Cook Time*	*Difficulty*
9 huge cookies	20 minutes *Inactive Time* 30 minutes to overnight	About 24 minutes	★★★☆☆ (This is a huge cookie to bake and assemble.)

For the cookies

- 2 ½ cups (300 g) all-purpose flour
- ⅔ cup (85 g) cake flour
- ½ teaspoon ground cardamom
- ½ teaspoon baking soda
- ¼ teaspoon kosher salt
- 6 tablespoons (89 g) neutral oil
- ½ cup | 1 stick (113 g) unsalted butter, softened
- ½ cup plus 2 tablespoons (120 g) granulated sugar, plus more for shaping the cookies
- ½ cup (60 g) confectioners' sugar
- 1 large egg
- 1 teaspoon mango extract or rose water
- A few drops of yellow food coloring gel (optional)

For the frosting

- One 8-ounce (226 g) block cream cheese, softened
- ½ cup (120 g) Greek yogurt
- 2 tablespoons (28 g) unsalted butter, softened
- ½ cup (60 g) confectioners' sugar
- ½ teaspoon ground cardamom
- Pinch of kosher salt

For topping the cookies

- Diced fresh mango
- Finely chopped pistachios
- Sea salt flakes
- Saffron threads (optional)

Lassi, a yogurt-based drink, has been a staple in Indian cuisine for centuries, tracing back to at least 1000 BCE, and mango lassi is especially beloved and timeless. I've always loved it, and any time I go to an Indian restaurant, I order a glass and watch Philip's eyes light up as he savors the hints of cardamom and rose water.

Each bite of this decadent cookie is sweet with subtle warmth from ground cardamom. The rich yogurt frosting is a nod to lassi, with a glorious crowning of fresh diced mango, a pop of jade from pistachios, and, if you're willing to splurge a little, a pinch of saffron to complete this sunny cookie. I hope you enjoy one with coffee or chai and with a loved one.

1. **Make the cookies.** Whisk the all-purpose flour, cake flour, cardamom, baking soda, and salt together in a medium bowl. Set aside. Using a stand mixer fitted with the paddle attachment (or in a large bowl with a hand mixer, whisk, or spatula), cream the oil, butter, and sugars together until light and fluffy. Scrape down the sides and bottom of the bowl. Add the egg, mango extract or rose water, and food coloring, if using, and mix until well incorporated. Again, scrape the bowl as needed. Add the flour mixture and mix on low speed just until a dough forms. Cover and chill the dough in the refrigerator for 30 minutes to overnight.

2. About 25 minutes before baking, adjust a rack to the middle position and preheat the oven to 350°F. Line two baking sheets with parchment paper.

3. Scoop about 3.2 ounces (90 g) of dough and place on one of the prepared baking sheets. Repeat, leaving about 3 inches between each portion. You should have enough dough to make nine very large cookies. Press down on each dough ball using the sugar-coated bottom of a glass or measuring cup until the edges begin to crack.

RECIPE *continues* →

Cookie Tip
I've provided a guide on how to pipe the frosting, but there's room to be creative. Maybe pipe rosettes, as pictured. Or simply spread the frosting over the cookie with an offset spatula.

Substitution
Instead of diced mango, you can use mango puree or jam to top the frosting or mix directly into the frosting.

Storage
Store the cookies in an airtight container at room temperature for up to 2 days.

4. Bake one sheet at a time (while the other sheet chills in the fridge) until the edges are crispy and golden brown, about 12 minutes. Let the cookies set on the baking sheet for a few minutes before transferring to a wire rack to cool completely.

5. **Make the frosting.** Whip the frosting ingredients together until fluffy and a good piping consistency. Transfer to a piping bag fitted with a large round tip. Start at the center of a cookie and pipe a spiral, working outward. If using a star tip, you can pipe rosettes instead of the spiral. Top the cookies with diced mango, pistachios, sea salt flakes, and a pinch of saffron, if using.

ONDEH-ONDEH MACARONS

Makes
about 35 assembled macarons

Prep Time
25 minutes

Inactive Time
About 2 hours, plus 20 to 30 minutes for the macaron shells to dry

Cook Time
About 30 minutes

Difficulty
★★★★★
(If you can master these macarons, you can make anything in this book.)

For the white ganache

- 1⅓ cups (225 g) high-quality white chocolate chips or chopped white chocolate
- 6 tablespoons (90 g) coconut milk
- 1 teaspoon red miso

For gula aren caramel

- ¼ cup (60 g) gula aren (palm sugar)
- 1½ tablespoons (20 g) water
- ¼ cup (60 g) heavy cream
- 2 tablespoons plus 1 teaspoon (30 g) unsalted butter
- 1 teaspoon red miso

For the macaron shells

- 3 large egg whites, room temperature
- ⅓ cup plus 1 tablespoon (80 g) granulated sugar
- ¼ teaspoon cream of tartar
- ¾ cup (90 g) almond flour, sifted
- ¾ cup plus 1 tablespoon (90 g) confectioners' sugar, sifted
- ½ teaspoon pandan extract or 5 g pandan powder
- Pinch of kosher salt

Shredded coconut, placed in a shallow bowl, for topping

Longtime Subtle Asian Baking member Gunawan Wu is a renowned Indonesian chef known for his beautiful pastries and fun desserts, like Indomie instant noodle and chicken satay-flavored macarons. He shared one of his mother's recipes for my book *Modern Asian Kitchen*, and this time he offers up his ondeh-ondeh (or klepon) macarons recipe, which I have adapted. Ondeh-ondeh is an Indonesian kuih, a Southeast Asian cake or sweet treat that's usually steamed, grilled, or baked. These pandan-flavored treats are coated in grated coconut and filled with a gula aren (palm sugar) caramel, offering delightful caramel notes. Like ondeh-ondeh, these macarons have a beautiful coconutty, pandan taste while bursting with sweet caramel flavor from within.

Gunawan's original recipe uses the French meringue method to make macarons, and in the past, I've only had about a 55 percent success rate with this method. Instead, we'll be using the Swiss meringue method. While this involves an extra step of heating the egg whites in a double boiler and using a digital or candy thermometer, I've found the technique to be more foolproof. The shells also take less time to dry before baking. The result is a pretty jade macaron with a delicate shell, beautiful feet, chewy interior, and a flavor that, I feel, captures the essence of ondeh-ondeh. Thank you for the inspiration, Gunawan!

1. **Make the white ganache.** Place the white chocolate in a medium bowl. In a saucepan, heat the coconut milk and miso until just bubbling at the edges. Pour the hot coconut milk mixture over the white chocolate. Let it rest for a few minutes, then use a rubber spatula to mix until all the chocolate is melted and the ganache is smooth. Cover the bowl with plastic wrap, ensuring it touches the surface of the ganache to prevent a skin from forming. Refrigerate until the ganache is set, about 2 hours. Once set, beat it with a hand mixer or stand mixer until fluffy. Cover and refrigerate until ready to use.

RECIPE *continues* →

2. **Make the gula aren caramel.** In a small saucepan, cook the gula aren and water over medium heat until the sugar has dissolved. Stir in the cream, butter, and miso and reduce the heat to medium-low. Cook until thickened like caramel sauce, a few minutes. Set aside to cool.

3. **Make the macaron shells.** Line two large baking sheets with parchment paper. Using a double boiler, heat the egg whites and granulated sugar until the mixture reaches 120°F and no higher, as that would cook the egg whites. Transfer the mixture to a stand mixer fitted with a whisk attachment. Add the cream of tartar and beat on medium-high speed until stiff, glossy peaks form, at least 5 minutes. Add the almond flour, confectioners' sugar, pandan extract or powder, and salt, but to properly combine these ingredients with the meringue and achieve the right consistency, perform macaronage with a rubber spatula: Gently fold the dry ingredients into the meringue batter. Start by folding from the bottom of the bowl upward, then press the flat side of the spatula through the center of the batter. Repeat this process, gently folding then pressing, until the batter becomes shiny and flows like molten lava. The goal is for the batter to fold into itself smoothly, leaving a thick ribbon that slowly blends back into the batter after about 10 seconds. When lifted with the spatula, the batter should fall in a smooth, continuous flow, allowing you to draw a figure 8 without the batter breaking off abruptly. Don't overmix/macaronage the batter, as it will deflate, and your macarons will crack or be flat.

4. Transfer the batter to a piping bag fitted with a medium to large round tip and pipe 1½-inch rounds onto the prepared baking sheets, evenly spaced. You should have enough meringue to make 70 shells. Tap the sheet against the counter a few times to release any air bubbles. Use a toothpick to pop any visible air bubbles and smooth out the tops of the shells. Let them rest until a skin forms on top of each macaron shell and they are no longer wet to the touch, 20 to 30 minutes. (In dry and cool conditions, the shells may dry out faster than that.)

5. About 25 minutes before baking, adjust a rack to the middle position and preheat the oven to 300°F.

◂ Stiff peaks on a whisk.

RECIPE *continues* →

Cookie Tip
Gula aren (palm sugar) usually comes in rock or paste form and is often available in Asian supermarkets and online.

Substitution
If you can't find gula aren, substitute brown sugar or coconut sugar one to one.

Storage
Store the macarons in an airtight container in the refrigerator for up to 4 days.

6. Bake one sheet of the macaron shells until firmed, the feet are set, and they peel away from the parchment paper when lifted, about 15 minutes. Set aside to cool completely directly on the baking sheet. Bake the second sheet and repeat this step.

7. **Assemble the macarons.** Add a dollop of ganache to the bottom side of one shell. (Assign uglier macaron shells as the bottom sides.) Add a little dab of gula aren caramel to the middle of the ganache. Sandwich together with a similarly sized macaron shell. Roll the macaron, like a wheel, in the coconut. Sprinkle the coconut all over the assembled macarons.

THIRD-CULTURE WHOOPIE PIES

Makes
about 12 whoopie pies

Prep Time
20 minutes

Cook Time
About 12 minutes

Difficulty
★★★★☆
(Multiple steps are involved, including browning butter, piping batter, and assembling the whoopie pies.)

For the bay leaf brown butter

½ cup | 1 stick (113 g) unsalted butter, cubed

3 bay leaves

For the cookies

2 cups plus 2 tablespoons (260 g) all-purpose flour

¾ cup (75 g) unsweetened Dutch-processed cocoa powder, sifted

½ teaspoon ground Vietnamese cinnamon

½ teaspoon baking soda

¼ teaspoon baking powder

½ cup | 1 stick (113 g) unsalted butter, cubed and softened

¾ cup (150 g) granulated sugar

1 large egg

1 tablespoon light soy sauce

1¼ cups (300 g) buttermilk

For the marshmallow filling

4 ounces (113 g) cream cheese (half of an 8-ounce block), softened

¼ cup (30 g) Marshmallow Fluff

1¼ cups (150 g) confectioners' sugar, plus more for dusting

1 teaspoon ube extract (for flavor and color)

1 teaspoon soy sauce

The first time this Cantonese Vietnamese American girl from Brooklyn had a whoopie pie was during a middle school trip to Pennsylvania Dutch Country, which is apparently the birthplace of these delightful treats. Legend has it that when Amish wives packed these soft cookie sandwiches in their husbands' lunches, the happy hubbies would exclaim, "Whoopie!"

Inspired by this tradition, I wanted to make whoopie pies for Jake, who is a third-culture kid like me. My whoopie pie incorporates flavors from our childhoods, with Vietnamese cinnamon and light soy sauce in the soft, cakey cookies and bay leaves and ube in the sweet filling. While Jake didn't say "whoopie," when seeing them, his taste buds did approve, and so did Philip's, our third-culture child. (Or is it fourth culture?)

1. Adjust two racks to the upper- and lower-middle positions of the oven. Preheat the oven to 375°F. Line two baking sheets with parchment paper.

2. **Make the bay leaf brown butter.** Cook the butter in a saucepan over medium heat while whisking continuously, until the butter foams, the foam subsides, the butter is golden, and brown (not black) bits form on the bottom, at least 5 minutes. You're looking for a nutty aroma and not a burnt smell. Stir in the bay leaves, remove from the heat, and set aside to cool. You will use this for the filling later. Once cooled, fish out the bay leaves and compost them.

3. **Make the cookies.** Whisk the flour, cocoa powder, cinnamon, baking soda, and baking powder together in a medium bowl. Set aside. Using a stand mixer fitted with the paddle attachment (or in a large bowl with a hand mixer, whisk, or spatula), cream the butter and sugar together until light and fluffy, about 2 minutes. Scrape down the sides and bottom of

RECIPE *continues* →

Cookie Tips
Since these whoopie pies come straight from my heart, I make them heart shaped. However, it's not an easy feat as the cookies puff up in the oven and can become misshapen, so feel free to simply pipe 2- to 2 ½-inch rounds to create the standard saucer-shaped whoopie pies.

Storage
Store the whoopie pies in an airtight container at room temperature for up to 3 days.

the bowl as needed. Add the egg and soy sauce and mix until well incorporated. Add the flour mixture to the batter in two additions, alternating with the buttermilk and finishing with flour. Mix at low speed until just combined.

4. Transfer the batter to a piping bag fitted with a medium to large round tip. Pipe batter onto one of the prepared baking sheets, creating a 3-inch diagonal line downward. Pipe another diagonal line to meet the first, forming a V-shaped heart approximately 3 inches wide at the top. Repeat to make about 24 hearts, spacing them at least 2 inches apart on the two baking sheets. Using a clean, wet finger, smooth out the tops of the cookies.

5. Bake all the cookies, switching the sheets between top and bottom racks and rotating front to back once halfway through, until puffy and set, about 12 minutes. Remove from the oven and let the cookies set on the baking sheets for a few minutes before transfering them to a wire rack to cool completely.

6. **Make the filling.** Transfer the bay leaf brown butter to the bowl of a stand mixer fitted with the paddle attachment. Add the cream cheese, Marshmallow Fluff, confectioners' sugar, ube extract, and soy sauce and cream until light, fluffy, and combined, about 2 minutes. Scrape the bottom and sides of the bowl as needed with a rubber spatula.

7. **Assemble the whoopie pies.** Working one at a time, pipe or spoon 1 to 2 tablespoons of the filling onto the flat side of one cookie. Top the filling with another cookie. Repeat until you've assembled about 12 whoopie pies. Dust the tops of the whoopie pies with confectioners' sugar, if desired.

PINEAPPLE BUN COOKIES

Makes
about 12 cookies

Prep Time
10 minutes

Inactive Time
2 hours to overnight

Cook Time
About 14 minutes

Difficulty
★★☆☆☆
(The only difficulty lies in scoring the pineapple pattern.)

- 1½ cups (180 g) cake flour
- 2 tablespoons custard powder or milk powder
- ½ teaspoon baking powder
- ½ teaspoon baking soda
- Pinch of kosher salt
- ¾ cup | 1½ sticks (170 g) unsalted butter, softened
- 2 tablespoons (28 g) lard, softened
- ½ cup (57 g) confectioners' sugar
- 2 large egg yolks
- ¼ cup (50 g) coarse or demerara sugar, placed in a shallow bowl for coating
- 1½ tablespoons (30 g) pineapple jam
- 1 large egg, beaten

Every time we visit a Chinese bakery, Philip always asks for pineapple buns. I love them too, but let's be honest, it's the sweet cookie crust on top that I really enjoy snacking on, rather than the bun in its entirety—unless it comes with a cold slab of butter. So, as a treat for myself, I made pineapple bun cookies, inspired by the bun, but mainly its cookie crust top.

Pineapple buns, or bolo bao in Cantonese, originated in Hong Kong. Despite their name, there's no pineapple in pineapple buns. The name comes from the golden, cross-hatched cookie crust that resembles a pineapple's exterior. Both pineapple buns and Japan's melon pans, which have no melons in them but look like them, reflect colonial and Western influences. To add a twist, and a bit of irony, I incorporate some pineapple jam directly into the egg wash and brush it liberally over the cookies before baking. Please note that these cookies are meant to be delicate and crumbly, just like the cookie crust atop pineapple buns.

1. Whisk the cake flour, custard or milk powder, baking powder, baking soda, and salt together in a medium bowl. Set aside.

2. Using a stand mixer fitted with the paddle attachment, cream the butter, lard, and confectioners' sugar together until light and fluffy. Scrape down the sides and bottom of the bowl as needed. Add the egg yolks and mix until well incorporated. Add the flour mixture and mix on low speed just until a cookie dough forms. Cover and refrigerate for 2 hours to overnight.

3. About 25 minutes before baking, adjust a rack to the middle position and preheat the oven to 350°F. Line a baking sheet with parchment paper.

4. Scoop about 2 tablespoons of dough and roll into a smooth ball, then roll in the coarse or demerara sugar to coat thoroughly. Repeat to form and coat 12 balls. Flatten each ball slightly between your palms, then use a knife or bench scraper

RECIPE *continues* →

Cookie Tip
If you have baker's ammonia handy, whisk a pinch of it into the dry ingredients. It will make the cookies crispier.

Substitution
If you don't have lard, you can use the same amount of shortening or unsalted butter.

Storage
Store the cookies in an airtight container at room temperature for up to 3 days, although they will get softer over time. You can reheat them in a toaster oven for a few minutes to help recrisp them.

to score the top with a crosshatch pattern, wiping the knife or scraper as needed. Make sure the pattern is well-defined, or most of it will disappear as the cookies bake in the oven. Place the cookies on the prepared baking sheet, spaced evenly about 2 inches apart

5. In a small bowl, whisk the pineapple jam and beaten egg together until combined for an egg wash.

6. Bake the cookies for 5 minutes. Remove from the oven and brush the tops of each cookie generously with the egg wash. Bake again until the tops and edges are lightly golden brown, about 9 minutes.

7. Let the cookies set directly on the baking sheet for a few minutes before transferring to a wire rack to cool completely.

LAURA'S MATCHA LANGUES DE CHAT

Makes
about 25 langues de chat

Prep Time
20 minutes

Inactive Time
2 hours

Cook Time
A few minutes for the ganache; 12 to 14 minutes for the cookies

Difficulty
★★★½☆
(There are multiple steps and assembly is required.)

For the matcha-white chocolate ganache

1 cup (170 g) white chocolate chips or chopped white chocolate

⅓ cup (80 g) heavy cream

1 tablespoon culinary-grade matcha

For the cookies

¾ cup (90 g) all-purpose flour

1 tablespoon culinary-grade matcha

Pinch of kosher salt

½ cup | 1 stick (113 g) unsalted butter, softened

1 cup (120 g) confectioners' sugar

1 teaspoon almond extract

3 large egg whites

1 to 2 drops green food coloring gel

Laura McCarthy, who tested the bulk of the recipes in this book, first tried a Mint Milano cookie when her college boyfriend (now husband), Conor, introduced them to her. She told me how she was instantly in love—and that the cookie was wonderful, too. Mint Milano cookies are based on the French cookie called langue de chat or cat's tongue cookie. Delicious and with an adorable shape, they are a favorite of many. Then, while living in Japan, Laura and Conor were happy to discover a brand of cookies called Shiroi Koibito (which means white sweetheart or lover) from Hokkaido, a square version of langues de chat with either a white chocolate or milk chocolate filling.

Filled with matcha and white chocolate ganache, Laura's charming verdant cookies are an interpretation of both the Milano and Shiroi Koibito cookies she fell in love with. They are divine, and I'm sure you'll fall in love with them, too.

1. **Make the ganache.** Place the white chocolate in a medium bowl. Heat the cream in a saucepan just until it bubbles. Pour the hot cream over the white chocolate and let rest for a few minutes. Mix with a rubber spatula until all the chocolate melts and the ganache is smooth. Add the matcha and mix until thoroughly combined. Cover the bowl with plastic wrap touching the ganache (to prevent a skin from forming) and refrigerate until the ganache is set, about 2 hours.

2. **Make the cookies.** Adjust two racks to the upper- and lower-middle positions of the oven. Preheat the oven to 325°F. Line two baking sheets with parchment paper.

3. Whisk the flour, matcha, and salt together in a medium bowl. Set aside. Using a stand mixer fitted with the paddle attachment (or in a large bowl with a hand mixer, whisk, or spatula), cream the butter, sugar, and almond extract until super light and fluffy. Add the egg whites, one at a time, and mix until

RECIPE *continues* →

Cookie Tips
Since the ganache takes time to set, always make it first. Warm the ganache piping bag between your hands to make it easier to pipe.

Variation
For a white chocolate ganache filling, omit the matcha in the ganache.

Storage
Store the cookies in an airtight container at room temperature for up to 2 days.

well incorporated after each addition, then add the green food coloring gel. It's okay if the mixture curdles at this point. Add the flour mixture and mix on low just until the batter is well combined and smooth. Don't overmix.

4. Transfer the batter to a piping bag fitted with a ½-inch tip and pipe about fifty 3-inch-long oblongs (or "cat tongues") onto the prepared baking sheets, leaving about 2 inches of space between each. Note these cookies will flatten as they bake in the oven.

5. Bake all the cookies, switching the sheets between top and bottom racks and rotating front to back once halfway through, until golden brown, 12 to 14 minutes. Remove from the oven and let the cookies set on the baking sheets for a few minutes before transferring them to a wire rack to cool completely.

6. **Assemble the matcha langues de chat.** Use a whisk or immersion blender to whip the chilled ganache until smooth and thick like frosting. Transfer the ganache to a piping bag fitted with a large round piping tip. Pipe a thick line of ganache on the flat side of one cookie, about ¼ inch from the edge. Sandwich with another cookie. Repeat until you've assembled about 25 matcha langues de chat.

BLACK SESAME-WHITE CHOCOLATE COOKIES

Makes
12 to 15 large cookies

Prep Time:
15 minutes

Inactive Time:
30 minutes to overnight

Cook Time:
About 15 minutes

Difficulty:
★★★½☆
(Multiple steps are involved.)

- ½ cup | 1 stick plus 1 tablespoon (120 g) unsalted butter, cubed
- ½ cup plus 1 tablespoon (120 g) packed dark brown sugar
- ¼ cup (50 g) granulated sugar
- 1 ¼ cups (160 g) all-purpose flour
- ⅓ cup (45 g) toasted black sesame seeds
- ½ teaspoon baking soda
- ¼ teaspoon baking powder
- ¼ cup (60 g) black sesame paste
- 1 large egg
- 1 tablespoon Japanese whisky or maple syrup
- 1 teaspoon red miso
- 6 ounces (170 g) high-quality white chocolate, chopped, plus more for topping the cookies
- Sea salt flakes, for garnish

In 2022, Elaine Du (@eat.laine on Instagram), a Subtle Asian Baking member, showed off her gorgeous black sesame and white chocolate cookies in our group, and I couldn't get those beauties out of my head. With a rich nuttiness from the brown butter and black sesame, it's a delightful treat, a cookie filled with so many nuanced flavors.

I knew I had to adapt Elaine's recipe here. Originally, she used salt and vanilla extract, but of course I had to give it an Asian twist with miso and Japanese whisky. The sweetness of white chocolate perfectly balances the cookie's overall not-too-sweet nature, and a sprinkle of sea salt flakes at the end is a crowning touch. Honestly, more cookies should be made with black sesame.

1. To make the brown butter, cook the butter in a heavy saucepan or pot over medium heat while whisking continuously, until the butter foams, the foam subsides, the butter is golden, and brown (not black) bits form on the bottom, at least 5 minutes. You're looking for a nutty aroma and not a burnt smell. Transfer the butter to a heatproof mixing bowl. Add the sugars and mix until dissolved. Set aside to cool. A few minutes in the freezer will hasten cooling.

2. Whisk the flour, black sesame seeds, baking soda, and baking powder together in a medium bowl. Set aside.

3. Add the black sesame paste, egg, Japanese whisky or maple syrup, and miso to the cooled brown butter and mix with a whisk or hand mixer until fully incorporated, paler in color, and thickened. (You can also use a stand mixer fitted with a paddle attachment.) Add the flour mixture and mix until homogenous. Fold in the white chocolate. Cover the dough and refrigerate for 30 minutes to overnight.

RECIPE *continues* →

Variations

Try rolling the cookie dough balls in a mixture of black sesame seeds and granulated sugar before baking. This will add a crunchy exterior and an extra burst of black sesame flavor to each cookie.

Substitute tahini for the black sesame paste and white sesame seeds for the black. Or use dark or semisweet chocolate instead of white chocolate.

Storage

Store the cookies in an airtight container at room temperature for up to 3 days.

4. About 25 minutes before baking, adjust two racks to the upper- and lower-middle positions of the oven. Preheat the oven to 350°F. Line two baking sheets with parchment paper.

5. Scoop about 2 tablespoons of the dough and roll into a smooth ball. Repeat to make 12 to 15 balls, placing them 2 inches apart on the prepared baking sheets. Press a chunk or two of white chocolate onto the top of each dough ball.

6. Bake all the cookies, switching the sheets between top and bottom racks and rotating front to back once halfway through, until the edges and bottoms are golden brown, about 15 minutes. The cookies are meant to be set with gooey middles.

7. Sprinkle the cookies with sea salt flakes. Allow the cookies to set on the baking sheets for a few minutes before transferring to a wire rack to cool completely.

COFFEE BEAN COOKIES

Makes
about 38 small cookies

Prep Time
14 minutes

Cook Time
About 25 minutes

Difficulty
★★½☆☆
(You need a little finesse when making the coffee bean shapes and adding the lines to the cookies.)

For the cookies

- About 1 tablespoon (8 g) instant coffee
- 1½ tablespoons hot water
- 1 cup (120 g) cake flour
- 2 tablespoons (16 g) cornstarch
- 1½ tablespoons (12 g) unsweetened Dutch-processed cocoa powder
- 1 tablespoon milk powder
- About ⅓ cup | ⅔ stick (75 g) unsalted butter, softened
- ½ cup plus 1 tablespoon (70 g) confectioners' sugar
- 1 teaspoon red miso
- 1 large egg yolk
- 1 teaspoon hazelnut extract (optional)

For the white chocolate glaze

- 2 tablespoons (30 g) heavy cream
- 1 tablespoon unsalted butter
- About ½ cup (75 g) high-quality white chocolate chips or chopped white chocolate
- ½ teaspoon red miso
- ½ teaspoon hazelnut extract (optional)

For optional toppings

- Sea salt flakes
- Confectioners' sugar

These coffee bean cookies were all the rage among Subtle Asian Baking members, especially during 2020. The true origin of the cookies? Unknown. But I've always thought of them as being subtly Asian and have found their shape and aesthetic irresistible and adorable: The melt-in-the-mouth cookies taste like coffee while looking like coffee beans. What's not to love about them?

I hope these coffee bean cookies remind you of lattes and other coffee drinks, like Vietnamese iced coffee.

1. **Make the cookies.** Adjust a rack to the middle position and preheat the oven to 325°F. Line a baking sheet with parchment paper.

2. Dissolve the instant coffee in the hot water and set aside. Whisk the cake flour, cornstarch, cocoa powder, and milk powder together in a medium bowl. Set aside.

3. Using a stand mixer fitted with the paddle attachment (or in a large bowl with a hand mixer, whisk, or spatula), cream the butter, sugar, and miso together until light and fluffy, about 1 minute. Scrape down the sides and bottom of the bowl as needed. Add the instant coffee mixture, egg yolk, and hazelnut extract, if using, and mix until well incorporated. Add the flour mixture and mix on low speed just until a soft dough forms.

4. Portion about 1½ teaspoons (8 grams) dough and shape into a small oval to resemble a coffee bean. Press a line in the center of the oval with the back of a knife blade or use a toothpick. Repeat to make about 38 coffee bean shapes, placing them on the prepared baking sheet. (The cookies don't spread much, so just space them evenly apart.)

5. Bake the cookies until set and no longer glossy, about 14 minutes. Let cool for a few minutes, then transfer the cookies to a wire rack to cool completely.

RECIPE *continues* →

Cookie Tip
Adjust the amount of instant coffee granules (or powder), depending on your taste preference.

Variations
Substitute the hazelnut extract with another flavor you commonly find in lattes, such as lavender. Or, instead of extract, add your favorite spices, like ½ to 1 teaspoon cardamom, cinnamon, or nutmeg, for a warmer coffee bean cookie.

Storage
Store the cookies in an airtight container at room temperature for up to 3 days.

6. **Make the glaze.** Meanwhile, gently heat the cream and butter in a small saucepan until it just begins to simmer. Remove from the heat and add the white chocolate, miso, and hazelnut extract, if using. Stir with a spatula until the chocolate has completely melted.

7. Dip the cooled cookies into the glaze or drizzle the glaze over the cookies. Then, if you like, top with sea salt flakes, or simply dust the cookies with confectioners' sugar.

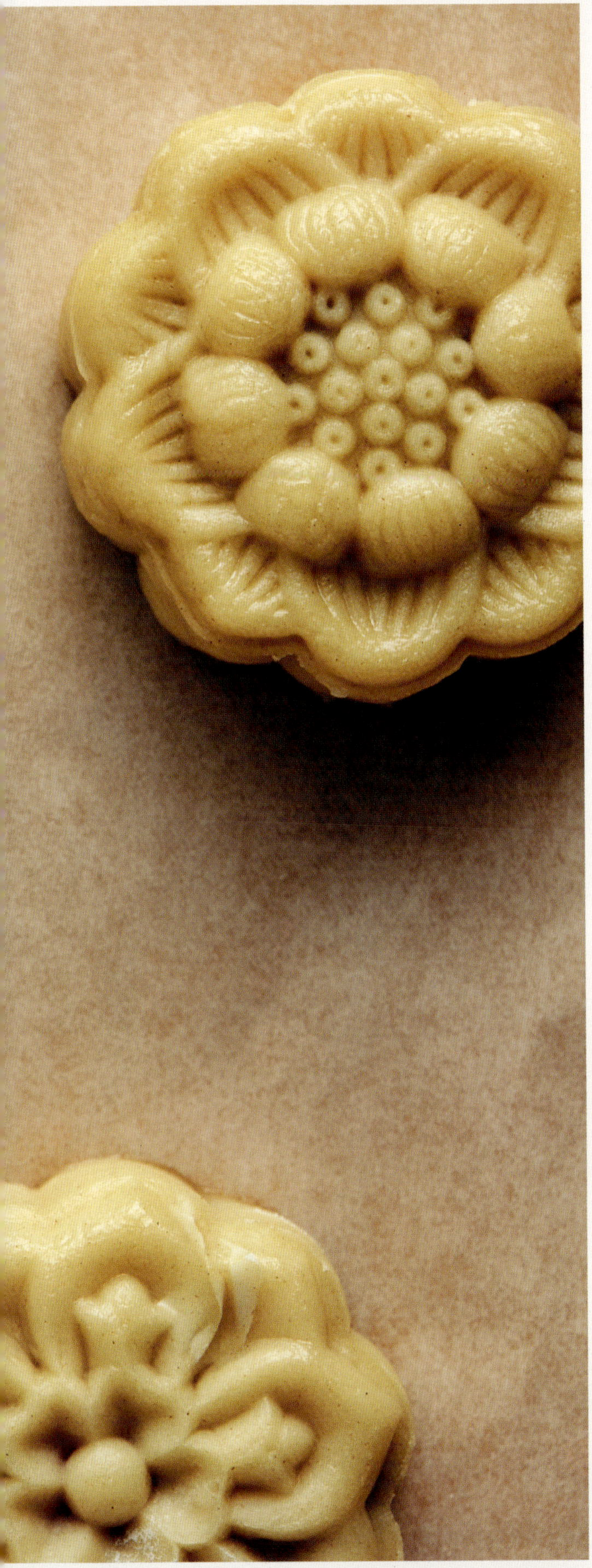

VII

SPECIAL OCCASION AND HOLIDAY COOKIES

Cookies and treats to enjoy on special occasions and share with loved ones during the holidays

While I never baked cookies from scratch with my family when I was growing up in Brooklyn, cookies and sweet treats were always part of our celebrations and holidays. Being a third-culture kid meant celebrating multiple holidays—both the major American and most of the East Asian ones. This always made me feel special, and I got to enjoy a wide variety of cookies throughout the year.

Mooncakes of all kinds were always a given during the Mid-Autumn Festival, and I decided to challenge myself. How could I turn mooncakes into stuffed cookies one can enjoy year-round? Let me introduce you to the White Lotus Mooncakes with Salted Duck Eggs, but Cookies recipe on page 326.

One of my favorite cookies during Christmastime is gingerbread. It's warm, comforting, and super fun to decorate. When developing my Lemongrass and Masala Gingerbread Cookies (page 333), I nurtured my inner child and drew inspiration from the lemongrass chai my good friend Suraj always makes when we visit his house.

Another must-make cookie from this chapter is my Black Forest Cookies (page 317). Black Forest cake was my father's favorite, and is now my son's. It's funny how they share the same name and have a similar palate! We've always had Black Forest cake for their birthdays, so I wanted to create a cookie that would capture the essence of those celebrations. While it's a Western dessert, Asian bakeries have embraced their own versions of Black Forest cakes for decades, if not longer, making it a perfect blend of cultures for birthdays and everyday enjoyment.

LAURA'S CHINESE WEDDING COOKIES

Makes	**Prep Time**	**Cook Time**	**Difficulty**
about 35 cookies	20 minutes **Inactive Time** About 1 hour	About 36 minutes	1 of 5

For the cookie dough

2 cups (240 g) all-purpose flour

1 cup (96) almond flour

½ teaspoon five spice powder

Pinch of kosher salt

1 cup | 2 sticks (226 g) unsalted butter, softened

½ cup (57 g) confectioners' sugar

2 teaspoons almond extract

For the dragon fruit powdered sugar

¾ cup (90 g) confectioners' sugar

½ cup (50 g) pink pitaya (dragon fruit) powder

Edible gold leaf, for decorating (optional)

This cookie, Laura's second in the book, is an Asian spin on Mexican wedding cakes (or cookies), a holiday treat she often made as a little girl with her mother and then with her own kids. She and her children spent many happy hours together making Christmas cookies, including these buttery, melt-in-your-mouth cookies that look like snowballs. Laura says that they are always the first to disappear from her annual Christmas cookie plate.

For this recipe, she gives her go-to Mexican wedding cookie recipe an update, replacing ground cinnamon with five spice powder. And inspired by Chinese wedding aesthetic, where red symbolizes prosperity and luck and gold symbolizes wealth and fortune, she adds pink pitaya powder to the confectioners' sugar, and asks that you "fancy the cookies up" with edible gold leaf. For added flavor complexity, she also recommends adding a splash of Rèmy Martin XO cognac (a common gift and drink at Chinese weddings) or brandy to the cookie dough.

Laura hopes it will become a family tradition for all of you! Thank you for sharing this lovely recipe with us, Laura! (Pictured on page 305.)

1. Whisk the all-purpose flour, almond flour, five spice powder, and salt together in a medium bowl. Set aside.

2. Using a stand mixer fitted with the paddle attachment (or in a large bowl with a hand mixer, whisk, or spatula), cream the butter, confectioners' sugar, and almond extract together until light and fluffy. Scrape down the sides and bottom of the bowl as needed. Add the flour mixture and mix on low speed just until a dough forms. Wrap the dough in plastic wrap and refrigerate until cold, about 1 hour.

3. About 30 minutes before baking, adjust a rack in the center and preheat the oven to 350°F. Line two baking sheets with parchment paper.

Cookie Tip

The dough may be kept in the refrigerator up to 2 days before rolling into balls and baking.

Variations

Use 1 teaspoon cognac, rum, or Japanese whisky in place of the almond extract.

Storage

Store the cookies in an airtight container at room temperature for up to days.

4. Scoop about 2 teaspoons (about 20 grams) dough and shape into a ball. Repeat to make about 35 balls, placing them on the prepared baking sheets about 1 inch apart. Bake the cookies, one sheet at a time, until the tops are lightly golden and the bottoms are golden brown, about 18 minutes. Cool the cookies for 5 minutes on the baking sheets.

5. **Make the dragon fruit powdered sugar.** While the cookies bake, mix the confectioners' sugar and dragon fruit powder together in a medium bowl. Set aside.

6. Using a spoon, gently toss the warm cookies in the dragon fruit sugar to coat completely. Transfer the coated cookies to a wire rack and cool completely. Reserve the remaining pink powdered sugar to sift over the cookies or to roll once more before serving.

7. If you like , dot the cookies with edible gold leaf for an extra fancy touch, fit for an extravagant Chinese wedding.

TARO AND UBE PINWHEEL COOKIES

Makes
about 2 dozen cookies

Prep Time
30 minutes

Inactive Time
1 hour to overnight

Cook Time
About 18 minutes

Difficulty
★★★★☆
(The rolling and slicing parts make this a relatively difficult recipe. Be sure to roll up the dough tightly.)

For the cookie dough

1½ cups (180 g) all-purpose flour

¼ cup (30 g) confectioners' sugar

2 tablespoons (14 g) taro powder

¼ teaspoon kosher salt

½ cup | 1 stick (113 g) unsalted butter, cold and cubed

4 ounces (113 g) cream cheese (half of an 8-ounce block), cold and cubed

1 tablespoon Japanese whisky

1 drop purple food coloring gel (optional)

Milk or cream, if needed

For the filling

About ¼ cup (65 g) ube halaya, plus more as needed

1 tablespoon unsalted butter, melted

1 teaspoon red miso

⅓ cup (40 g) toasted walnuts, finely chopped

½ cup (60 g) toasted white sesame seeds

For topping the cookies

¼ cup (50 g) coarse sugar or sanding sugar, or more as needed, placed in a shallow bowl

This is a whimsical cookie because I deliberately combined taro with ube, two tubers people often mistake for each other, even though they look and taste different. Taro has a light lavender, almost gray hue when cooked, whereas ube's flesh is strikingly purple. Both are mellow and earthy in flavor, though taro is starchier with notes of chestnut and ube has subtle hints of vanilla.

The pretty cookies make for a fantastic holiday treat and will definitely brighten up any cookie tray or box. With taro powder in the cookie dough, you'll have a pale purple and buttery cookie housing deep purple swirls of ube halaya. The combination of different shades makes these cookies visually stunning and perfect for festive occasions. They are especially cherished by the Filipino and Chinese members of my family as they bring together beloved flavors and cultural heritage in a delightful treat.

1. **Make the cookie dough.** Pulse the flour, confectioners' sugar, taro powder, and salt in a food processor for a few seconds to combine. Add the butter, cream cheese, Japanese whisky, and purple food coloring gel, if using. (Or omit the food coloring if you'd like lightly colored cookies.) Pulse continuously until a ball of dough forms. At first, it'll be crumbly but should come together into one ball. If the dough is too crumbly or dry, mix in a teaspoon or two of milk or cream. Cover and refrigerate the dough for 1 hour to overnight.

2. About 25 minutes before baking, adjust a rack in the center and preheat the oven to 350°F. Line a baking sheet with parchment paper.

3. **Make the filling.** In a small bowl, mix the ube halaya, melted butter, and miso until well combined. Keep the bowl close by.

RECIPE *continues* →

Cookie Tip
Instead of a food processor, you can mix the dough using a stand mixer fitted with a paddle attachment, but the butter and cream cheese must be softened first.

Substitution
Feel free to omit the Japanese whisky or substitute 1 teaspoon almond extract.

Storage
Store the cookies in an airtight container at room temperature for up to 3 days.

4. Turn the dough onto a lightly floured large sheet of parchment paper. Using a rolling pin, roll the dough into a rectangle measuring approximately 10 by 14 inches. If desired, trim the edges to create a straight and even rectangle (save the dough scraps to bake later as a baker's snack). Spread the ube halaya mixture evenly over the dough. If needed, use more ube halaya to achieve an even layer. Sprinkle the chopped walnuts and sesame seeds evenly over the ube halaya layer.

5. Starting from one of the long edges, carefully roll the dough into a tight and even log, similar to rolling a jelly roll. Use the parchment paper to help guide and lift the dough as you roll, ensuring the filling stays evenly distributed. Once rolled, gently press the seam to seal the log and smooth out any imperfections. Cover and chill the roll in the freezer for 10 minutes (this will make the dough easier to slice).

6. Using a sharp knife, cut the roll into ½-inch-thick slices. You may need to carefully wipe the knife between each slice. Dip one side of each slice into the coarse sugar, then arrange the slices, sugar side up, on the prepared baking sheet, spaced evenly.

7. Bake the cookies until the edges are golden brown, about 18 minutes. Let the cookies set directly on the baking sheet.

MATCHA MELTING MOMENTS WITH STRAWBERRY BUTTERCREAM

Makes about 14 assembled melting moments

Prep Time 25 minutes

Inactive Time About 20 minutes

Cook Time About 15 minutes

Difficulty ★★★☆☆ (Some assembly required.)

For the cookies

1 ½ cups (180 g) all-purpose flour

½ cup (64 g) cornstarch

1 tablespoon culinary-grade matcha

1 cup | 2 sticks (226 g) unsalted butter, softened

½ cup (57 g) confectioners' sugar

2 tablespoons (30 g) heavy cream

1 teaspoon red miso

For the buttercream

6 tablespoons (85 g) unsalted butter, cubed and softened

1 ½ cups (170 g) confectioners' sugar

1 tablespoon freeze-dried strawberry powder

1 teaspoon lemon juice

Pinch of kosher salt

Confectioners' sugar or matcha, or a mix of both, for dusting (optional)

Sometimes, there's just nothing better than a melt-in-your-mouth cookie that's also a little old school. And melting moments cookies (shortbread cookie sandwiches that originated in Australia where there's a huge population of Asian diasporas) truly live up to their name. Infusing the dough with matcha and sandwiching the cookies with a strawberry buttercream, they're a nod to the blossoming and transient flavors of the season and all the delicious matcha-strawberry desserts I enjoyed during my family trips across Japan.

Note that the cookie dough is meant to be wet and a little messy when you roll it into balls with your hands. Flouring and re-flouring your hands while shaping the dough will keep the dough from sticking to your fingers. So go ahead, embrace the mess—it's all part of the charm before you experience that quintessential melting moment, when time seems to pause just as these cookies disappear from the plate.

1. **Make the cookies.** Line two baking sheets with parchment paper. Whisk the flour, cornstarch, and matcha together in a medium bowl. Set aside. Using a stand mixer fitted with the paddle attachment (or in a large bowl with a hand mixer, whisk, or spatula), cream the butter, confectioners' sugar, heavy cream, and miso together until light and fluffy. Scrape down the sides and bottom of the bowl as needed. Add the flour mixture in thirds and mix on low speed just until a soft dough forms.

2. Lightly flour your hands. Scoop a tablespoon of dough and shape into a smooth ball. Repeat to make 28 balls, placing them 2 inches apart on the prepared baking sheet. Dip a fork

RECIPE *continues* →

Variation
Instead of sandwiches, you can enjoy these melting moments as frosted cookies.

Storage
Store the cookies in an airtight container at room temperature for up to 2 days.

into flour and use the tines to flatten the cookies into ½-inch-thick discs and indent a pattern over the tops. (Or use a wet fork, which also will not stick to the cookies.) Chill the cookies, uncovered in the freezer, for 20 minutes.

3. Adjust two racks to the upper- and lower-middle positions of the oven. Preheat the oven to 350°F.

4. Bake all the cookies, switching the sheets between top and bottom racks and rotating front to back once halfway through, until the cookies are set and the edges and bottoms are light golden brown, about 15 minutes. It's okay if the cookies are a little cracked around the edges. Let the cookies set and cool directly on the baking sheets.

5. **Make the buttercream.** Meanwhile, using a stand mixer fitted with the paddle attachment, cream all the buttercream ingredients together until light and fluffy, a few minutes. Transfer the buttercream to a piping bag fitted with a medium or large round piping tip and refrigerate until ready for use.

6. Once the cookies are fully cooled, pipe buttercream onto the bottoms of half of the cookies and sandwich the frosting with the remaining unfrosted cookies. If you like, dust the cookies with confectioners' sugar or matcha.

HUG FROM HALMEONI COOKIES

Makes	*Prep Time:*	*Cook Time:*	*Difficulty:*
9 large cookies	15 minutes *Inactive Time:* 30 minutes	11 to 13 minutes	★★☆☆☆ (Halmeoni would say these are not too sweet and not too hard to make.)

½ cup (60 g) dried jujube fruits (red or Chinese dates)

About 1¼ cups (145 g) all-purpose flour

1½ teaspoons ground cinnamon

½ teaspoon kosher salt

½ teaspoon baking powder

¼ teaspoon baking soda

4 tablespoons (57 g) unsalted butter, softened

⅔ cup (80 g) unpacked light brown sugar

3 tablespoons (40 g) granulated sugar

1 tablespoon high-quality sesame oil, plus more to coat your hands and brush on the cookie dough balls

1 large egg

⅓ cup (50 g) peeled roasted chestnuts, chopped

¼ cup (35 g) pine nuts

⅓ cup (45 g) toasted sesame seeds (white, black, or both), placed in a small bowl

Sea salt flakes (optional)

Over the holidays a few years ago, Subtle Asian Baking member Angie Chung (@angie_extract on Instagram) shared a heart-warming video of her enjoying these cookies with her halmeoni (Korean for paternal granny). The cookies, Angie explained, represented a bridge between two worlds of her and her halmeoni.

Angie remembers that after dinner, instead of American-style cakes or freshly baked cookies, her halmeoni would hand her family large plates of sliced fruit, a handful of dried jujube dates, and a bowl of mixed nuts. To recapture these memories, she developed a cookie that wholly encapsulates traditional Korean flavors. Like the Korean treat yaksik (or yakbap), which is made of steamed sticky rice, dark syrup or brown sugar, cinnamon, sesame oil, chestnuts, jujube dates, and pine nuts, these are slightly sweet, but also have balancing savory notes from both the sesame oil and toasty seeds.

When we asked what Halmeoni thought about the cookies, Angie shared that she was so very touched by how Angie was able to encapsulate so many traditional Korean flavors into what she considers a normally "too sweet" American dessert. And now you can feel Halmeoni's hug, too!

1. Bring 1 cup water to a boil in a small saucepan. Remove from the heat, add the dried jujube fruits, and let rehydrate for about 30 minutes. Drain and pat dry, then chop and set aside.

2. Adjust a rack to the middle position and preheat the oven to 375°F. Line a baking sheet with parchment paper.

3. Whisk the flour, cinnamon, salt, baking powder, and baking soda together in a medium bowl. Using a stand mixer fitted with the paddle attachment, cream the butter, sugars, and sesame oil together until light and fluffy. Scrape down the sides and bottom of the bowl as needed. Add the egg and mix until well incorporated. Add the flour mixture and mix on low speed just until a cookie dough forms. Fold in the chopped jujube fruits, chestnuts, and pine nuts.

RECIPE *continues* →

Cookie Tips
If banging a hot baking sheet against the counter is not your style, before baking, flatten the dough balls with the bottom of a measuring cup or a glass.

Storage
Store the cookies in an airtight container at room temperature for up to 3 days.

4. Lightly coat your hands with some sesame oil. Portion about 2 tablespoons (55 g) dough, shape into a ball, and roll in the bowl of sesame seeds until generously coated. Repeat to form and coat 18 balls, placing them 2 inches apart on the prepared baking sheet. Brush the tops with sesame oil.

5. Bake until the cookies are lightly golden brown around the edges and puffy, 11 to 13 minutes. Remove from the oven and drop the baking sheet on the counter to slightly flatten the cookies. If you like, sprinkle the tops with sea salt flakes. Allow the cookies to cool and set on the baking sheet.

▲ Angela (Angie) Chung and her halmeoni

BLACK FOREST COOKIES

Makes
24 cookies

Prep Time
15 minutes

Inactive Time
30 minutes

Cook Time
About 10 minutes

Difficulty
★★☆☆☆
(The cacao nibs may fall off so be sure to press them into the cookie with more pressure as needed.)

For the cookies

1 cup (120 g) all-purpose flour

½ cup (40 g) unsweetened Dutch-processed cocoa powder, sifted

½ teaspoon baking powder

½ teaspoon baking soda

½ cup | 1 stick (113 g) unsalted butter, softened

⅔ cup (133 g) packed dark brown sugar

⅓ cup (67 g) granulated sugar

1 tablespoon red miso

1 large egg

1 tablespoon Japanese whisky

One 4-ounce (113 g) bar semisweet chocolate, chopped

1 cup (150 g) chopped dried cherries

For coating and decorating the cookies

¼ cup (30 g) cacao nibs, or more as needed, placed in a shallow bowl

¼ cup (50 g) granulated sugar, or more as needed, placed in a shallow bowl

12 Amarena or maraschino cherries, stemmed and halved

Confectioners' sugar, for dusting

You're probably asking, what's so Asian about Black Forest desserts? Black Forest cake, after all, is a dessert traditionally associated with Germany and the West. But for as long as I remember, you could find Black Forest cakes in East Asian bakeries. It was always a little funny to see this cake next to mooncakes, pork floss buns, and egg tarts, like it was an outlier, or an "other." Kind of like me growing up, the only Asian girl in my entire elementary school cohort.

My father always chose Black Forest cake as his favorite, and now, my son has the same love. It's the cake he wants for all his birthdays. Naturally, I couldn't help but turn the favorite of both my late father and my son into a cookie and include it in this celebration chapter.

1. **Make the cookies.** Whisk the flour, cocoa powder, baking powder, and baking soda together in a medium bowl and set aside. Using a stand mixer fitted with the paddle attachment (or in a large bowl with a hand mixer, whisk, or spatula), cream the butter, sugars, and miso together until light and fluffy. Scrape down the sides and bottom of the bowl as needed. Add the egg and Japanese whisky and mix until well incorporated. Add the flour mixture and mix on low speed just until a soft dough forms. Fold in the chocolate and dried cherries. Cover and refrigerate the dough for at least 30 minutes.

2. About 30 minutes before baking, adjust two racks to the upper- and lower-middle positions of the oven. Preheat the oven to 350°F. Line two baking sheets with parchment paper.

3. Scoop a tablespoon of dough and shape into a ball. Roll in the cacao nibs to coat thoroughly, and then roll in the granulated sugar. Repeat to form and coat 24 balls, placing them on the prepared baking sheets about 2 inches apart. Press an Amarena or maraschino cherry half into the center of each dough ball.

RECIPE *continues* →

Variations
Rum, cognac, whiskey, or bourbon can be substituted for the Japanese whisky. For a more tender cookie, use cake flour instead of all-purpose flour.

Storage
Store the cookies in an airtight container at room temperature for up to 3 days.

4. Bake all the cookies, switching the sheets between top and bottom racks and rotating front to back once halfway through, until the cookies are set and the tops have dried, about 10 minutes. The centers are meant to be soft.

5. Remove from the oven and tap the baking sheets against a counter to flatten the cookies slightly. Allow the cookies to set on the baking sheets for a few minutes before transferring them to a rack to cool completely. Dust the cookies with confectioners' sugar to represent the cream in Black Forest cakes.

SLICE-AND-BAKE JAPANESE SWEET POTATO COOKIES

Makes
12 to 16 cookies, depending on how thin your slices are

Prep Time:
20 minutes

Inactive Time:
1 hour to overnight

Cook Time:
15 to 18 minutes

Difficulty:
★★★★☆
(Multiple steps are involved and you'll need a bit of fine motor skills.)

For the cookies

- 4 tablespoons plus 1 teaspoon (65 g) unsalted butter, softened
- ¼ cup plus 1 teaspoon (35 g) confectioners' sugar
- 1 large egg
- 1 tablespoon Japanese whisky
- 1 teaspoon red miso
- 1 small (about 50 g) Japanese sweet potato, roasted (see Yaki Imo Bars on page 139) and mashed
- ⅞ cup (110 g) all-purpose flour, sifted, plus more for dusting
- ½ teaspoon baking soda
- 1 to 2 tablespoons milk or plant-based milk, for brushing dough log
- ¼ cup (30 g) purple sweet potato powder, or more as needed, sifted and placed in a shallow bowl
- Roasted black sesame seeds, for topping

For the miso-honey butter glaze

- 1 tablespoon unsalted butter, melted
- 1 tablespoon honey
- 1 tablespoon light brown sugar
- ½ teaspoon red miso

Since it takes over an hour to roast sweet potatoes to caramelized perfection in the oven, every time I make them, I make sure to prepare a bigger batch. Then, I store them in the freezer to enjoy cold for lunch, dinner, or even dessert—or to use in recipes like my Yaki Imo Bars with Miso-Honey Caramel (page 139) and these slice-and-bake cookies. Each bite has a slight crispness that quickly gives way to a buttery, tender crumb. Plus, there's something incredibly fun about transforming a vegetable into cookies that look just like it.

1. **Make the cookies.** Using a stand mixer fitted with the paddle attachment (or in a large bowl with a hand mixer, whisk, or spatula), cream the butter, confectioners' sugar, egg, Japanese whisky, and miso together until light and fluffy, about 1 minute. Scrape down the sides and bottom of the bowl. Add the mashed sweet potato and mix until incorporated. Add the flour and baking soda and mix until a cookie dough forms. Turn the dough out onto a lightly floured surface. Knead and then shape it into a log about 6 inches long and 1½ to 2 inches thick. Cover and refrigerate for 1 hour to overnight.

2. About 25 minutes before baking, adjust a rack in the center and preheat the oven to 350°F. Line a baking sheet with parchment paper.

3. Brush the dough log all over with the milk or plant-based milk. Roll the log in the sweet potato powder to cover thoroughly (to resemble the sweet potato's skin). Place the log on a cutting board and use a sharp knife to cut ½-inch-thick slices. Or, for crispier cookies, cut thinner slices.

RECIPE *continues* →

Substitutions
You may omit the Japanese whisky; ube powder or taro powder can be substituted for the sweet potato powder.

Storage
You can store the cookies in an airtight container at room temperature for up to 2 days but they are best eaten the day they're baked.

4. Transfer the cookies to the prepared baking sheet, spaced evenly apart. Thanks to the sweet potato, these cookies don't spread much but you still want to give them space for circulation and even baking. Sprinkle a few black sesame seeds on top of the center of each cookie.

5. **Make the miso-honey butter glaze.** Mix all the glaze ingredients together in a small bowl until combined. Brush the glaze over each cookie. You can be generous with the glaze.

6. Bake the cookies until set and the bottoms and edges are golden brown, 15 to 18 minutes, or 13 to 14 minutes for thinner cookies. Let the cookies cool on the baking sheet for a few minutes, then transfer to a wire rack to cool completely.

MATCHA AND PANDAN PEANUT BUTTER BLOSSOMS

Makes
about 4 dozen cookies

Prep Time
15 minutes

Inactive Time
30 to 60 minutes

Cook Time
About 24 minutes

Difficulty:
★★½☆☆
(Fun and therapeutic. The colorful sugars nurture the inner child.)

1 ¾ cups (210 g) all-purpose flour

1 tablespoon culinary-grade matcha

1 teaspoon baking soda

½ cup | 1 stick (113 g) unsalted butter, softened

½ cup (100 g) granulated sugar

½ cup (110 g) packed light brown sugar

2 teaspoons red miso

½ cup (130 g) peanut butter (smooth or chunky)

1 tablespoon heavy cream

1 large egg

1 teaspoon pandan extract

For rolling and topping the cookies

About ⅓ cup (67 g) turbinado or granulated sugar

About ¼ cup (50 g) green and/or red sanding sugars (optional)

4 dozen dark chocolate kisses from a 10-ounce bag

Peanut butter blossoms were first called Black-Eyed Susans when Freda Smith entered her cookies into the 1957 Pillsbury Bake-Off. Since then, peanut butter blossoms haven't really evolved over the years. Why change something that's already spectacular? But, in the spirit of bake-offs—which, as the founder of Subtle Asian Baking, I've hosted online many times—I thought it'd be fun to reimagine these cookies a little. Since they are usually baked and enjoyed during the holidays, I make them green with matcha and pandan to give them a Grinchy spin. Plus, matcha's earthy, grassy, and vegetal flavors really shine through when paired with peanut butter. In the spirit of the holidays, I also use red and green sanding sugar to add festive color.

1. Whisk the flour, matcha, and baking soda together in a medium bowl. Set aside.

2. Using a stand mixer fitted with the paddle attachment, cream the butter, sugars, and miso together until light and fluffy, about 2 minutes. Scrape down the sides and bottom of the bowl as needed. Add the peanut butter, cream, egg, and pandan extract and mix until well incorporated. Add the flour mixture and mix on low speed just until a cookie dough forms. Cover the dough and chill in the refrigerator for 30 to 60 minutes.

3. While the dough is chilling, adjust a rack to the middle position and preheat the oven to 375°F. Line two baking sheets with parchment paper.

4. Place the turbinado or granulated sugar and the sanding sugars in separate shallow bowls.

RECIPE *continues* →

Substitutions
Mini peanut butter cups, white chocolate kisses, or any other chocolate candy of your liking can be swapped in for the dark chocolate kisses.

Storage
Store the cookies in an airtight container at room temperature for up to 3 days.

5. Portion a 1-inch piece of dough, shape into a smooth ball, and roll in your choice of sugar until thoroughly covered. Repeat to form and coat 48 balls, placing them 2 inches apart on the prepared baking sheets.

6. Bake, one sheet at a time, until the cookies are lightly browned and slightly cracked, about 10 minutes. Remove from the oven and press a chocolate kiss into the middle of each cookie, cracking the cookie. Bake again until the chocolate is glossy, about 2 minutes. Let the cookies set and cool on the baking sheet. It's best to enjoy these cookies while still warm.

WHITE LOTUS MOONCAKES WITH SALTED DUCK EGG, BUT COOKIES

Makes
14 mooncakes

Prep Time
45 minutes

Inactive Time
60 minutes to overnight

Cook Time
20 to 25 minutes

Difficulty
★★★★☆
(Multiple steps and molding are required.)

For the mooncake cookie crust

- 9 tablespoons (126 g) unsalted butter
- ¼ cup (30 g) confectioners' sugar
- 1 tablespoon Japanese whisky
- 1 teaspoon red miso
- 1 large egg
- 1 ¼ cups (150 g) cake flour

For the filling

- 1 ½ cups (350 g) sweetened white lotus paste, refrigerated so it's cold
- 14 cooked salted duck egg yolks

- Cornstarch, for dusting as needed
- 1 large egg beaten with 1 tablespoon milk or water, for egg wash
- Edible gold flakes or foil, for garnish
- Sea salt flakes, for garnish

I have a confession: I have yet to make a traditional mooncake using lye water and golden syrup. I thought I would finally tackle the traditional mooncake, but then I saw these matcha cookie-crust mooncakes, with a red bean filling and a salted egg yolk center, by my online friend Jacinta Halim of jajabakes.com: I knew I had to create my own. Inspired by her creation, my cookie mooncakes have a white lotus filling (my favorite), a salted egg yolk center, and a brown butter cookie crust.

While not traditional, I think this standout mooncake-cookie hybrid is a fitting addition to the mooncake repertoire. Please note you will need a 75-gram plastic mooncake press mold to make the cookies, which you should be able to source easily online. As for the sweetened white lotus paste, the best place to find it is in a Chinese grocery store or Asian supermarket, and it's also available online. Or you could always make your own lotus paste from scratch. I have a recipe on modernasianbaking.com.

1. **Make the mooncake cookie crust.** To make brown butter, cook the butter in a small saucepan over medium heat while whisking continuously, until the butter foams, the foam subsides, the butter is golden, and brown (not black) bits form on the bottom, at least 5 minutes. You're looking for a nutty aroma and not a burnt smell. Remove the brown butter from the heat and chill in the freezer, uncovered, for a few minutes to cool.

2. Using a stand mixer fitted with the paddle attachment (or in a large bowl with a hand mixer, whisk, or spatula), mix the brown butter, confectioners' sugar, Japanese whisky, and miso together until well incorporated. Scrape down the sides and bottom of the bowl as needed. Add the egg and mix until combined. Add the cake flour and mix on low speed just until a soft dough forms. Cover and refrigerate for 30 minutes to overnight.

Substitution
Feel free to use sweetened red bean as the filling instead of white lotus paste.

Storage
Store the mooncake cookies in an airtight container at room temperature for up to 3 days.

3. About 25 minutes before baking, adjust a rack to the middle position and preheat the oven to 350°F. Line a baking sheet with parchment paper.

4. **Make the filling.** Divide the lotus paste into 14 equal portions, about 1 ½ tablespoons (25 grams) each. Working one at a time, roll each portion into a smooth ball, then flatten into a thin disc, 2 ½ to 3 inches in diameter. Wrap one disc around a salted egg yolk, sealing it completely, and gently push the lotus paste around to cover the egg yolk as needed. Roll in your hands to make a smooth ball. Repeat to make 14 lotus paste-covered egg-yolk-filled balls.

5. Divide the cookie dough into 14 equal portions, each 24 to 25 grams. Shape one portion into a smooth ball and flatten into a disc about 3 inches in diameter. Wrap the dough disc around a filling ball, sealing it completely. Roll in your hands to make a smooth ball. Repeat to make 14 filled dough balls ready for molding.

6. Dust the inside of a 75-gram mooncake mold press with cornstarch. Dust a filled ball all over with cornstarch before stuffing it inside the mooncake mold press. Press down on a flat surface or the counter. Push on the plunger to shape and imprint the pattern, then release the mooncake by lifting the mold off the work surface. Push the plunger or handle to pop the mooncake out. Repeat until you have molded all 14 mooncakes.

7. Transfer the mooncakes to the prepared baking sheet, spaced evenly. Chill in the freezer, uncovered, for 30 minutes.

8. Bake the mooncakes for 10 minutes. Remove from the oven and brush the tops with the egg wash. Return the mooncakes to the oven and bake until golden brown all over, 10 to 15 minutes. Let the mooncakes set on the baking sheet for a few minutes before transferring to a wire rack to cool completely.

9. Decorate the mooncakes with edible gold flakes or foil and top with sea salt flakes. Enjoy with a hot cup of oolong or jasmine tea.

1 2 Wrap the cookie dough over the yolk-filled lotus paste ball.

3 4 Stuff assembled mooncake into the mold.

5 6 7 Press down on a flat surface or the counter.

8 Freeze the mooncakes before baking.

MISO AND HOT-CHOCOLATE BROWNIE COOKIES

Makes
12 to 14 cookies

Prep Time
20 minutes

Cook Time
About 10 minutes

Difficulty
★★★☆☆
(You'll have to melt chocolate, then allow it to cool to make these drop cookies.)

About ¼ cup (40 g) glutinous rice flour
¼ cup (20 g) unsweetened Dutch-processed cocoa powder
½ teaspoon baking soda
½ teaspoon baking powder
1 large egg
¼ cup (55 g) packed light or dark brown sugar
1 teaspoon red miso
½ cup (100 g) chopped semisweet chocolate
2 tablespoons (28 g) unsalted butter
¼ cup (40 g) semisweet chocolate chips
Miniature marshmallows, for topping
Sea salt flakes, for garnish

I met and married Jake before I became an avid home baker, but baked goods were always part of our love story. For many Christmases during our earlier years together, I would gift him brownies from Fat Witch Bakery in NYC. And every Valentine's Day I made him brownies, like the Red Velvet Brownies with Doubanjiang on page 148. Jake's love for brownies and cookies is profound and deep, like an underground spring, so when I started baking I figured, why not merge two of his favorite treats (hot chocolate and brownies) into one? During the holidays these days, I bake him these special cookies. They're like a warm hug. Not too sweet thanks to the miso addition and melty on the inside, they remind us of hot chocolate, especially with the gooey marshmallows on top.

1. Line a baking sheet with parchment paper. Adjust a rack to the middle position and preheat the oven to 350°F.

2. Whisk the glutinous rice flour, cocoa powder, baking soda, and baking powder together in a small bowl. Set aside.

3. Using a stand mixer fitted with the whisk attachment, whisk the egg, brown sugar, and miso on high until pale, fluffy, thick, and doubled in volume, about 2 minutes. Set aside.

4. Melt the chopped chocolate and butter in the top of a double boiler over simmering water, in a saucepan over low heat, or in a microwave in a medium heatproof bowl in 30-second bursts. Mix until well combined and no chocolate lumps remain.

5. Check the temperature of the chocolate mixture; it should be 115°F to 122°F. If it's too hot, allow it to cool down to the right temperature. Pour the mixture into the bowl of the stand mixer and mix at low speed until well combined. Scrape down the sides and bottom of the bowl with a spatula. Add the flour

RECIPE *continues* →

Cookie Tip
A dusting of confectioners' sugar will make these cookies festive.

Variation
Substitute gochujang for the miso to make spicy brownie cookies. Just double-check the labels first to be sure the gochujang is gluten-free if that is a concern.

Storage
Unknown, Jake always eats them all.

mixture and mix on low speed until just combined. Gently fold in the chocolate chips.

6. Scoop about 1 tablespoon of dough and drop onto the prepared baking sheet. Repeat to make 13 cookies, spacing them at least 1 inch apart to allow for minimal spreading. Smooth out the tops with a wet finger.

7. Bake the cookies until their tops are glossy and exhibit a crinkled, cracked appearance, about 10 minutes. Remove from the oven and promptly press a mini marshmallow or two into the top of each hot cookie. Garnish the cookies with a small pinch of sea salt flakes. Transfer the cookies to a wire rack to cool completely.

LEMONGRASS AND MASALA GINGERBREAD COOKIES

Makes
12 to 16 cookies, depending on the size of your cookie cutter

Prep Time
About 20 minutes

Inactive Time
15 minutes

Cook Time
16 to 24 minutes

Difficulty
★★★½☆
(Many steps are involved: rolling out and chilling the dough, cutting out shapes, and decorating the cookies.)

For the cookies

1 cup (120 g) all-purpose flour
⅓ cup (40 g) cake flour
½ teaspoon baking powder
¼ teaspoon baking soda
1 tablespoon plus ½ teaspoon ground ginger
1 teaspoon garam masala
½ teaspoon ground cinnamon
¼ teaspoon nutmeg
½ cup | 1 stick (113 g) unsalted butter, softened
½ cup (95 g) unpacked dark brown sugar
1 teaspoon red miso
1 large egg
1½ tablespoons (30 g) unsulfured dark molasses
2 teaspoons store-bought lemongrass paste; or 1 tablespoon finely minced fresh lemongrass

For decorating the cookies

Fondant
Royal icing or cookie icing
Edible sprinkles or glitter
Melted chocolate

Whenever we visit my friend Suraj, he greets us with his exceptional lemongrass chai—a brew so captivating and delightful that I featured the recipe in *Modern Asian Baking at Home*. His chai, with its soulful blend of lemongrass and black tea, sparked the creation of these masala gingerbread cookies.

These cookies symbolize a celebration of friendship and also represent an almost perfect third-culture fusion, melding Southeast and South Asian flavors with classic European gingerbread. Make these and enjoy with a cup of lemongrass chai, naturally!

1. Adjust a rack to the middle position and preheat the oven to 350°F. Line two baking sheets with parchment paper.

2. Whisk the all-purpose flour, cake flour, baking powder, baking soda, ginger, garam masala, cinnamon, and nutmeg together in a medium bowl. Set aside.

3. Using a stand mixer fitted with the paddle attachment (or in a large bowl with a hand mixer, whisk, or spatula), cream the butter, brown sugar, and miso together until light and fluffy. Scrape down the sides and bottom of the bowl as needed. Add the egg, dark molasses, and lemongrass paste or minced lemongrass and mix until well incorporated. Add the flour mixture and mix on low speed just until a soft dough forms.

4. Roll out the dough between two sheets of parchment paper to a ¼-inch thickness. Chill in the freezer, uncovered, for 15 minutes. Use a gingerbread man cookie cutter to cut out shapes. Gather the scraps, re-roll, and continue cutting until all the dough is used. Place the cookies on the prepared baking sheets, spaced at least 1 inch apart.

RECIPE *continues* →

Cookie Tip
Chilling the dough in the freezer or refrigerator before cutting shapes and after gathering and re-rolling the scraps ensures well-defined edges.

Variation
Add a pinch of black pepper with the other spices in step 2 for an extra spicy kick.

Storage
Store the cookies in an airtight container at room temperature for up to 3 days.

5. Bake one sheet at a time (while the other sheet chills in the freezer or fridge) until the edges of the cookies are golden brown, 8 to 12 minutes, depending on the size of the cookies.

6. Let the cookies set on the baking sheet for a few minutes, then transfer to a wire rack to cool completely. Decorate with royal icing, fondant, melted chocolate, edible glitter, sprinkles, or other decorations as desired.

INDONESIAN SNOW WHITE COOKIES (Kue Putri Salju)

Makes	*Prep Time*	*Cook Time*	*Difficulty*
about 24 cookies	15 minutes *Inactive Time* 10 minutes	About 30 minutes	★★☆☆☆ (Nothing too challenging here. I've already lowered the difficulty too by making these rounded instead of crescent-shaped.)

- 1 ⅔ cups (200 g) all-purpose flour
- About ½ cup (50 g) cornstarch
- Pinch of ground black pepper
- 9 tablespoons (120 g) unsalted butter, softened
- 2 tablespoons (30 g) cream cheese, softened
- 5 tablespoons (60 g) granulated sugar
- 1 large egg
- 1 teaspoon ube extract (with color) (optional)
- ½ cup (60 g) grated Parmesan cheese
- ½ cup (60 g) shredded white cheddar cheese
- Milk or water, if needed

For coating the cookies

- About ⅓ cup (67 g) granulated sugar, placed in a shallow bowl or plate
- About ⅔ cup (85 g) confectioners' sugar, placed in a shallow bowl or plate

These snowy cookies are like a warm embrace on a cold day, packed with flavor and history. They draw inspiration from kue putri salju (Indonesian snow white or princess cookies) that are often shared during Eid and Lunar New Year and symbolize festivity. Though they traditionally take a crescent shape, I prefer shaping my cookies into playful snowballs (mainly because I'm lazy).

While modern and traditional Indonesian cookies often prominently feature cheese, kue putri salju traditionally do not. My addition of cheese marks a reclaiming of the culinary narrative, since Dutch colonization introduced Western foods like cheese to Indonesia. Finally, if you decide to add the optional ube extract for subtle floral and vanilla-like essence, the inside will be a lovely purple hue. Note that mine as pictured are without the ube extract, keeping them like traditional kue putri salju.

1. Adjust a rack to the middle position and preheat the oven to 300°F. Line a baking sheet with parchment paper.

2. Whisk the flour, cornstarch, and black pepper together in a medium bowl. Set aside.

3. Using a stand mixer fitted with a paddle attachment, cream the butter, cream cheese, and granulated sugar together until light and fluffy. Scrape down the sides and bottom of the bowl as needed. Add the egg and ube extract, if using, and mix until well incorporated. Add the cheeses and mix until well combined. Add the flour mixture and mix on low speed until a smooth dough forms. If the dough is too dry, add about a teaspoon of milk or water. Cover the dough with plastic wrap and chill in the freezer for 10 minutes.

RECIPE *continues* →

Cookie Tip
Light on time? Instead of rolling the cookies in granulated and confectioners' sugar, you can simply dust them with confectioners' sugar.

Variation
For a green, pandan-flavored cookie, substitute pandan extract for the ube extract.

Storage
Store the cookies in an airtight container at room temperature for up to 3 days.

4. Scoop about a walnut-sized portion of dough (20 to 25 grams) and shape into a smooth ball. Repeat to make 24 portions, placing them 1 inch apart on the prepared baking sheet.

5. Bake until the cookies are lightly golden, about 30 minutes. Let the cookies rest on the baking sheet for a few minutes before transferring them to a wire rack to cool completely.

6. Once completely cooled, roll each cookie thoroughly in the granulated sugar, then repeat in the confectioners' sugar. Lightly shake off excess confectioners' sugar.

ASIAN S'MORES BARS

Makes
24 bars

Prep Time
15 minutes

Cook Time
About 25 minutes

Difficulty
★★★☆☆
(There are many components, browning butter, and assembly with some chill time in between.)

For the matcha blondies

½ cup | 1 stick (113 g) unsalted butter, cubed

¾ cup (165 g) packed light brown sugar

1 ¼ cups (145 g) all-purpose flour

1 tablespoon culinary-grade matcha, plus more for optional dusting

½ teaspoon baking soda

1 large egg

1 tablespoon milk

1 tablespoon maple syrup

1 teaspoon red miso

For topping the blondies

About two 4-ounce (113 g) bars semisweet or dark chocolate, chopped into squares

¼ cup (37 g) toasted white sesame seeds

12 regular-sized marshmallows, halved

Lotus Biscoff cookies or graham crackers, crushed into pea-sized crumbles, for topping (optional)

Sea salt flakes, for garnish

After four decades of living in America, I still haven't gone camping or glamping. Despite this *blasphemy*, I've always loved s'mores, the all-American sweet snack emblematic of the great outdoors. What makes s'mores great are the different textures and temperatures—roasted marshmallows and melty chocolate sandwiched between two crispy graham crackers.

My take on s'mores is more like cookie bars than cookie sandwiches. But one taste and you'll see these s'mores bars are not fully American and not fully Asian, a duality that resonates with my own experience as a third-culture kid.

1. Adjust a rack to the middle position and preheat the oven to 350°F. Crumple, then uncrumple a large sheet of parchment paper and use it to line an 8-inch square cake pan with some overhang. Smooth and press down the parchment paper with your hands.

2. To make the brown butter, cook the butter in a heavy saucepan or pot over medium heat while whisking continuously, until the butter foams, the foam subsides, the butter is golden, and brown (not black) bits form on the bottom, at least 5 minutes. You're looking for a nutty aroma and not a burnt smell. Remove from the heat and transfer to a heatproof mixing bowl. Add the brown sugar and mix until dissolved. Set aside to cool. A few minutes in the freezer will aid in cooling.

3. Whisk the flour, matcha, and baking soda together in a medium bowl. Set aside.

4. To the cooled brown butter, add the egg, milk, maple syrup, and miso and mix with a rubber spatula until fully incorporated. Add the flour mixture and mix until homogenous.

5. Transfer the batter to the prepared pan. Use an offset spatula or butter knife to spread the batter evenly. Bake until the edges

RECIPE *continues* →

Cookie Tip
Coating a sharp knife with neutral oil will prevent melted marshmallow from sticking to the blade as you slice through the bars.

Storage
Store the bars in an airtight container at room temperature for up to 2 days.

are brown and a toothpick or bamboo skewer inserted into the middle comes out clean, about 23 minutes.

6. Remove the blondies from the oven. Immediately and carefully lay the chocolate evenly over the top of the blondies and allow a few minutes for the chocolate to melt. Use an offset spatula to spread the chocolate evenly across the blondie surface. Evenly sprinkle the sesame seeds on top. Quickly arrange the marshmallows in a single layer on top of the melted chocolate, with the uncut sides facing up. If the marshmallows aren't sticking to the chocolate, return the blondies to the hot oven for a few minutes to heat up, then try adding the marshmallows again. Set the broiler to high. Place the bars 4 to 5 inches under the broiler to toast the marshmallows for 1 to 2 minutes, making sure they don't burn to a blackened crisp. If you're prone to burning food, use the low setting.

7. Flatten all the marshmallows with a spatula. If you like, sprinkle the bars with crushed cookies or graham crackers and dust with matcha. Transfer to a wire rack to cool completely.

8. Carefully coat the blade of a sharp knife with neutral oil, then slice into 24 equal squares for serving. To round out all the flavors, sprinkle sea salt flakes over the s'mores.

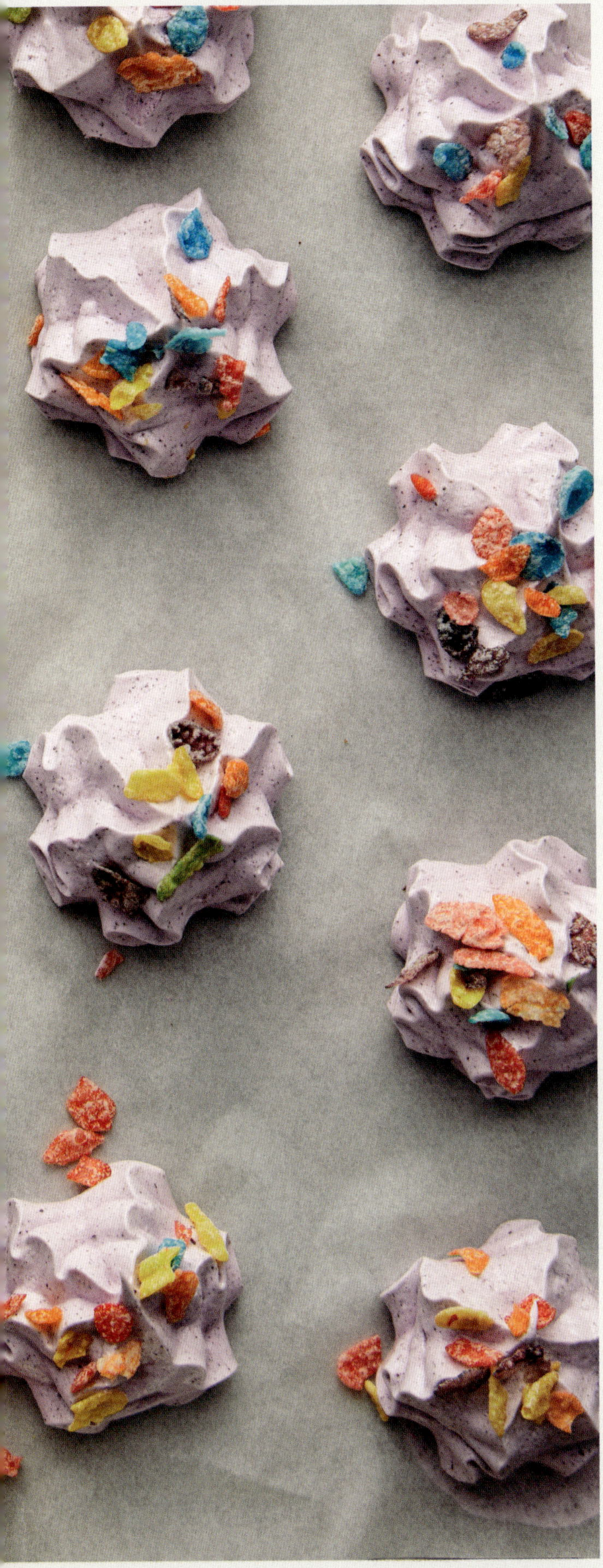

VIII

LIFE IS A BOX OF NOT-TOO-SWEET TREATS

Cookies and their non-cookie cousins that can hold their own on a cookie tray

I can't remember a time when my grandparents didn't feed me. When I was growing up in Montreal, Ah Ma taught me how to cook and shop for the freshest fruits and veggies. In turn, ZeZe would whisk us away to Indian buffets and Japanese restaurants, introducing me to spices, matcha, wasabi, and many other ingredients and flavors early on. This early exposure fostered my lifelong open-minded approach to food.

But, my relationship with food hasn't always been simple. As a teenager, I often felt conflicted: torn between the joy of eating and the pressure to conform to societal standards of thinness. Food has always been my family's love language, and yet it became a source of guilt and resentment. Sometimes, I would overeat, feel ashamed, and then cry my eyes out about it. This terrible cycle took years to break.

Reclaiming my love for food, learning to play with it, create with it, and ultimately find peace with it, has been a journey—a journey reflected in the recipes I share with you now. These recipes are a mix of old and new, each one carrying a piece of my story. Some are nods to the past, like my Salted-Egg-Yolk Cornflake Haystacks (page 348). Other recipes are ones that I developed in honor of my family, especially the two biggest cheerleaders in my life (and my favorite Filipinos): my son and husband.

Not everything is a cookie-cookie in this chapter, including my Cookie Dough Milk Bread (page 350) or my Edible Cookie Dough (with Miso, of Course) on page 355. It's safe to eat raw and super delicious.

Finally, a recipe dedicated to Ah Ma. It's an exquisite cookie and a labor of love. Patience and care are qualities she valued deeply. She demanded a lot from her children and grandchildren, and I think this recipe, my Durian Tea Sandwich Cookies for Ah Ma (page 380), would make her proud.

This chapter is more than just a collection of recipes; it's a journey through my memories and a celebration of the sweet—and not-so-sweet—moments that have shaped who I am today.

JOLLIBEE-INSPIRED PEACH-MANGO DUMPLINGS

Makes
18 dumplings

Prep Time:
15 minutes

Inactive Time:
1 hour

Cook Time:
About 10 minutes for the filling; 25 to 30 minutes for the dumplings

Difficulty:
★★★☆☆
(For me, sometimes pastry dough becomes a bit too soft after thawing it. And while baking, these dumplings can come apart.)

1 cup (150 g) diced ripe mango
½ cup (125 g) canned peaches, drained and diced
2 tablespoons (30 g) syrup from the peach can
¼ cup (50 g) packed light brown sugar
1 tablespoon calamansi juice
1 tablespoon unsalted butter
1 tablespoon red miso
1 tablespoon cornstarch
1 teaspoon ground cinnamon
2 sheets (about 250 g) frozen puff pastry, thawed
1 large egg, beaten with 1 teaspoon milk or heavy cream, for egg wash
Shredded coconut, for garnish
White sesame seeds, for garnish

Before smartphones became ubiquitous, I used to flip through print magazines like *Better Homes & Gardens*. I loved the scratch-and-sniff coffee stickers in the magazine, and all the tips on how to be the best homemaker. I also remember seeing an “apple dumplings” recipe. Being young at that time, I was surprised those dumplings weren’t wontons or gyozas, but rather baked pastries.

Apple dumplings are, I later learned, a retro classic dessert from Pennsylvania Dutch Country that evokes simpler times with their rustic appeal. Instead of making apple dumplings for this book, however, here I made peach-mango ones inspired by Jollibee’s delicious peach mango pie, one of Philip and Jake’s favorite desserts. (Jollibee, if you don’t know, is a Filipino fast-food chain hugely popular in America and across the world. Imagine that McDonald’s and KFC had a baby that sells fried chicken, burgers, and Filipino food.)

Jollibee’s pies are deep-fried, and I try to avoid deep-frying whenever I can. These peach and mango dumplings are easy to put together and bake and can hold their weight on any cookie tray. They’re not exactly the traditional baked dumplings, swimming in a sweet sauce, and they’re not exactly pies or cookies, either. But who knows? Maybe one day, a kid will be flipping through a magazine, online zine, or this book, see this recipe, and feel inspired. (Pictured on page 345.)

1. In a saucepan, combine the mango, peaches, syrup from the can, brown sugar, calamansi juice, butter, miso, cornstarch, and cinnamon and stir continuously over medium heat until the mixture comes to a boil. Reduce the heat to low and simmer until slightly reduced and thickened, about 6 minutes. Cover and refrigerate for 1 hour to cool completely.

Cookie Tips

Have toothpicks handy to keep the pastry in place as it bakes.

Look for canned peaches that come in light syrup rather than juice.

Storage

Store the dumplings in an airtight container at room temperature for up to 3 days. It's best to reheat them in the toaster oven.

2. About 30 minutes before baking, adjust a rack in the center and preheat the oven to 400°F. Line a baking sheet with parchment paper.

3. Roll out the sheets of puff pastry and cut each into nine 3-inch squares. Transfer the squares to the prepared baking sheet. Using a clean finger, paint the outside ½ inch of each square with a little egg wash.

4. Add a heaping tablespoon (or up to 2 tablespoons) of the cooled filling to the center of each square. Fold each corner of the square over the filling so they meet in the center, forming a square dumpling. Press the edges of the pastry together to seal. Note that the edges will spread apart once you bake these dumplings. You can insert a toothpick through the center where all the corners meet, ensuring it goes through the folded layers of pastry, to keep the pastry in place as it bakes.

5. Evenly space the dumplings on the prepared baking sheet, brush the tops with egg wash, and sprinkle with shredded coconut. Crown with some white sesame seeds. Bake until the pastry is crispy and golden brown, 25 to 30 minutes.

6. Let the dumplings set on the baking sheet for a few minutes before transferring to a wire rack to cool completely.

SALTED-EGG-YOLK CORNFLAKE HAYSTACKS

Makes
about 18 haystack cookies

Prep Time
10 minutes

Inactive Time
About 30 minutes

Cook Time
About 20 minutes

Difficulty
★★☆☆☆
(I've made these a bunch of times already. They get easier and easier with each new batch.)

Especially across Malaysia and China, salted-egg-yolk cornflakes have become a popular snack during Lunar New Year. The snack features garlicky, umami-ful salted egg yolk flavored with curry leaves and chili peppers and covered with cornflakes. It's a snack that is enjoyed not by the spoonful but by the handful. I thought it'd be fun to make haystack cookies with salted egg yolks.

Haystack cookies have been popular in America since the Great Depression, first using melted butterscotch or chocolate chips instead of peanut butter and corn syrup to bind the haystacks together with chow mein noodles or pretzel sticks to give them their signature crunch and haystack-like appearance. By baking the cornflakes first, we keep these haystacks nice and crunchy.

For the salted-duck-egg-yolk cornflakes

4 tablespoons (57 g) unsalted butter

6 cooked salted duck egg yolks, mashed finely, 1 tablespoon reserved to sprinkle over the haystacks

½ teaspoon chicken powder

Dash of MSG

¼ cup (35 g) toasted white sesame seeds

6 cups (about 180 g) cornflakes

For the haystacks

1 cup (320 g) light corn syrup

1 cup (250 g) creamy peanut butter

½ cup (100 g) granulated sugar

Sea salt flakes, for garnish

Finely minced fresh curry leaves, for garnish (optional)

1. **Make the salted-duck-egg-yolk cornflakes.** Adjust a rack in the center and preheat the oven to 300°F. Line a baking sheet with parchment paper.

2. In a large saucepan, melt the butter over medium heat until it starts to brown lightly, a few minutes. Add the mashed salted duck egg yolks, chicken powder, and MSG, then stir to combine with the butter. The mixture should resemble yellow foam. Reduce the heat to low and stir in the sesame seeds and cornflakes. Gently stir until the cornflakes are evenly coated with the butter and yolk mixture. Remove from the heat and spread the cornflakes onto the prepared baking sheet. Bake until crispy and golden, about 10 minutes. Set the baking sheet on a wire rack to cool the cornflakes.

3. **Make the haystacks.** Combine the corn syrup, peanut butter, and granulated sugar in the same saucepan you used earlier and cook over medium-high heat, stirring constantly, until the mixture comes to a boil. Remove from the heat, add the cooled cornflakes, and stir until evenly coated.

Cookie Tip
We have two recipes in one here. Give the salted-egg-yolk cornflakes a taste. If you enjoy them as they are, you can always skip turning them into haystack cookies and have lots of delicious "chips" for snacking. Or use the prepared cornflakes as add-ins to other cookies in this book, like the Cowboy Cookies, but Asian (page 38).

Variation
You can replace ½ cup of cornflakes with ½ cup of your favorite nuts.

Storage
Store the haystacks in an airtight container at room temperature for up to 3 days.

4. Use a cookie or ice cream scoop to drop about 18 mounds of the mixture onto the previously prepared baking sheet with the used parchment paper. These cookies are called haystacks because the mounds resemble little haystacks. You will need to compact the mounds with a spoon or your hands when they are cool enough to touch, so the components stick together. Top the haystacks with the reserved mashed salted egg yolks, sea salt flakes, and minced curry leaves, if using. Let the haystacks set for about 30 minutes at room temperature before serving. You can also refrigerate the haystack cookies, which will make them firmer and help develop the flavors more. I personally enjoy these haystacks more the next day.

COOKIE DOUGH MILK BREAD

Makes
16 buns

Prep Time
45 minutes

Inactive Time
About 2 hours

Cook Time
35 to 40 minutes

Difficulty
★★★★☆
(This recipe can be a bit difficult if you've never made bread before.)

For the tangzhong

¼ cup (30 g) all-purpose flour

½ cup (120 g) milk or plain plant-based milk

For the bread dough

½ cup (120 g) milk or plain plant-based milk

Pinch of granulated sugar

One ¼-ounce packet or 1 heaping teaspoon (8 grams) active dry yeast

2 ½ cups (300 g) bread flour, plus more as needed

½ cup (90 g) packed light brown sugar, plus more for topping the bread

Pinch of kosher salt

1 large egg

3 tablespoons (43 g) unsalted butter, softened

½ cup (90 g) chocolate chips, placed in a shallow bowl, plus more as needed

1 large egg, beaten, mixed with 1 tablespoon milk, for egg wash

First off, these are milk bread buns that are meant to *look like* cookie dough balls. The buns do not include cookie dough. Anyway, I know you already love cookies because you bought this book (or maybe you bought the book because you love me), but if you also adore bread, this is the recipe for you.

Recipes like this one really define me, I feel, as they fuse what I loved growing up as an American, like Chips Ahoy! cookies, with what I cherish from the East, like fluffy milk bread made with tangzhong or yudane (flour roux or paste incorporated into the dough to lock in moisture). So, grab that apron to bake up some fusion magic, and don't worry if you've never made bread before. Even if you mess up somewhere along the way, delicious bread buns will still come out of the oven.

1. **Make the tangzhong.** In a saucepan over low heat, whisk the all-purpose flour and milk together until smooth. Cook until thickened, like sticky, gluey mashed potatoes, about 5 minutes. Remove from the heat and stick the saucepan in the freezer to cool for a few minutes. You can also cover and rest the tangzhong overnight in the refrigerator, mimicking what bakers do in Asian bakeries.

2. **Make the bread dough.** In a medium heatproof bowl, combine the milk and granulated sugar. Microwave in 30-second bursts until the milk reaches 110°F. Stir in the active dry yeast and set aside for 5 minutes to allow the yeast to bloom (foam and bubble).

3. In the bowl of a stand mixer fitted with the bread hook attachment, mix the bread flour, brown sugar, and salt for a few seconds. Add the milk mixture, egg, and butter and mix on low speed for 5 minutes. Add the tangzhong and mix for another 5 minutes. Cover and let the sticky dough rest for 10 minutes. Uncover and mix again on low speed for 5 additional minutes. If the dough is still too sticky at this point, mix in a little bread flour,

RECIPE *continues* →

1 Shape the dough.

2 Roll into discs.

3 Add chocolate to the discs.

4 Fold over the chocolate and roll into ball.

5 Top with more chocolate.

6 Place on the baking dish.

Bread Tip
Instead of a stand mixer, you can mix and knead this dough by hand; just note it will take considerably more time and effort.

Storage
Store the buns in an airtight container at room temperature for up to 3 days. If serving on the third day, warm in the toaster oven for a few minutes.

a tablespoon at a time, up to an extra 12 tablespoons (100 g) bread flour, but no more than that. You can stop mixing when the dough is elastic and stretchy, like chewed bubble gum.

4. Lightly dust your hands with flour, shape the dough into a smooth ball, and transfer the dough to a lightly greased or buttered bowl. You can also keep the dough in the stand mixer bowl. Cover and proof in a warm place (or use the oven's "Proof" function if available) until roughly doubled in size, about 1 hour.

5. Crumple, then uncrumple a large sheet of parchment paper and use it to line a 9-inch square baking pan with some overhang. Smooth and press down the parchment paper with your hands.

6. Degas (deflate) the dough with one swift, cathartic punch, and turn it out onto a floured work surface. Divide it into 16 equal pieces, about 45 grams each. Working with one piece at a time, flatten into a disc 2 to 3 inches in diameter. Scoop a small handful of chocolate chips onto the center of the disc. Fold the dough disc to form a ball shape, enclosing the chips. Pinch and tuck the seam to seal, then roll the dough to form a smooth ball. Repeat with the remaining pieces of dough, placing the balls on the prepared baking pan in a close-together 4-by-4 array.

7. Press chocolate chips onto the tops of the buns. The buns need to rise a second time, so let proof, covered, until puffy and roughly one and a half times larger, another hour.

8. About 25 minutes before baking, adjust a rack in the center and preheat the oven to 350°F.

9. Brush the egg wash evenly over the tops of each bun. Sprinkle the tops with some brown sugar. Bake, covering the top with an aluminum foil tent about 15 minutes into baking, until the tops are golden brown, 30 to 35 minutes. Let the buns cool in the baking pan for 5 minutes before transferring to a wire rack. Serve while the buns are still warm and toasty, especially when the chocolate is still melty.

EDIBLE COOKIE DOUGH (with Miso, of Course)

Makes
1 pint jar of edible cookie dough

Prep Time
10 minutes

Inactive Time
15 minutes to overnight

Cook Time
About 20 seconds

Difficulty
(Even without a stand mixer, this recipe comes together easily and quickly.)

- 1½ cups (150 g) almond flour
- ½ cup | 1 stick (113 g) unsalted butter or vegan butter, cubed and softened
- ½ cup (110 g) packed light brown sugar
- 2 tablespoons (25 g) granulated sugar
- 2 teaspoons red miso
- 2 teaspoons milk or plant-based milk
- 2 teaspoons hojicha powder
- ½ cup (90 g) chocolate chips or chocolate chunks
- ⅓ cup (50 g) any chopped nuts or dried berries
- Sea salt flakes

There's something undeniably rebellious about eating cookie dough, like you're breaking a small rule, but in the best way possible. However, unless you heat-treat wheat flour and use pasteurized eggs to make cookies, never, ever eat raw cookie dough. Salmonella and E. coli infections are no joke. When I was developing an edible cookie dough recipe, I turned to nut and plant flours like almond and coconut flour, which are relatively safe to consume raw (unless, of course, you're allergic to them). Still, I recommend heat-treating your nut or plant flour first before ingesting it raw.

Now that my short PSA is over (it's more for me than for you, because I'm always tempted to eat my raw cookie dough), let's talk about this edible cookie dough dish. I honestly can eat this by the tablespoonful. I feel this makes up for lost time and my childhood, which was devoid of baking cookies from scratch and bravely trying cookie dough.

Variation
Chocolate lovers can melt some semisweet chocolate for dipping the edible cookie dough balls into, or simply drizzle over the dough. Then top with sea salt flakes and let the chocolate set before enjoying.

Storage
Store the edible cookie dough in an airtight container or a lidded jar in the refrigerator for up to 1 week.

1. Heat-treat the almond flour: Spread it evenly on a heatproof plate and microwave for 20 seconds on high. Set it aside to cool.

2. Using a stand mixer fitted with the paddle attachment (or in a large bowl with a hand mixer, whisk, or spatula), cream the butter, sugars, miso, and milk together until light and fluffy. Scrape down the sides and bottom of the bowl. Add the hojicha powder and heat-treated almond flour until a cookie dough forms. Fold in the chocolate chips and nuts or dried berries, or a mix of both. Transfer the cookie dough to a pint-size jar or airtight container and refrigerate for 15 minutes to overnight.

3. Serve the cookie dough by scooping from the jar by the spoonful; or you can roll into 1-tablespoon balls. Sprinkle sea salt flakes over the dough and enjoy.

THAI-TEA ICE CREAM SANDWICH COOKIES

Makes
72 cookies; 36 assembled ice cream sandwiches

Prep Time
Over 1 hour in total

Inactive Time
Several hours to overnight

Cook Time
About 10 minutes

Difficulty
★★★★☆
(There are multiple steps, especially if you make the ice cream, and assembly is required.)

For the Thai-tea ice cream

2 cups (480 g) heavy cream

¼ cup (about 30 g) Thai tea mix

1 tablespoon Thai tea leaves

1 cup (300 g) sweetened condensed milk, or more to taste

For the wafer cookies

1¼ cups (150 g) cake flour

½ cup (50 g) unsweetened Dutch-processed cocoa powder

¼ cup (25 g) black cocoa powder

½ teaspoon baking powder

¼ teaspoon baking soda

6 tablespoons (85 g) unsalted butter, melted, plus more if needed

¾ cup (150 g) unpacked light brown sugar

1 large egg

1 teaspoon red miso

For coating the cookie rims

½ cup (75 g) toasted white sesame seeds, plus more as needed, placed in a shallow bowl

I'm a sucker for a good ice cream sandwich, and I'm a little old school, so my favorite ice cream sandwich cookie has got to be a delicate chocolate wafer. As for the ice cream, I want to highlight one of my favorite drinks, Thai tea, and turn it into an easy no-churn ice cream to use as the filling for the cookies.

Thai tea is usually a strong black tea or Ceylon tea flavored with spices like cardamom and tamarind seed. As an ice cream, Thai tea's intensity mellows and balances the chocolate wafer's rich, bitter-sweet notes.

1. **Make the Thai-tea ice cream.** Combine the cream, Thai tea mix, and Thai tea leaves in a saucepan. Stir occasionally over medium heat until the cream starts to simmer. Remove from the heat, cover, and let the mixture steep for 15 minutes. Strain the tea-flavored cream into a bowl through a fine-mesh sieve, pressing the tea leaves with a spoon to extract as much flavor as possible. If desired, strain again through a finer sieve to avoid small brown flecks in the ice cream, although I love it when ice cream has some impurities. Cover the bowl and refrigerate until very cold, at least 2 hours or overnight.

2. Line a loaf pan or an 8-inch square cake pan with plastic wrap, leaving an overhang on all sides.

3. Transfer the very cold tea-flavored cream to the bowl of a stand mixer fitted with a whisk attachment. Whip until soft peaks form. Add the condensed milk (using the whole can if preferred) and beat until firm to stiff peaks form. You may not achieve completely stiff peaks with the sweetened condensed milk added, but the mixture should be firmer than soft peaks. Transfer to the prepared pan and spread evenly. Cover and freeze until fully set, at least 4 hours or overnight.

RECIPE *continues* →

4. **Make the cookies.** Whisk the cake flour, cocoa powder, black cocoa powder, baking powder, and baking soda together in a medium bowl. In a large mixing bowl, whisk the melted butter with the brown sugar until the sugar dissolves. Add the egg and miso and whisk until combined. Gradually sift in the flour mixture, then fold with a rubber spatula until just combined and no dry flour spots remain. If the dough is too crumbly, consider adding a bit more melted butter. Use a rubber spatula rather than a whisk to mix the dough. Squeeze the dough with your hands to form a ball, and wrap it well in plastic wrap. Cover and refrigerate for 30 minutes.

5. About 25 minutes before baking, adjust two racks to the upper- and lower-middle positions of the oven. Preheat the oven to 350°F. Line two baking sheets with parchment paper.

6. Divide the dough into three equal portions. Roll out one portion on parchment paper or a silicone baking mat to a thickness of 1/16 to 1/8 inch. (Keep the other portions covered in the refrigerator.) With a 2-inch scalloped cookie cutter, cut the rolled-out dough into rounds. Gather the scraps, re-roll, and continue cutting to make about 24 rounds. (Alternatively, use a sharp knife and a ruler to cut each sheet of cookie dough into 24 equal rectangles.) Carefully place the cut cookies on the prepared baking sheets, spacing them evenly.

7. Bake all the cookies, switching the sheets between top and bottom racks and rotating front to back once halfway through baking, until set and the tops have a sheen, about 10 minutes. Set the baking sheets on a wire rack to cool the cookies completely.

8. **Assemble the ice cream sandwiches.** Let the ice cream soften slightly on the counter for about 5 minutes. Line a baking sheet with parchment paper and place in the freezer.

9. Take a cooled cookie and place a scoop of the ice cream on the flat side. Top with another cookie, flat side down, to create a sandwich. Roll the edges of the ice cream sandwiches in the

Substitution
If you'd prefer to use ice cream you already have at home, that's fine. You'll always have an easy no-churn Thai tea ice cream recipe to turn to here whenever you run out of ice cream.

Storage
Store the assembled sandwich cookies, individually wrapped in parchment paper, in an airtight container in the freezer for up to 6 months. Let the frozen ice cream sandwiches soften a little on the counter before enjoying.

toasted sesame seeds, pressing lightly to adhere. For more even ice cream distribution, consider freezing the ice cream in a plastic-lined sheet pan and cutting out circles of ice cream with a cookie cutter.

10. Place the assembled ice cream sandwiches on the prepared baking sheet in the freezer immediately after assembling each one to prevent melting. Freeze for at least 15 minutes before serving.

BUKO PANDAN MELTAWAY COOKIES

Makes
about 20 cookies

Prep Time
20 minutes

Inactive Time
About 30 minutes

Cook Time
About 14 minutes

Difficulty
★★½☆☆
(Not a difficult recipe, per se, but there are multiple steps, so read through the recipe first before starting.)

For the cookies

- 1 cup | 2 sticks (226 g) unsalted butter, softened
- ⅓ cup (40 g) confectioners' sugar
- 1 tablespoon red miso
- 1 tablespoon pandan extract
- 1 cup (120 g) all-purpose flour
- ¾ cup (90 g) cornstarch, sifted
- ¼ cup (about 45 g) kaong (sugar palm seeds), drained, wiped dry, and diced

For the frosting

- 4 ounces (113 g) cream cheese (half an 8-ounce block), cubed and softened
- 2 tablespoons (28 g) unsalted butter, softened
- 2 teaspoons coconut extract
- 1 teaspoon red miso
- ¼ cup plus 2 tablespoons (55 g) confectioners' sugar

For the topping

- 20 pieces of nata de coco, drained and dried with a paper towel, plus more as needed
- Shredded coconut or desiccated coconut
- Toasted pinipig (optional)

Retro meltaways are a playful cross between shortbread and cotton candy. They dissolve in the mouth and leave a delightful surprise, like the chopped kaong, or sugar palm seeds, we add to the dough here.

Why buko pandan, you ask? Well, Jake, Philip, and I recently had buko pandan (a refreshing Filipino dessert with a sweet, creamy base) at a Filipino restaurant, and the boys asked me to make a cookie version. Capturing the essence of buko pandan in a cookie was a little challenging, especially since many of the core components are quite wet, like sago, nata de coco (jelly made from fermented coconut water), and sugar palm seeds, translucent, jelly-like seeds harvested from the fruit of the sugar palm tree which usually come housed in a sugar syrup. But I succeeded with a mild pandan-flavored cookie paired with a coconut cream cheese frosting generously topped with toppings you usually find in buko pandan. Keep these cookies refrigerated and feel free to serve them cold, just like how we serve the dessert that inspired this recipe.

1. **Make the cookies.** Using a stand mixer fitted with the paddle attachment (or in a large bowl with a hand mixer, whisk, or spatula), cream the butter, confectioners' sugar, miso, and pandan extract together until well combined. Scrape down the sides and bottom of the bowl. Add the flour and cornstarch and mix on low speed just until a cookie dough forms. Fold in the diced kaong. Cover the dough and refrigerate for 30 minutes.

2. About 30 minutes before baking, adjust a rack to the middle position and preheat the oven to 350°F. Line a baking sheet with parchment paper.

3. Scoop a tablespoon of dough and shape into a smooth ball. Repeat to make 20 balls, placing them about 1 inch apart on the prepared baking sheet. Press down on each ball with a clean

RECIPE *continues* →

Variation
Latik (Filipino toasted coconut milk curds) would go nicely as a topping for these cookies.

Storage
Store the cookies in an airtight container at room temperature for up to 2 days.

hand or the bottom of a glass coated in granulated sugar, just until the cookie edges begin to crack. Bake until set and the edges are lightly golden brown, about 14 minutes.

4. Let the cookies set on the baking sheet for a few minutes, then transfer to a wire rack to cool completely.

5. **Make the frosting.** While the cookies are cooling, using a stand mixer fitted with the paddle attachment (or in a medium bowl with a hand mixer), beat the cream cheese, butter, coconut extract, and miso together until smooth and creamy. Gradually add the confectioners' sugar, a small portion at a time, and beat until fully incorporated, smooth, and spreadable.

6. Spread or pipe frosting on top of each cooled cookie. Finish assembling the cookies by arranging a nata de coco in the center of each cookie, then sprinkle with shredded or desiccated coconut and pinipig, if using.

DOUBLE BUDDY BREAD

Makes	***Prep Time***	***Difficulty***
10 to 12 assembled double buddies	10 minutes ***Cook Time*** 12 to 15 minutes	(A relatively straightforward recipe, written with Jake in mind so he can make these whenever he has a craving, without depending on me!)

- 3 cups (360 g) all-purpose flour
- 2 teaspoons baking powder
- 2 tablespoons (16 g) milk powder (optional)
- 4 tablespoons (57 g) unsalted butter, softened
- 2 tablespoons (28 g) margarine, cold
- 1 cup (240 g) water
- 1 large egg
- 1 cup (220 g) packed light brown sugar
- 1 tablespoon red miso
- 2 teaspoons ube extract or a few drops of lavender food coloring gel
- Shredded or desiccated coconut, and/or sesame seeds, for topping (optional)
- About ⅓ cup (75 g) margarine, softened
- A few tablespoons sweetened condensed milk, for drizzling
- Milk powder, for dusting

While watching contestants mess up their macarons on season 10 of *MasterChef*, Jake mentioned how a specific set of puffy, fat macarons reminded him of double buddy (or body) bread, or lambingan bread, a favorite treat from his childhood in the Philippines. Jake described these big and filling breads which are an everyday, everyman snack as a lesser-known pan de sal, a Filipino bread roll and staple often topped with bread crumbs.

Double buddies involve two flatbreads, sandwiching a generous amount of sweetened margarine. Sometimes, they are crispy like cookies. When I was working on this book, Jake, knowing my penchant for re-creating treats, kept raving about double buddies, hinting to me how much he loved the yellow and purple versions. Since I'm dedicated to healing and nurturing everyone's inner child, especially my husband's, this recipe was born. One bite and he was 6 again, back at home in Bacolod City. His eyes welled up and I knew I had successfully baked a homemade double buddy for my forever buddy.

1. Adjust a rack to the middle position and preheat the oven to 350°F. Line two baking sheets with parchment paper.

2. Whisk the flour, baking powder, and milk powder, if using, together in a medium bowl. Set aside.

3. Using a stand mixer fitted with the paddle attachment (or in a large bowl with a hand mixer, whisk, or spatula), mix the butter, cold margarine, water, egg, brown sugar, and miso together until small chunks of butter and margarine are floating in the mixture, like cheese curds, about 2 minutes. Scrape down the sides and bottom of the bowl as needed. Add the ube extract or food coloring gel and the flour mixture and mix on low speed just until a cohesive and sticky batter forms.

4. Working one at a time, drop about 2 tablespoons of batter onto the baking sheet, spaced 2 inches apart, to make 20 to

RECIPE *continues* →

Variations
To make each buddy a different color, split the batter into two equal portions. To each portion, add distinct food coloring or flavor extracts according to your taste, or choose to leave one part unaltered.

Storage
Store double buddies in an airtight container at room temperature for up to 2 days.

24 portions. Smooth out the tops with a clean, wet fingertip. Alternatively, transfer the batter to a piping bag fitted with a large star tip and pipe 2-inch round or oblong shapes. If you like, decorate the tops with the coconut shreds or sesame seeds, or both.

5. Bake all the double buddies until the edges are golden brown and the middles are puffy and set, 12 to 15 minutes. Remove from the oven and let the breads set for a few minutes before transferring them to a wire rack to cool completely.

6. Spread the softened margarine evenly over the flat sides of all the cooled double buddies. Drizzle a little condensed milk in the middle. Assemble the sandwiches by piecing two together, then dust the tops with milk powder.

MELT-ON-THE-TONGUE NAMA CHOCOLATES

Makes
36 truffles

Prep Time
10 minutes

Inactive Time
4 hours to overnight

Cook Time
5 to 10 minutes

Difficulty
★★☆☆☆
(Trust the process and keep whisking that chocolate; the ganache will come together smoothly as long as your cream is heated to the right temperature.)

- 3 ¼ cups (470 g) high-quality (couverture) semisweet chocolate
- 1 cup (240 g) heavy cream
- 2 tablespoons (28 g) unsalted butter
- About 4 teaspoons (30 g) sweetened condensed milk
- 1 teaspoon red miso (gluten-free if that is a concern)
- Pinch of sea salt
- Pinch of nutmeg (optional)
- 2 tablespoons (30 g) Japanese whisky, bourbon, or a liquor of your choice (optional)
- Unsweetened Dutch-processed cocoa powder, for dusting
- Sea salt flakes, for garnish (optional)
- Edible gold foil, for garnish (optional)

According to my son, Philip, if you want to know what heaven tastes like, have one of these nama chocolates. Nama chocolates are Japanese truffles with a velvety, rich, creamy texture and intense chocolate flavor thanks to high-quality semisweet chocolate, butter, and fresh cream usually from Hokkaido. The Japanese word nama (生) means "raw" or "fresh." While they are more confectionery than cookie, they are still perfect on a cookie tray or nestled in a holiday cookie tin.

While there are many brands, I always buy Royce' nama chocolates. Whenever we are in Japan, we pick them up at Narita Airport. While you can also find Royce' chocolates in the States, they cost almost double what you would pay abroad, so it makes sense to make decadent nama chocolates at home. After all, life is always sweeter with a bit of chocolate, especially the good kind.

1. Crumple, then uncrumple a large sheet of parchment paper and use it to line an 8-inch square cake pan with some overhang. Smooth and press down the parchment paper with your hands. Add the chocolate to a large heatproof bowl and set aside.

2. In a heavy saucepan, heat the cream, butter, condensed milk, miso, salt, and nutmeg, if using, over medium heat until the mixture reaches 120°F, about 5 minutes. Do not overheat, as your chocolate will not temper correctly if this mixture is too hot. Remove from the heat.

3. Microwave the chocolate in two 30-second bursts until softened. Pour the heated cream mixture over the softened chocolate. Stir with a rubber spatula, then use a whisk to mix thoroughly. Once homogenous, smooth, and glossy, stir in the liquor, if using. Pour the chocolate mixture into the prepared

RECIPE *continues* →

Truffle Tips
You will need a candy or digital thermometer for this recipe. Also, because we're not adding stabilizers and emulsifiers, the chocolates will soften quickly at room temperature.

Substitution
You can use a blend of chocolates. I didn't have enough semisweet chocolate, so I mixed in some milk chocolate chips. Just don't use white chocolate for this recipe.

Storage
Store the nama chocolates in an airtight container in the refrigerator for up to 6 days, and indefinitely in the freezer.

baking pan and smooth the top with an offset spatula. Cover and refrigerate for 4 hours or overnight.

4. Take the chocolate out of the baking dish. Dip the blade of a sharp knife into hot water and carefully wipe off the water. Slice the chocolate into 36 equal squares (or cut them bigger or smaller). It's best to dip the knife back into the hot water and wipe it before each cut.

5. Dust the chocolates with cocoa powder. If you like, sprinkle sea salt flakes over the chocolates and decorate with edible gold foil. Enjoy with hot tea and be sure to let the chocolate melt on your tongue.

FILIPINO SWEET RICE CAKES (Palitaws)

Makes about 12 sweet rice cakes

Prep Time 10 minutes

Cook Time About 10 minutes to boil all the palitaws if splitting into batches

Difficulty: ★★☆☆☆ (Be careful since we're working with boiling water. Supervise children as needed.)

For the palitaws

- 2 cups (300 g) glutinous rice flour, plus more as needed
- Pinch of kosher salt
- ½ cup (120 g) coconut milk
- ½ cup (120 g) coconut water or water, plus more as needed
- 2 tablespoons (30 g) maple syrup
- 1 tablespoon ube extract (with color) (optional)
- ⅔ cup (50 g) sweetened shredded coconut, plus more as needed

For coating the palitaws

- ¼ cup (36 g) toasted white sesame seeds, plus more as needed
- ¼ cup (50 g) granulated sugar, plus more for serving
- ¼ cup (35 g) ground peanuts or finely chopped peanuts or cashews
- ⅔ cup (50 g) shredded coconut (unsweetened or sweetened), placed in a shallow bowl, plus more as needed

During a family trip to Bacolod City, we had palitaws, sweet Filipino rice cakes. They remind me of the Hokkien/Teochew dessert, muah chee (麻糍), or peanut mochi, which was a staple throughout my childhood. Back at home, to remind us of our trip, I developed this recipe so we can snack on them whenever we want. Because we only occasionally expose Philip to his Filipino side, these little reminders and flavors of the Philippines are very important to us.

While traditional palitaws don't usually include peanuts, I add them because they evoke the muah chee I cherished as a kid. Now, when eating these, Philip can taste and appreciate the richness of his mixed Chinese and Filipino heritage.

1. **Make the palitaws.** Mix the glutinous rice flour, kosher salt, coconut milk, coconut water or water, maple syrup, and ube extract, if using, together in a medium bowl until a cohesive, smooth, pliable dough forms. It should resemble mashed potatoes that come together. If the dough breaks apart, work in a little water, a few teaspoons at a time. If the dough is too watery, add more glutinous rice flour until the dough can hold together.

2. Scoop about 2 tablespoons of the dough and roll into a smooth ball. Gently flatten into a disc ¼ to ½ inch thick. Alternatively, you can also flatten them into long ovals. Repeat to make about 12 rice cakes.

3. Line a baking sheet with parchment paper. Bring a heavy saucepan or pot of water to a rolling boil over medium-high heat. Boil the rice cakes, a few at a time without overcrowding, until the rice cakes float to the top, about 4 minutes. Use a slotted spoon or spider strainer to remove the cooked rice cakes from the saucepan or pot and transfer to the prepared baking sheet, then arrange in a single layer to cool.

RECIPE *continues* →

Variations
Feel free to make these smaller, with 1- to 1½-tablespoon dough balls. Also, you can split the dough, so half are ube-flavored, and half are not.

Instead of white sesame seeds, use black sesame seeds. Feel free to replace the ground peanuts with any other ground nuts, or use black sesame powder instead.

Storage
Palitaws are best enjoyed fresh.

4. **Coat the palitaws.** Whisk the sesame seeds, granulated sugar, and ground peanuts or finely chopped peanuts together in a shallow bowl. Place the shredded coconut in a separate shallow bowl. While the rice cakes are still warm (not hot), and working one at a time, roll the rice cakes in the shredded coconut to thoroughly coat, then toss in the sesame seed mixture.

5. Before serving, and don't skip this step, heat the palitaws for 30 to 60 seconds in the microwave and serve warm. This way, they are perfectly soft and gooey. Spoon any extra sesame seed mixture over the palitaws.

TARO MERINGUE COOKIES

Makes
24 to 30 meringue cookies

Prep Time
15 minutes

Inactive Time
2 hours to overnight

Cook Time
90 minutes

Difficulty
★★★☆☆
(Anything can go wrong with whipping egg whites into meringue, which adds challenge to this recipe.)

- 4 large egg whites, room temperature
- ¼ teaspoon cream of tartar
- ½ cup (100 g) granulated sugar
- ¼ cup (30 g) confectioners' sugar
- Drops of purple or violet food coloring gel (optional, but recommended)
- 2 tablespoons (15 g) taro powder
- 1 teaspoon cornstarch
- ¼ cup (15 g) Fruity Pebbles cereal, for garnish, or more as needed

Meringue Tip
The meringues need to dry out in the oven a few hours to overnight. Because they take so much time to make, you may want to double the ingredients and make a larger batch.

Substitutions
Substitute desiccated coconut or sesame seeds for the Fruity Pebbles, or a combination of different toppings.

Storage
Store the meringue cookies in an airtight container in a cool, dry place for up to 2 weeks. To crisp them up again, bake at 200°F for 15 minutes.

When Ah Ma whipped up eggs to make a chiffon cake for my fifth birthday, the scent of meringue filled the air. With the rest of the egg whites, Ah Ma baked cookies. They were crispy at first bite, then melted in my little mouth. Everything just seems more magical when you're a kid.

Wanting to re-create some of that magic for my son, I created these taro meringue cookies. Taro is nutty, sweet, and earthy all at once, and these were flavors I grew up with. For whatever reason, the women in my family all love taro—my grandmother, my mother, and me. Philip is starting to like it more, and I love how I can introduce things I cherish from my childhood to his. Long after I'm gone, I hope every taro treat reminds him of me and his happy childhood, just as I am reminded of Ah Ma and the goodies she made for me.

1. Adjust a rack in the lower third of the oven and preheat the oven to 210°F. Line a baking sheet with parchment paper.

2. Using a stand mixer fitted with the whisk attachment, beat the egg whites and cream of tartar on high speed until white and frothy, about 2 minutes. In increments, gradually add the granulated and confectioners' sugars, then whisk on high speed until stiff, glossy peaks form, at least 6 to 8 minutes. If you like, add purple food coloring gel and whisk until combined, a few seconds. Sift in the taro powder and cornstarch and gently fold with a rubber spatula until combined.

3. Transfer the meringue to a piping bag fitted with a large open star tip (or feel free to experiment with other tips). Pipe the meringue into 2-inch-diameter cookies onto the prepared baking sheet, each about 1½ inches high and spaced evenly. Sprinkle Fruity Pebbles cereal, or other toppings as desired, generously on top of each meringue cookie.

4. Bake the cookies for 1½ hours, then turn off the oven and leave the cookies in the oven for at least 2 hours to overnight, or until they're completely dry.

MANGO-STICKY RICE SCONES

Makes	*Prep Time*	*Cook Time:*	*Difficulty*
12 scones	20 minutes *Inactive Time* 60 to 90 minutes	10 to 12 minutes for the ganache; about 22 minutes for the scones	★★★★☆ (The difficulty is higher because there are multiple steps and processes involved.)

For the sticky rice ganache

- One 4-ounce (113 g) bar high-quality white chocolate, chopped; or 4 ounces white chocolate chips
- ½ cup (120 g) heavy cream
- 1 tablespoon unsalted butter
- 1 teaspoon red miso
- 1 teaspoon coconut extract
- ⅓ cup (65 g) Thai sticky rice, washed
- ⅔ cup (160 g) coconut water

For the scones

- 1 cup (120 g) all-purpose flour
- 1 cup (120 g) bread flour
- ⅓ cup (67 g) granulated sugar
- ⅓ cup (50 g) toasted white sesame seeds, plus more for topping
- ⅓ cup (30 g) desiccated coconut
- ⅓ cup (40 g) dried mangoes, chopped finely
- 1 tablespoon baking powder
- 6 tablespoons (85 g) unsalted butter, cold and cubed
- ⅓ cup (80 g) Greek yogurt
- 2 large eggs
- 1 tablespoon red miso
- 1 teaspoon coconut extract (optional)
- ⅔ cup (100 g) diced fresh or thawed frozen mango, plus more for topping

Since mango sticky rice (or khao niao mamuang in Thai) is one of my favorite desserts, I stayed up many nights trying to turn it into a cookie. Again and again, I failed because the mango made the cookie dough too wet and cakey. And trying to find a way to incorporate sticky rice was also a challenge. As the weather turned warmer, my family visited the Washington State Fair and we shared tender, fruity scones. They weren't wedge shaped like my kimchi scones on page 207, but classically round and somewhat rustic. Those scones gave me the epiphany to make a mango-sticky rice scone for this book. As for the sticky rice whipped ganache that goes with the scones, we have Subtle Asian Baking member Rosie Tran (@theasianfooddiary) to thank for the idea.

1. **Make the sticky rice ganache.** Add the white chocolate to a medium heatproof mixing bowl. Heat the cream, butter, and miso in a small saucepan until boiling, then pour over the white chocolate. Cover and let stand for 5 minutes. Add the coconut extract and stir until all the chocolate is melted. Cover with plastic wrap touching the ganache (so a skin doesn't form) and refrigerate until cold, at least 1 hour. (Or chill in the freezer for about 30 minutes to speed up the process.)

2. Meanwhile, combine the sticky rice and coconut water in a medium microwave-safe bowl and cover with an upside-down plate. Microwave on high for 2 minutes. Carefully remove the bowl from the microwave and fluff the rice with a paddle or fork. Cover and cook the rice for 2 minutes and fluff again. Repeat fluffing and microwaving the rice in 2-minute bursts, until the rice is soft and translucent, and all the water is gone, 3 to 4 bursts total. Set aside.

3. Using a stand mixer fitted with the whisk attachment (or by hand with a whisk or hand mixer), whip the ganache if using, until fluffy, about 1 minute. Fluff the sticky rice so it becomes

RECIPE *continues* →

Scone Tip
Instead of dropping the dough onto a baking sheet, you can bake the scones in a greased muffin tin.

Storage
Store the scones in an airtight container at room temperature for up to 3 days. The ganache, without the sticky rice, can be refrigerated for up to 5 days.

loose, then add it to the ganache and whip for a few seconds to combine. Cover and refrigerate.

4. **Make the scones.** Whisk the all-purpose flour, bread flour, sugar, sesame seeds, coconut, chopped dried mango, and baking powder together in a large mixing bowl. Add the butter and chop it into the dry ingredients with a pastry cutter or fork. Alternatively, use clean hands to rub or smear the butter into the flour between your fingers. Either way, work in the butter until pea-sized pieces of flour-coated butter remain.

5. Form a well in the center of the flour mixture. Add the yogurt, eggs, miso, and coconut extract, if using, to the well and mix just until the ingredients come together. Add the fresh or thawed frozen mango, mixing until thoroughly combined into a sticky and wet dough. Cover and refrigerate for 30 minutes.

6. About 25 minutes before baking, adjust a rack to the middle position and preheat the oven to 375°F. Line a baking sheet with parchment paper.

7. Working one at a time, use a ¼ cup measuring cup to drop dough directly onto the prepared baking sheet, making about 12 scones and spacing them about 1 inch apart.

8. Bake the scones until set and golden brown, about 22 minutes. Let the scones set on the baking sheet for a few minutes, then transfer to a wire rack to cool completely.

9. To serve, either top the scones with a layer of the sticky rice ganache, or slice each scone crosswise in half and sandwich a layer of ganache between the halves. Either way, top the ganache with some chopped mango and sesame seeds, if desired.

CUTE PINEAPPLE TARTS

Makes
about
36 pineapple tarts

Prep Time
45 minutes

Inactive Time
30 minutes to overnight

Cook Time
About 30 minutes to cook the pineapple jam filling; about 20 minutes to bake the tarts

Difficulty
★★★★★
(As difficult as any of the recipes here can get.)

For the pineapple jam filling

Three 20-ounce cans sliced pineapples, drained; or about 2 large fresh pineapples (1.7 kg total), peeled, eyes and cores removed, and diced

½ cup (100 g) granulated sugar, plus more if needed

¼ cup (55 g) unpacked light brown sugar

1 tablespoon rum

1 tablespoon red miso

1 teaspoon cornstarch

1 teaspoon ground cinnamon

¼ teaspoon ground cloves

For the pastry dough

¼ cup (150 g) cake flour

1 tablespoon cornstarch

1 ½ teaspoons culinary-grade matcha

⅓ cup plus 1 tablespoon (80 g) unsalted butter, cubed and room temperature

3 tablespoons (40 g) granulated sugar

1 tablespoon sweetened condensed milk

1 teaspoon red miso

1 small egg

Drops of green food coloring gel

Black sesame seeds, for frog eyes

1 large egg, beaten with 1 teaspoon milk, for egg wash

My family loves pineapple tarts. For many years, before going to work, my father ate store-bought ones for breakfast, those rectangular-shaped ones Taiwan is famous for. We always rejoice when our friends bring back pineapple tarts from Taiwan.

There's also Southeast Asia's versions of pineapple tarts, where the pineapple jam is a topping rather than a filling. I love pineapple tarts of all kinds and wanted to make a version that didn't involve using molds. I also wanted to make the tarts cute, like the ones Subtle Asian Baking members show off during Lunar New Year.

Frog-shaped desserts always call to me, so I developed a cute froggy pineapple tart, one that is guaranteed to put a smile on the eater's face. While they will be delicious they will also most definitely be silly-looking, unless you're great at sculpting or have experience molding clay or Play-Doh.

If you're able to source fresh pineapple, use it to make the jammy filling; it will make quite a difference. You can make the jam a day or two in advance; otherwise, it will take a good chunk of an afternoon to fully assemble these tarts. Still, they'll be worth it!

1. **Make the pineapple jam filling.** Pulse the pineapple in a blender or food processor until the mixture resembles applesauce, 10 to 15 seconds. Discard the excess pineapple juice by straining the pineapple in a fine-mesh strainer and transfer the pineapple to a saucepan. Mix in the sugars, rum, miso, cornstarch, cinnamon, and cloves. Cook over medium heat, stirring continuously, until the mixture darkens like a deep honey and thickens to a dry and sticky jam, about 30 minutes. The jam is ready when it is spreadable yet firm and can hold its shape. Be sure to taste test along the way to see if the jam is sweet enough. If it's not, feel free to stir in a little more sugar. Remove from the heat and transfer the jam to a medium bowl, cover, and cool completely in the refrigerator.

RECIPE *continues* →

Substitutions
You can omit the rum in the jam. Instead of using black sesame seeds as pupils, you can use melted chocolate.

Storage
Store the pineapple tarts in an airtight container at room temperature for up to 3 days.

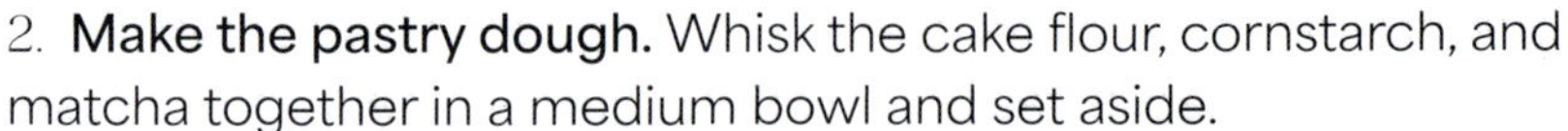

2. **Make the pastry dough.** Whisk the cake flour, cornstarch, and matcha together in a medium bowl and set aside.

3. Using a stand mixer fitted with the paddle attachment (or in a large bowl with a hand mixer, whisk, or spatula), cream the butter, sugar, condensed milk, and miso together until light and fluffy, about 1 minute. Scrape down the sides and bottom of the bowl. Add the egg and green food coloring gel and mix until well incorporated. Add the flour mixture and mix on low speed just until a cookie dough forms. Cover the dough and chill in the refrigerator for 30 minutes to overnight.

Add faces to the froggy tarts.

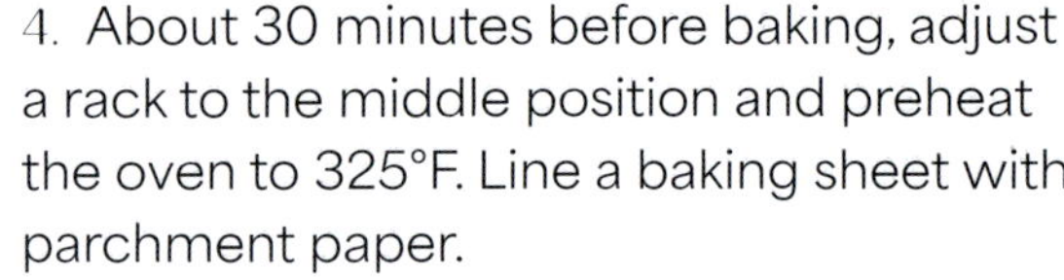

4. About 30 minutes before baking, adjust a rack to the middle position and preheat the oven to 325°F. Line a baking sheet with parchment paper.

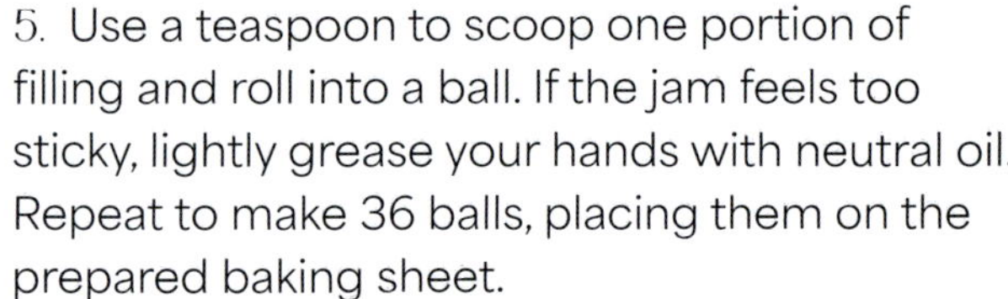

5. Use a teaspoon to scoop one portion of filling and roll into a ball. If the jam feels too sticky, lightly grease your hands with neutral oil. Repeat to make 36 balls, placing them on the prepared baking sheet.

6. On a lightly floured work surface, shape the dough into a log and cut into 39 small portions, each about ⅔ tablespoon or 10 grams. Reserve three portions to use as the frog eyes.

7. Working one at a time, roll a piece of dough into a smooth ball and flatten into a 2-inch disc. Place a ball of jam filling in the center of the disc and wrap the dough around the filling. Pinch the seams and roll into a smooth ball. Transfer to the prepared baking sheet. Continue until you've wrapped all the jam filling with pastry dough.

8. To make frog eyes, pinch small pea-sized pieces of dough from the reserved pastry dough pieces and roll into small balls. Use a little water to moisten the tops of the larger dough balls, then gently press two small balls on top of each larger ball, spacing them about

¼ inch apart to resemble a pair of frog eyes. Press a black sesame seed into the center of each small ball to create the pupils. Use a bamboo skewer or toothpick to draw a mouth or other designs on your froggy pineapple tarts.

9. Using a pastry brush, brush the cute pineapple tarts with the egg wash. Bake all the tarts until the edges are golden brown, about 20 minutes. Transfer the tarts to a wire rack to cool completely.

DURIAN TEA SANDWICH COOKIES FOR AH MA

Makes
12 tea sandwich cookies

Prep Time
20 minutes

Inactive Time
A few hours to overnight

Cook Time
About 1 hour to toast the sugar; 13 to 15 minutes to bake the cookies; a few minutes to melt the chocolate for the frosting

Difficulty
★★★★☆
(Each part is easy to make, but there's a lot of planning ahead and assembly required.)

For the toasted sugar

2 cups (400 g) granulated sugar (or as much as needed), sifted

For the cookies

½ cup | 1 stick (113 g) unsalted butter, room temperature

1 teaspoon red miso

1 small egg

1 cup (120 g) all-purpose flour

¼ cup (35 g) toasted white sesame seeds

For the filling

⅓ cup (80 g) fresh ripe durian flesh

4 tablespoons (57 g) unsalted butter, softened

⅔ cup (80 g) confectioners' sugar

1 tablespoon Japanese whisky

For the chocolate frosting

¼ cup (45 g) semisweet chocolate chips

1 tablespoon olive oil

¼ cup (45 g) finely crushed toasted walnuts, placed in a shallow bowl

Confectioners' sugar, for dusting (optional)

Saving the best for last, I wanted to end the book with a cookie that would have impressed my granny, Ah Ma, who taught me how to whip egg whites into beautiful meringue, how to make chiffon cakes, mooncakes, and cream puffs, along with the best Vietnamese food, and how to appreciate durian and turn it into the most delicious ice cream (which Ah Ma had stored for years in her freezer!). During my childhood summers in Montreal, Ah Ma would take me, my sister, and cousin all over Chinatown to enjoy baked goodies and dim sum. As we both got older, Ah Ma and I became phone pals, until she could no longer answer the phone.

Ah Ma was so strong, stubborn, intelligent, and creative that I feel nothing I bake would have impressed her. After all, in her youth, she learned all about French baking and pastries when France occupied her homeland. What would impress Ah Ma if I ever got to bake for her again? It would have to be something that required more than a little thought, effort, and a whole lot of heart. While there are many steps, including toasting sugar to add more complex flavor, putting it all together is relatively simple and worth it for teatime with a beloved. Ah Ma, I dedicate these cookies to you. I hope you are proud of me. I love you and thank you for everything. May you rest in peace.

1. **Make the toasted sugar.** Adjust a rack to the middle position and preheat the oven to 300°F. Line a baking sheet with parchment paper. Spread the granulated sugar in an even layer on the prepared baking sheet. Toast in the oven, stirring occasionally with a wooden spoon or rubber spatula, until it resembles light brown sugar, about 1 hour. Let the sugar cool completely at room temperature directly on the baking sheet. Once cooled, reserve ½ cup for the cookies and store the rest of the toasted sugar in an airtight container.

2. **Make the cookies.** Using a stand mixer fitted with the paddle attachment (or in a large bowl with a hand mixer, whisk, or

RECIPE *continues* →

spatula), cream the ½ cup toasted sugar, butter, and miso together until light and fluffy, about 1 minute. Scrape down the sides and bottom of the bowl. Add the egg and mix until well incorporated. Add the flour and mix on low speed just until a cookie dough forms. Fold in the toasted sesame seeds. Cover and chill the dough in the refrigerator for 2 hours to overnight.

3. About 30 minutes before baking, adjust a rack to the middle position and preheat the oven to 325°F. Line a baking sheet with parchment paper.

4. Scoop a tablespoon of the dough and roll into a smooth ball. Repeat to make 24 balls, placing them 1 inch apart on the prepared baking sheet. Use the bottom of a glass coated in sugar to flatten each dough ball into a ¼-inch-thick disc.

5. Bake the cookies until the edges and bottoms are golden brown, 13 to 15 minutes. Let the cookies set on the baking sheet for a few minutes before transferring to a wire rack to cool completely.

6. **Make the filling and fill the cookies.** By hand with a whisk (or with a stand mixer fitted with the paddle attachment), beat the durian and butter until combined. Add the confectioners' sugar and Japanese whisky and cream the mixture until fluffy and spreadable.

7. Spread the bottoms of half of the cookies with 2 to 3 teaspoons of filling (use less filling if you like thinner cookies). Spread the filling thin with a butter knife or offset spatula. Top with the remaining cookies to make sandwiches.

8. **Make the chocolate frosting and finish assembling the cookies.** Melt the chocolate with the olive oil, using either a double boiler or in the microwave in 20-second bursts. Stir the melted mixture until smooth and homogenous. Transfer to a shallow bowl.

Substitution
Ah Ma loved walnuts, but feel free to swap them out for your favorite nuts.

Storage
Store the cookies in an airtight container at room temperature for up to 2 days.

9. Roll the edges of each sandwich cookie in the chocolate mixture to make a chocolate rim. Then roll in the finely chopped walnuts. Transfer the cookies to a wire rack to allow the chocolate to set. (For faster setting, refrigerate the cookies.)

10. Dust with confectioners' sugar if desired. Enjoy these with your favorite tea, and with a loved one. Brush your teeth before you kiss any non-durian lovers (or smooch them anyway because love is unconditional).

ACKNOWLEDGMENTS

TO THE AMAZING VORACIOUS TEAM: Vivian Lee, Morgan Wu, Thea Diklich-Newell, Jessica (Jess) Chun, Juliana (Jules) Horbachevsky, Arik Hardin, Deri Reed, Jennifer Noon Hess, Katherine Akey, Lauren Ortiz, and Michael Szczerban—thank you for being my sounding board, my greatest cheerleaders, and for helping bring *108 Asian Cookies* to life. Your invaluable guidance and unwavering support have shaped this book into something truly special. Sometimes I pinch myself to see if I'd wake up from a dream. From the very beginning, you believed in this project and steered it with such love, expertise, and care. It was especially meaningful to me to pick Vivian's brain on the nuances of Cantonese pronunciations and idioms. If it were up to me alone, I would never have been able to sound out and spell words like baat bóu faahn or 八宝飯! Thank you also to Toni Tajima and Kirin Diemont for their design work on the interior and the cover, respectively.

To my beautiful literary agent, **Katherine Latshaw**, thank you! From the moment I queried you and you responded to my email enthusiastically within what felt like minutes later, I knew our partnership was meant to be. For decades, I've dreamed of having a literary agent, and it's like God answered by sending me the best one ever. Thank you for everything, for believing in this book, and in me. I can't wait to work on a next book together, be it another cookbook or a spicy rom-com!

To my fabulous team of recipe testers: Seriously, what would I have done without my incredible recipe testers? Julia Child once said, "A cookbook is only as good as its poorest recipe." Thanks to your invaluable help, not a single one of my recipes falls short. Your dedication, feedback, and support have been instrumental in bringing this project to life. Thank you for making every cookie the best it can be!

Rachel Gascon:
Rachel, you've tirelessly tested recipes from two of my cookbooks, and made sure I got my feedback in time even when you were sick, busy, or life was throwing you a few curveballs! I'll always remember how good you are to me. The moment you came back from your amazing Japan trip, you reached out to me to remind me to send recipes for you to test. You kept me on track, and I am just so grateful to you!

Sharon Hsu:
Sharon, Sharon, Sharon, my little sister from another mister. What can I say? I love and appreciate you and I am so teary writing this. Despite a busy schedule working and navigating your new career in the food industry, you developed two recipes for this book and tested a handful. Not only that, you've supported Subtle Asian Baking tirelessly. You've flown two years in a row to Seattle from Queens to support our events and to see me! Your soul is so kind and gentle and you will always be my sunshine and sparkles, even on the grayest of days! Never change, my dear friend! I will always be your cheerleader, as you have been mine.

Shannon Kish:
Shannon, thank you once again for testing recipes for me! I love how we connected on Instagram and you really came to my rescue when I needed recipes tested. I will always appreciate your thoughtful feedback and enthusiasm.

Susan H. Louangsaysongkham:
Susan, you've tested recipes for all three of my cookbooks, and are always so thorough, supportive, warm, and friendly. You fill me with joy whenever you tell me how much your beautiful children enjoy the cookies you've tested, and you helped saved so many of my recipes. God sends us angels and light, and you're both an angel and light to me. I thank you from the bottom of my heart.

Laura and Conor McCarthy:
Laura, it's like God knew I would need help with this book, and he sent me you. You kept me on track and reminded me to work on this book and tested recipes during a heat wave, house renovations, and a busy life as a doting mother and wife. You sent me encouraging messages and checked up on me when you just knew my mental health was struggling. Not only did you test the bulk of the recipes in this book, you developed two wonderfully delicious recipes, and shared cookies with Conor, the love of your life and your "wonderful and honest #1 taster." Conor, I'd like to thank you for your amazing feedback as well! Before reading Laura's notes, I always thought

to myself, "I hope Conor approved!" Additionally, Laura, thank you to your friends at F45 Dumbarton gym who enthusiastically tasted every cookie you brought them, even the early ones with too much fish sauce or questionable teeth-cracking textures! Do they know, however, that Conor hoarded some of the cookies, LOL? Finally, I hope you and I can work together again and who knows, maybe I'll be testing recipes for your cookbooks one day!

Hannah Park:
Hannah, thank you once again for testing a cookbook for me. You're so dedicated and your feedback is so precise and precious to me. You've saved me a lot of headaches, helping test some of my more "difficult" cookies and brainstorming changes for both the coffee bean cookies and mango lassi cookies. Without your help, I would have had to scrap a few recipes and start from scratch again! You radiate with passion for food science. Never change, queen!

Wilson Pu:
Wilson, you light up the room with your infectious smile and I'm so glad we connected at Microsoft! I love your scientific and technical feedback, which I always looked forward to reading. Tweaking my recipes based off your notes was a breeze. Bro, you have a knack for this, so I hope you continue to test recipes! Thank you for your support and showing up at my events in Seattle! It means so, so much to me and I'm so touched by your words, that you just want to support my dreams. Getting teary writing this!

Judy Shertzer:
I am so incredibly grateful for your unwavering support. Your feedback has always been detailed, insightful, and kind. Thank you for testing the recipes in not just one but two of my books. It means the world to me. When you found my books at a local library in South Bend and during your trip to NYC at Strand Books, and you enthusiastically told me about your discovery, it filled me with so much warmth and pride. Beyond testing recipes, you've been there to check up on me, send kind notes (especially the ones about my late father, as you knew how much I always miss and think about him), and keep my spirits high. If you're up for it, I'd be honored to have you continue testing recipes for all my future books. From the bottom of my heart, thank you, dear Judy!

Kanney "Nini" Wong:
Nini, you are so amazing, and from the moment you showed up to our remote interview in a full suit, I knew so many great things will be waiting for you in life. Thank you for being a wonderful intern and testing recipes even when you didn't have an oven in your dorm. You went out of your way to a friend's kitchen to make the cookies. PS: Thank you for spending a day with us in Seattle during the photo shoot!

To my Subtle Asian Baking family: This is, again, our book! I hope you are proud of all we've achieved together through the years!

▾ Kat and Laura McCarthy in Renton, 2024

◂ Wilson Pu

▾ Rachel Gascon

▴ Judy Shertzer

◂ Susan's kiddos and taste testers. :)

▾ Nini and Kat at the cookbook photo shoot, Seattle, 2024

▾ Sharon and Kat at the 2024 IACP Summit and Awards Ceremony

▲ From left to right: Theresa, Kat, Charity, and Tyler, Seattle, 2024

To my photography team: Thank you, Charity Burggraaf, Theresa Gilliam, and Tyler Hill. This amazing team worked so tirelessly (even through a heat wave in Seattle!) to ensure all the photos in this book came out spectacular, and they did! Your dedication, talent, and passion breathed life into this book. Every time I flip through these pages, I am still in awe, and I can't wait to work again together on another project!

To every cookie lover out there: Thank you for celebrating cookies with me. This book was made for you, and may it inspire endless batches and happy memories.

And last but not least, to my loving neighbors and friends, and my beloved family, Jake, Philip, Mom, Panda, and Escargot (my five-year-old pet snail): You are everything to me.

Every celebration, every win, every up and down, my beloved family is beside me.

▲ From left to right: Kat, Phil, and Mom

▸ From left to right: Mom, Phil, Avery, Jake, Austin, Kat, Karthik, and Yashika

INDEX

Note: Page references in *italics* indicate photographs.

R

S

T

ABOUT THE AUTHOR

KAT LIEU is an award-winning author, food writer, recipe developer, content creator, and the visionary behind Subtle Asian Baking (SAB), the largest global online group focusing on spreading the love and joy of Asian baking. SAB is more than a hobby group online; collectively, SAB members have raised over $101,000 for charities such as Welcome to Chinatown, the Very Asian Foundation, and the Wing Luke Museum.

Drawing inspiration from culinary icons like Julia Child and Martha Stewart, Kat aspires to carve her own niche in the food world (without ever ending up in federal prison like Martha). When she's not in the kitchen, Kat enjoys video games, unwinds to lo-fi beats, writes silly rom-coms during ungodly hours, and cherishes moments with family and pets, a black and white shih-poo named Panda and a snail named Escargot. Note how she's super creative when it comes to naming her pets. She is the proud author of the best-selling *Modern Asian Baking at Home* and *Modern Asian Kitchen*. Now that her third cookbook, *108 Asian Cookies*, is out in the world, Kat is manifesting that by her fourth cookbook, she can grace the cover with her silly face and still see it fly off the shelves.

ABOUT THE PHOTOGRAPHY TEAM

Charity Burggraaf is a food and lifestyle photographer based in the Pacific Northwest, with over thirty cookbooks under her belt. When she isn't in the studio, she enjoys growing flowers in her garden, throwing pottery, or cooking something up in her kitchen.

By the age of 10, **Theresa Gilliam** had already discovered a passion for cooking and photography. Although she grew up amid the flat expanses of the Chicago suburbs, she always dreamed of relocating to the mystical Pacific Northwest. Today, as a seasoned food and beverage stylist based in Seattle for over a decade, she has turned those childhood dreams into a reality.

Tyler Hill is a food and beverage stylist hailing from a small town in West Virginia. Growing up in his father's pizza shop inspired him to work in the restaurant and hospitality industry, leading him to follow his dreams of becoming a food stylist in New York City. His favorite food to eat and style is ice cream, and he currently lives in Seattle, Washington.

Growing up as a Canadian-born Vietnamese Chinese American, Kat Lieu sought comfort in the flavors of her youth, like taro and black sesame. But she struggled to find a home for herself as a third-culture baker in American bakeries, online, or in cookbooks. In the auspiciously titled *108 Asian Cookies,* Lieu honors the varied and rich tapestry of Asian cultures and ingredients that inspired these recipes. And with help from members of Subtle Asian Baking, the online baking group she founded, she presents a diverse array of original and member-submitted drool-worthy recipes for cookies and other bakes, incorporating ingredients from the diaspora—including gochujang, ube, miso, fish sauce, sambal, tahini, matcha, and MSG—stirred into each batter and dough.

At many Asian tables, "not too sweet" is the highest compliment one can give—so whether these recipes are comfortingly familiar or new discoveries, *108 Asian Cookies* will be sure to delight even the most discerning palates for years to come.